The Reconstruction of Southern Debtors

For Catherine and Michael
With great appreciation
for your friendship.

For Maryann and Myles
With great appreciation
for your friendship.

W.

STUDIES IN THE LEGAL HISTORY OF THE SOUTH

Edited by Paul Finkelman, Kermit L. Hall, and Timothy S. Huebner

This series explores the ways in which law has affected the development of the southern United States and in turn the ways the history of the South has affected the development of American law. Volumes in the series focus on a specific aspect of the law, such as slave law or civil rights legislation, or on a broader topic of historical significance to the development of the legal system in the region, such as issues of constitutional history and of law and society, comparative analyses with other legal systems, and biographical studies of influential southern jurists and lawyers.

The Reconstruction of Southern Debtors

Bankruptcy after the Civil War

ELIZABETH LEE THOMPSON

The University of Georgia Press • *Athens and London*

Published by the University of Georgia Press
Athens, Georgia 30602
© 2004 by Elizabeth Lee Thompson
All rights reserved
Designed by Walton Harris
Set in Minion by Bookcomp, Inc.
Printed and bound by Maple-Vail

The paper in this book meets the guidelines for
permanence and durability of the Committee on
Production Guidelines for Book Longevity of the
Council on Library Resources.

Printed in the United States of America
08 07 06 05 04 C 5 4 3 2 1

Library of Congress Cataloging-in-Publication Data

Thompson, Elizabeth Lee, 1967–
The reconstruction of southern debtors : bankruptcy after
the Civil War / Elizabeth Lee Thompson.
    p.   cm.
Includes bibliographical references and index.
ISBN 0-8203-2624-0 (Hardcover : alk. paper)
1. Bankruptcy—Southern States—History. I. Title.
KF1524.T48 2004
346.7307'8'09—dc22   2004005101

British Library Cataloging-in-Publication Data available

For David

CONTENTS

List of Illustrations   *xi*

List of Tables   *xiii*

Acknowledgments   *xv*

Introduction   *1*

1 An Act of Transcendent Importance   *13*

2 The Federal District Courts in Bankruptcy Cases   *31*

3 Southerners' Use of the 1867 Act   *52*

4 Southern Attorneys as Bankruptcy Counsel   *59*

5 Voluntary Bankruptcy Proceedings in the South   *73*

6 Involuntary Bankruptcy in Southern Tribunals   *93*

7 White Women and African Americans under the Bankruptcy Act   *105*

8 Bankrupt Partners and Corporations before the Federal Courts   *121*

9 Repeal of the 1867 Act   *135*

Appendix on Methodology   *143*

Notes   *147*

Sources Cited   *177*

Index   *187*

ILLUSTRATIONS

CHARTS

1 Bankruptcy cases commenced each year nationwide versus southern states 54

2 Average bankruptcy cases filed by district: U.S. courts versus southern federal courts 55

3 Bankruptcy cases filed: Districts of Southern Mississippi, South Carolina, and Eastern Tennessee 56

4 Bankruptcy cases filed: All U.S. courts, southern federal courts, and Districts of Southern Mississippi and South Carolina 57

5 Voluntary bankruptcy filings: Districts of Southern Mississippi, South Carolina, and Eastern Tennessee 57

6 Involuntary bankruptcy filings: Districts of Southern Mississippi, South Carolina, and Eastern Tennessee 58

7 Occupation of voluntary bankrupts at time of filing 88

8 Occupation of voluntary bankrupts at or near time of filing 88

9 Number of bankruptcy cases involving women 116

MAPS

1 Southern District of Mississippi voluntary bankruptcy filings by county 76

2 Southern District of Mississippi voluntary bankruptcy filings by county relative to population density 76

3 Southern District of Mississippi voluntary bankruptcy filings by county relative to white population density 77

4 Southern District of Mississippi valuation of property by county (1870 Federal Census) 77

5   District of South Carolina voluntary bankruptcy filings by county   *78*

6   District of South Carolina voluntary bankruptcy filings by county relative to population density   *78*

7   District of South Carolina voluntary bankruptcy filings by county relative to white population density   *79*

8   District of South Carolina valuation of property by county (1870 Federal Census)   *79*

9   Eastern District of Tennessee voluntary bankruptcy filings by county   *80*

10 Eastern District of Tennessee voluntary bankruptcy filings by county relative to population density   *80*

11 Eastern District of Tennessee voluntary bankruptcy filings by county relative to white population density   *81*

12 Eastern District of Tennessee valuation of property by county (1870 Federal Census)   *81*

13 Southern District of Mississippi involuntary bankruptcy filings: Residence of creditors filing against Mississippi debtors   *98*

14 District of South Carolina involuntary bankruptcy filings: Residence of creditors filing against South Carolina debtors   *98*

15 Eastern District of Tennessee involuntary bankruptcy filings: Residence of creditors filing against Tennessee debtors   *99*

TABLES

1. Leading debtor attorneys in voluntary cases   66
2. Leading attorneys for initiating creditors in involuntary cases   68
3. Incidence of voluntary bankrupts receiving discharge   85
4. Foreign-born voluntary bankrupts   87
5. Property ownership by voluntary bankrupts after discharge   90
6. Property ownership by wives and mothers of male voluntary bankrupts   91
7. Residence of filing creditors in involuntary bankruptcy cases   100
8. Marital status of women involved in bankruptcy cases   113
9. Characteristics of women involved in bankruptcy cases   114

ACKNOWLEDGMENTS

The debts that I have incurred in the course of this work are many. Numerous people and institutions have contributed in ways that I can never repay. George Forgie represents what every graduate student would hope for in a dissertation adviser: a scholar who possesses a wealth of knowledge and who is accessible, who is helpful no matter how large or small the question, and who is a strong advocate of rigorous scholarly inquiry. The other members of my dissertation committee proved similarly invaluable. Shearer Davis Bowman, William Forbath, Brian Levack, and James Sidbury all provided insightful comments. Their thorough, careful analysis enhanced my thinking regarding both the central themes involved and the details in the study. I also profited from various other professors and colleagues at the University of Texas at Austin, including Richard Graham, Kevin Kenny, and Tom Russell. Graduate coordinator Mary Helen Quinn repeatedly and unhesitatingly supplied advice and assistance. Financial support from the Dora Bonham Fund at the University of Texas at Austin funded my travel and costs associated with dissertation research.

I am thankful to Paul Finkelman, Kermit Hall, and Timothy Huebner, editors of the Studies in the Legal History of the South series at the University of Georgia Press, for endorsing this work for publication. I am particularly grateful to Paul Finkelman and to an outside reviewer for their incisive comments on a previous draft. Press staff Walton Harris, Sandra Hudson, Derek Krissoff, and Jennifer Reichlin provided valuable assistance as I transformed the dissertation into a book. Ellen Goldlust-Gingrich employed her superior copyediting skills to strengthen the manuscript.

I am also greatly indebted for advice and support from Lawrence Friedman, Michael Klarman, and Robert Weisberg during and after my time at Stanford Law School. David Bridgman, Paul Lomio, Richard Porter, and Erika Wayne of the Stanford Law School Library consistently provided prompt and indispensable access to various source materials. At the Center for the Study of Law and Society at the University of California at Berkeley, Rosann Greenspan, Robert Kagan, and Harry Scheiber welcomed me into a vibrant environment that encouraged my production of this book. I am also grateful for valuable comments from Jeff Hummel, Stanley Kutler, Erwin Surrency, and my colleague fellows at the American Society of Legal History's Willard Hurst Legal History Institute at the University of Wisconsin at Madison in 2001, which benefited from the insight of Lawrence Friedman at the helm. Harold Hyman provided an indispensable line-by-line review of an earlier draft of this work; his suggestions and accessibility were immensely beneficial. I also thank the *American Journal of Legal History* for allowing me to reproduce text from my article, "Reconstructing the Practice: The Effects of Expanded Federal Judicial Power on Postbellum Lawyers," in chapter 4.

Research for this project allowed me to profit from the knowledge of archivists and librarians at various institutions. The staff of the National Archives—Southeast Region in East Point, Georgia, supplied noteworthy assistance. Mary Ann Hawkins, Charles Reeves, Arlene Royer, and the late Gary Fulton each unhesitatingly pulled box after box of case files, directed me to notable bankrupts, and generously shared research resources concerning the case files as I came to grips with the large quantity of records. Arlene Royer in particular provided repeated assistance both on site and via E-mail and telephone calls concerning the data. At the National Archives in Washington, D.C., Robert Ellis, Mary Frances Morrow, and Aloha South likewise provided unfailing help as they provided me with troves of rich federal court documents. The Genealogy Department staff at the Dallas Public Library contributed knowledgeable eyes and direction as I studied the federal manuscript census schedules. Appreciation for helpful assistance also goes to Mike Widener, archivist of rare books and special collections at the Tarlton Law Library at the University of Texas Law School; Sidney Thomas of the U.S. Court of Federal Claims in Washington, D.C.; and staff at the Detroit Public Library, the Library of Congress, the Maryland Historical Society Library, the Mississippi Department of Archives and History, Southern Methodist University Law Library, and the U.S. District Courts for the District of South Carolina, Eastern District of Tennessee, and Southern District of Mississippi.

Some of my greatest debts are personal ones. Alisa and Clay Sell graciously allowed me to stay at their Washington, D.C., home, conveniently located within walking distance of the Library of Congress and the National Archives. Mete Yavuzcan contributed his expert knowledge of computer graphics to aid with the charts in the book, while John Huggins employed his fine cartographic skills to create the maps. Various friends—particularly Frances Albright, Erika Allen, John Burke, Kim Celeni, Cindy Conger, Julie Forrester, Carol Glendenning, Kandis Hodges, Leslie and Doug Hoy, Susan Hurd, Tiffany Jackson, Crozier Kimzey, Kathryn and Kam Kronenberg, Ellen and Steve Miura, Marlow Muldoon, Darian Reichert, Catherine Russell, and Tim Weil—supplied encouragement and interest as I worked on the written product. Tom Luce has been a valued supporter of my writing efforts and a facilitator for them. My parents, Nancy Beth and Harry Roberts, have proved unflagging in their support of my academic pursuits; their example and encouragement have enabled me to view the world with a broad and inquisitive outlook. My brother and his wife, Whit and Kristen Roberts; my husband's parents, Peggy and Jere Thompson; and my husband's siblings and their spouses—Debbie and Michael Thompson, Carolyn and Jere Thompson, Amy and Pat Thompson, Debbie and Bruce Nelson, Kim and Mark Thornton, and Susie and Chris Thompson—have likewise provided constant and appreciated backing throughout my years of graduate education and production of this book. My daughter, Elizabeth, who arrived between the completion of my dissertation and my work on the book, consistently reminds me of life's joys beyond scholarship. To my husband, David Thompson, I owe the largest debt of all. I have told him repeatedly that without his contribution of hours of computer expertise to the database and computer graphics and his astute advice, this book would not have been completed. His generosity knows no bounds, even when his wife is spending her days reviewing nineteenth-century court records in some distant archive. He is a true friend, a treasured soul mate, and an exceptional enabler.

The Reconstruction of Southern Debtors

Introduction

It is a bill for the relief, if I may be allowed so to speak, of southern debtors, of men and women in the rebel States, and they will be the parties who will most readily hasten to embrace its benefits. —Senator Jacob M. Howard of Michigan, in opposition to the 1867 Bankruptcy Act

"Perhaps no people in the history of the world have ever been so suddenly and completely ruined as this Southern people," lamented South Carolina state judge A. P. Aldrich in 1866. "The property is gone, the labor is very uncertain, the debts remain." Along with defeat in the Civil War, white southerners suffered depreciated property values, worthless Confederate currency, a loss of laborers through wartime casualties, and a substantial financial loss from slaves' emancipation. Yet the South did not emerge from Reconstruction with a transformed economic, social, and political hierarchy. White, former Confederates often maintained control of property and ultimately regained political power in the 1870s. Many factors contributed to what Eric Foner describes as the "unfinished revolution" of Reconstruction; this study explores one, previously unappreciated contributor: the Bankruptcy Act of 1867. Two principal contentions underlie scholarly assessments of nineteenth-century U.S. bankruptcy legislation. First, the three short-lived Bankruptcy Acts of 1800, 1841, and 1867 were failures. Congressmen during the 1870s described the 1867 Act as "a swindle to debtor and creditor" and "a scourge in its desolating course."[1] The few historians who have considered the 1867 legislation have accepted this view; Charles Warren describes how "the Act of 1867 almost from the outset proved a failure and unpopular everywhere."[2] The second position is that political ideology and regional concerns shaped the groups supporting and opposing the legislation. In particular, contemporaries contended and scholars have consistently maintained that southerners opposed federal bankruptcy laws as a threat to state autonomy and agrarian debtors, while northern creditors supported federal control and debt collection available through the bankruptcy laws. David Skeel refers to the "continuous opposition" to a federal bankruptcy regime, "especially from the South and West," during the century, and contends that the "strongest opposition to federal bankruptcy came from the South." Sectional opposition to the 1867 Bankruptcy Act was strong, William Wiecek argues, as "southerners and westerners voiced their instinctive fears of federal courts and national laws providing for the collection of debts." The 1867 Act allowed for both voluntary bankruptcy (whereby debtors declared themselves bankrupt) and involuntary bankruptcy (whereby creditors initiated the filing against debtors). In operation, the "voluntary bankruptcy provisions seem to have been most unpopular in the south and west," Wiecek states, "while northeastern creditors disliked the involuntary provisions, a reaction the opposite of what one might have expected."[3] However, these contentions concerning the failure of the Bankruptcy Act of 1867 and continuous southern opposition to the legislation oversimplify or do not apply to the statute's operation in the South.

During the nineteenth century, Congress employed its constitutional power to "establish . . . uniform Laws on the subject of Bankruptcies throughout the United States" on four occasions. The legislation was always passed in reaction to an economic crisis and when political parties whose representation included the economic interests of the Middle Atlantic and New England regions had control of both the presidency and Congress. The first three measures, enacted in 1800, 1841, and 1867, were short-lived, while the 1898 legislation remained the law for most of the twentieth century. The 1800 Act was meant only to benefit creditors, but according to one nineteenth-century bankruptcy lawyer, the U.S. measure was not adapted from the English system on which it was based "to the peculiar interests of commerce in this country." The 1841 law suffered from creditor complaints that it was too friendly to debtors. When the economic crises passed, Congress responded to these criticisms by repealing these Acts.[4]

The Bankruptcy Act of 1867 lasted for eleven years, the longest tenure of the first three measures. A Republican Congress passed the 1867 statute at the height of Radical Reconstruction; legislators expressly intended the Act to mollify the commercial upheavals brought about by the Civil War. Creditors would benefit from the equitable distribution of debtors' assets; debtors would gain economic resuscitation through discharge of their debts. But charges that the federal bankruptcy system was, in Lawrence Friedman's words, "cumbersome, badly administered, and a failure in operation" led to the measure's repeal in 1878. Congressmen who repealed the Act spoke out vehemently against its faults, and historians have continued to reflect these views.[5]

These disparaging characterizations of the popular opinions and actual workings of the 1867 Act were accurate in some senses. The 1870s saw a growing number of complaints from across the country regarding inefficiency, waste, and corruption in the law's administration by federal officials. The critics included many southerners, particularly during the 1870s, a phenomenon that combined with the region's traditional antipathy to federal intrusion to lead southern congressmen to support repeal. But a more nuanced and enlightening picture than previous historiography suggests lies below this surface and can be discerned through an investigation of federal case records in the South during the life of the 1867 Bankruptcy Act.

As scholars have recognized, there is no one definition for what area composes the U.S. South: the answer has changed over time as a result of white and African American population shifts and agricultural and technological developments, including the shift of slaves from the Upper to the Lower South after the creation of the cotton gin in the late eighteenth century. Historical studies of the Reconstruction period take different stances as to whether to consider the four Upper South slave states that did not secede from the Union as part of the immediate postwar South. By 1860, Delaware, Maryland, Missouri, and Kentucky were, in William H. Freehling's words, "ambiguously southern." The secession of the other eleven slave states and the events of the Civil War made these four states all the more distinct from their southern neighbors. A primary focus of this volume—the interplay of southern ideology (in those areas where it became so extreme that it resulted in secession) with self-interest (when aided by reaping benefits granted by the former foe)—calls for a study of residents in the former Confederate states. Thus, in this volume, the *South* refers to the eleven states that had formerly seceded from the United States and formed the Confederate States of America, and *southerners* are the residents of those eleven states. However, because the four Union slave states had particular ties to the Confederate South, this book notes instances involving Kentucky, Missouri, Delaware, and Maryland residents. References to the *Union* or *northern states* include all states that remained in the Union (including slave states), reflecting the line drawn during the Civil War and still distinct during the Reconstruction era.[6]

This book sets forth four central contentions. First, the 1867 Bankruptcy Act was not a failure from the perspective of white southerners. Rather, the Act represented a well-timed source of relief and opportunity. White residents of the South embraced the law right after its passage, flocked to the courts to file for voluntary bankruptcy at a higher rate than that seen nationwide in the late 1860s, and—viewing the law as a temporary measure to address the exceptional commercial turmoil that followed the Civil War—supported the measure's repeal in 1878. Thus, in the words of an 1881 American Bar Association reporter (referring to American attitudes toward bankruptcy), southerners viewed the law as a temporary "sponge, to wipe off a vast amount of hopeless debts, and give everybody a clean slate with which to start fresh." It was a "physic to be taken in a huge dose." Once the slates were clean, the law was properly repealed. This "brief and spasmodic effort . . . at legislation" served residents of the former

Confederate states quite well.[7] The federal law catered to white southerners' economic needs at the height of Radical Reconstruction, and the Act's repeal practically coincided with the political redemption of the South after the Compromise of 1877.

Second, ideological concerns about federal intrusion, which scholars contend drove southern opposition to a national bankruptcy regime during the era, did not govern the Act's practical workings in the South. Rather, self-interest drove southerners' warm reception of the bankruptcy legislation during the late 1860s, but this self-interest did not necessarily conflict with southerners' ideological beliefs. Instead, southerners' use of the 1867 Act reflects the historical evolution of states' rights ideology in the South and its complicated interaction with self-interest.

This conclusion, as well as the intense use of the Bankruptcy Act by residents of the South, particularly at the height of Radical Reconstruction in the late 1860s, contradicts traditional views of southern attitudes toward federal bankruptcy laws, including the 1867 measure. During debates considering repeal of the 1867 Bankruptcy Act, Ohio Representative John A. McMahon summed up this view: "A bankrupt law has therefore always been . . . against the sentiment of a great portion of the people of the South as a permanent institution." This view had its roots in a long history of southern opposition that stemmed from two sources: the positions that federal bankruptcy represented an unwelcome federal intrusion into areas traditionally reserved for the states and that a federal bankruptcy regime harmed the South's agrarian interests and benefited the North's commercial markets. Underlying antebellum sentiments against federal interference (and grounding southerners' adherence to states' rights) was the fear that federal incursions would threaten the regional institution of slavery. Southern congressmen helped defeat a proposed bankruptcy act in the early 1820s, founded, as Warren notes, "on their rigid views as to any extension of the power and jurisdiction of the Federal Government and its courts." Twenty years later, votes on bills leading to the 1841 Bankruptcy Act displayed sectional divisions, with southerners opposing the legislation. In considering the 1841 law, the Charleston Chamber of Commerce expressed fears regarding the prospect of "this law to bring into immediate liquidation, under the orders of the Court, the affairs of all the insolvent debtors of the country." The chamber concluded that leaving debt settlement to "the wise and humane compromises of a people naturally sagacious" would avoid the massive sacrifices of property that would probably result under the bankruptcy law. More than half a century later, during debates concerning the 1898 Bankruptcy Act, southerners were the principal opponents. Maintaining that the bill was of no benefit to farmers, southern legislators asserted that requests for the measure came "only from rich and powerful commercial corporations, wholesale dealers and boards of trade and associated jobbers." When their opposition to the measure's enactment failed and it became law, the South's representatives repeatedly attempted to repeal the legislation during the early twentieth century.[8]

Likewise, when Congress considered the repeal of the 1867 Bankruptcy Act during the late 1870s, southern statesmen were among the law's vocal detractors. "It has worked evil, and great evil," stated Senator Samuel Maxey of Texas. Charging that the law was cumbersome, hard to understand, and inefficient, Maxey contended, "while it has worked some good, yet upon the great principle that laws should be made for the greatest good to the greatest number, it has worked in my judgment infinitely more evil than good." Further, an underlying source of southerners' complaints in the 1870s was their objection to the accretion of federal judicial power that resulted from the law. As Warren recognizes, there "was the general prevalence in the West and South of the view that the whole course of legislation since the war had gone too far in increasing the powers and jurisdiction of the Federal Courts and in removing cases out of the State Courts."[9]

Yet although a traditional ideological aversion to federal bankruptcy existed in the South, practical necessity drove thousands of southerners to employ the 1867 Act. Indeed, post–Civil War bankruptcy filers included staunch former Confederates and strong advocates of southern redemption from federal and Republican control after the Civil War. Scholars have recognized how states' rights adherents have historically ignored that ideology when it was politically advantageous or in their self-interest to do so. As Friedman has well stated, "The same people who talk about devolving government to the states are quite eager for federal intervention when it suits them." Yet with respect to the 1867 Bankruptcy Act, white southerners ultimately sacrificed neither their states' rights beliefs nor their self-interest, as thousands received economic relief through the statute and then, when the number of filings trickled, southern congressmen supported repeal of the statute (and thus diminished federal jurisdiction) in 1878. As a result, southerners' reactions to the Bankruptcy Act of 1867 highlight how they maintained their states' rights ideology during Reconstruction, albeit in a somewhat altered form, since a central motivating force behind the belief system—the protection of the institution of slavery—no longer was at issue, and accommodated that ideology to their practical needs.[10]

Third, congressmen and southerners depicted the 1867 Bankruptcy Act as distinct from Reconstruction legislation, but the Act's effects were integrally related to the outcome of Reconstruction. As Scott Sandage notes, "By the spring of 1867, advocates of the bankrupt bill had believed that it would not pass unless they could extricate it from the controversies of Reconstruction."

But nevertheless, as Charles Fairman recognizes, "In various connections the Bankruptcy Act was entwined with Reconstruction."[11] Advancing the law as a measure of benefit to the commercial classes in all sections of the country, adherents with differing political agendas represented the Bankruptcy Act as relatively politically neutral. The law was far from neutral, however, both in its effect on federal-state relations and in whom it benefited. Because the primary beneficiaries of bankruptcy relief were white, male merchants, professionals, and planters, the Act stabilized and entrenched southern society's postwar class and race structure and thus bolstered the economic, political, and social power of the demographic that had formed the leading secessionists and Confederates. Those who were insolvent could receive discharges from their debts and move forward in their economic pursuits, free from the burden of past obligations. Further, through state and federal property exemptions, bankrupts maintained considerable amounts of property, and control of land enabled the owners to maintain political and social control of the region after the war. So the law benefited those who were already established with property and assets in the late 1860s and 1870s. The use of a bankruptcy law to profit the commercial class is unsurprising; bankruptcy legislation had historically applied only to merchants. Yet the timing of passage at the height of Radical Reconstruction is notable. Both white women and African American men and women sought greater recognition of their rights—including economic rights—during the period. Married women suffered from legal disabilities that restricted their economic rights to contract and own property; their rights under state law were unevenly granted and enforced. In Patricia Allan Lucie's words, women "could well have stood to gain from a definition of [women's economic] freedom."[12]

Freedpeople argued for an ownership stake in the land that they had worked without compensation for centuries, while some Radical legislators discussed possible confiscation of former Confederates' plantations. Instead, congressmen—in chambers dominated by Republicans friendly to the interests of the freedpeople and sitting without representatives from the former Confederate states present (except for Tennesseans)—enacted a law that would be unlikely to benefit former slaves. As slaves, the freedpeople had not been legally able to hold property or engage in commerce, so they did not have assets or debts right after the war. Unless they were among the small minority of black southerners who had been free before the war and had engaged in commerce, their need for bankruptcy legislation was minimal. Passage of the Bankruptcy Act occurred during the same period when federal legislators enacted numerous laws to protect freedmen's rights and promote their interests. Yet the Bankruptcy Act, the major piece of economic legislation to affect and benefit southerners during the era, did not address—much less expand—the economic rights of white women or African Americans. Instead, it ignored them.

In sum, the Bankruptcy Act represented a conservative approach to economic Reconstruction during the postwar era, for one of the law's consequences was the reinforcement of the South's economic hierarchy. As Eric Foner notes, the political revolution based on equality went forth, but the economic revolution that took place after emancipation failed "to address significantly the economic plight of the mass of black Americans."[13] The fact that the federal bankruptcy system benefited white male propertied southerners—the leading secessionists and influential Confederates—and did not profit the freedpeople is a telling indication of the complicated aims of Republicans in the late 1860s.

Yet the law as applied by southerners was political in another, more personal way. Most of those in the South who employed the Bankruptcy Act were of the group that Congress had intended to be its beneficiaries: white men of the merchant class. Yet these men used the Act in ways that Republican congressmen had not anticipated. For example, legislators expected creditors who used the Act to be northerners. But creditors who initiated involuntary bankruptcy claims against southerners were almost as frequently from the South as from the North. These southern creditors employed the legislation to bolster their postwar economic footing and, like northern creditors, often used involuntary proceedings as a negotiating tool to promote settlement rather than as an end in themselves. Further, white male merchants—and, to a lesser degree, professionals and farmers—were the predominant defendants in involuntary proceedings. At times, these debtors worked outside of the law to defeat creditors' claims by transferring or wasting assets. The 1867 Bankruptcy Act, then, was hardly just a static measure governing proceedings in federal court. Rather, it structured relationships between southern debtors and their creditors—who often were also southerners—through the federal courthouse; the parties then bent and stretched this legal structure to fit their purposes. In this way, the law shaped economic, social, and political power relationships between debtors and creditors.[14]

Fourth, scrutiny of thousands of bankruptcy filings in three southern federal judicial districts illuminates the various roles of the southern federal courts during Reconstruction. These tribunals did not simply act as enforcers of federal legislation in the recently defeated southern states; rather, the courts also served as instruments that southerners used for their benefit: to sue, to collect claims from the government, and to file for bankruptcy. Scholars have documented well the enforcement role of the Reconstruction federal courts; this book delves into the tribunals' instrumental role for southerners. An understanding of this multifaceted relationship between southerners and the judicial arm of the federal government is essential to fully grasp the dynamics of reunion and reconstruction that took place in the former Confederate states.

The arguments in this volume are based on a broad range of sources, including thousands of lower federal court case files, manuscript census records, congressional documents, and an array of other private and governmental papers. I have relied on empirical results derived from review of more than thirty-eight hundred bankruptcy cases filed in three southern federal district courts: the District of South Carolina, the Southern District of Mississippi, and the Eastern District of Tennessee.[15] These three districts represent a cross-section of the varied geographical, economic, and political conditions in the South but also demonstrate some common postwar regional characteristics.

In contrast to Mississippi and South Carolina, East Tennessee had historically been a poor region. With its mountainous topography and only portions of the area suitable for farming, "East Tennessee remained outside the mainstream of U.S. commercial agriculture." The district diverged from other areas of the South and the rest of Tennessee in having relatively low levels of staple crop production and of wealth, a relatively low percentage of slaves among the population, and a low percentage of slaveholding families. The Civil War greatly exacerbated poverty in the region. As the East Tennessee Relief Association noted in 1864, "The patriotism of our people and the tyranny of the rebels have, naturally enough, co-operated to impoverish our country." East Tennessee was also an area of entrenched Unionism: "The history of Unionism in East Tennessee is altogether marvelous," one Unionist asserted decades after the conflict. "It has no analogy anywhere in the country."[16]

The two Deep South states of Mississippi and South Carolina stood in sharp contrast with respect to loyalty to the Union and the strength of their antebellum economies. South Carolina merited the term "Cradle of the Confederacy" since it was the first state to secede; as late as 1867, a federal court referred to Charleston as "that treason-infected city." After traveling the state during late 1865 and early 1866, an *Atlantic Monthly* correspondent concluded, "In South Carolina there is very little pretence of loyalty." He calculated that he "found less than fifty men who admitted any love for the Union." Yet another correspondent testified in 1866 that he came across "in South Carolina a more virulent animosity existing in the minds of the common people against the government and people of the North than in any other State." Economically, however, South Carolinians could not afford to be too standoffish toward the rest of the Union. Before the war, South Carolina with its chief port, Charleston, had a well-developed plantation economy and commercial trade. Although relatively untouched by Civil War fighting, the war had left the state in "utter pecuniary prostration," as the *Charleston Daily Courier* put it in 1865. Charleston stagnated. And one northern reporter compared the economic devastation of Low Country planters to "the ruin of the French nobility at the first Revolution." Economic recovery across the state was slow.[17]

Like South Carolina, Mississippi possessed an antebellum plantation culture that was drastically affected by the Civil War. As the *Jackson Clarion* concluded in 1867, the state's population was composed of "impoverished people, staggering under the weight of debt contracted before the war." Likewise, Mississippi was one of the strongholds of Confederate sentiment, and, along with South Carolina, was not "redeemed" by southern Democrats from Republican control until well into the 1870s. Lying at almost the opposite end of the Deep South from South Carolina and in the more recently settled Southwest, however, Mississippi experienced a distinct situation. As William Harris concludes, "In some ways its [postwar] characteristics and experiences were an extreme form of those common to other states of the region." Unlike South Carolina, Mississippi experienced much physical destruction as a result of the Civil War. Further, this state that had been agriculturally fruitful during the antebellum years—producing more cotton than any other state in 1860—suffered from poor crop years immediately after the war. Consequently, many Mississippians felt the postwar economic crises: wrote one state resident in 1867, "The War and almost two years failure in crops, has brought at least half our population to want."[18]

Thus, the three judicial districts examined in this volume housed populations with diverse political feelings concerning the federal government and distinct bases for their economy. But all three experienced economic prostration during the postwar period. Thus, studying these geographically, politically, and culturally distinct areas allows for a cross-regional comparison of developments in various states as well as a broad perspective on trends across the South generally.

Further, to understand the people and dynamics involved in greater detail, I focus in some instances on filings from two counties in southern Mississippi, two counties in South Carolina, and (because of the smaller number of cases involved) all counties in East Tennessee. Of the selected counties in Mississippi and South Carolina, one contains the major metropolitan area of the judicial district (Vicksburg in Warren County, Mississippi, and Charleston in Charleston County, South Carolina). The other is an average county based on property values and population in the state (Lauderdale County, Mississippi, and Anderson County, South Carolina).[19] Thus, in addition to studying all 3,810 voluntary and involuntary filings in the three districts, this study concentrates in depth at times on the 864 bankruptcy cases involving residents of these areas.

Such a process—facilitated by detailed database records created for each case considered in depth—allows for conclusions on topics ranging from parties' occupations and birthplaces to gender and race to attorneys hired and whether discharges were obtained. The result is a comprehensive picture of the people who employed the 1867 Act and the outcomes of their efforts.

Previous historiography provides a thorough grounding in the historical development of bankruptcy and insolvency laws in American history, particularly the congressional debates associated with federal legislation. Warren's 1935 publication, *Bankruptcy in United States History,* assimilates more than a century of congressional deliberations concerning bankruptcy legislation. Peter Coleman briefly analyzes the short-lived nineteenth-century bankruptcy acts in his broad investigation of insolvency and bankruptcy, *Debtors and Creditors in America,* and Skeel's comprehensive study, *Debt's Dominion: A History of Bankruptcy Law in America,* "provide[s] a political history of U.S. bankruptcy law that explains where the distinctive features of the U.S. framework came from." Although Skeel offers a useful account of the earlier federal bankruptcy laws (in what he characterizes as a "brief survey"), he concentrates on the era from the 1898 Bankruptcy Act forward. In *Republic of Debtors: Bankruptcy in the Age of American Independence,* Bruce H. Mann presents the transformation of eighteenth-century attitudes toward debt from moral reprobation to increasing acceptance of bankruptcy as a consequence of commercial life.[20] In addition, two works— Edward Balleisen's *Navigating Failure: Bankruptcy and Commercial Society in Antebellum America* and Scott Sandage's dissertation, "Deadbeats, Drunkards, and Dreamers: A Cultural History of Failure in America, 1819–1893"—provide a valuable grounding in the nineteenth-century cultural, social, legal, and business dimensions of failure.[21] Balleisen uses rich empirical data concerning filers under the 1841 Bankruptcy Act in the Southern District of New York to trace how bankrupts responded to failure and carried on with their business endeavors. His approach permits specific, quantifiable conclusions, a methodology that I also employ with regard to a different regional and temporal focus. Sandage most expansively investigates the federal bankruptcy debates surrounding the 1867 Act, focusing on how debtors and legislators came to link the idea of failure to the idea of debt slavery.[22]

This volume expands beyond previous historiography by providing the first study of the use of federal bankruptcy during the post–Civil War years. I thus explore the role of the Bankruptcy Act of 1867 in the course and outcome of Reconstruction. Economic stress and crucial shifts in relations between citizens and the federal government occurred immediately after the Civil War. The

Bankruptcy Act of 1867 served as a significant component of the federal government's involvement in private economic recovery and thus of federal action that affected private affairs. How did the traditional sectional antipathy—particularly southerners' opposition to federal bankruptcy—that contemporaries noted and various scholars have identified play out in the application of bankruptcy legislation? What does the pattern of bankruptcy cases display about the relations between southerners and the federal courts and, in a larger sense, about the complex interactions between southerners and the federal government during the postwar period? Who specifically employed the Bankruptcy Act, and with what success? What do the answers reveal about the political, economic, and social impact of bankruptcy as the predominant piece of federal economic legislation by which Reconstruction-era southerners could obtain relief? In sum, this study focuses on the Bankruptcy Act of 1867 to establish the effect of the legislation and also to investigate broader themes concerning postwar reunion, federalism, and the process of Reconstruction.

The book begins with two chapters that set out the institutional structure of the 1867 Bankruptcy Act. The first considers the congressional debates that led to its passage and the terms of the statute. The second explores the interactions between federal courts and southerners during Reconstruction, using the lens of bankruptcy proceedings to shed light on this multifaceted relationship. The text then turns to southerners' embrace of the Bankruptcy Act of 1867 and the attorneys who represented bankrupts in the federal courts. During the late 1860s, when most filings took place, southerners crowded the federal bankruptcy dockets, with rates in the region surpassing the national average; the rates then fell dramatically in the 1870s. Attorneys did not bring about the high filing rates, however; most attorneys represented only a few bankruptcy parties, a pattern that establishes that lawyers were not filing bankruptcy cases en masse but rather points to individual southerners taking the initiative to employ the Bankruptcy Act (and thus the federal courts) for personal benefit.

The next four chapters investigate various segments of the southern population that used—or did not use—the Bankruptcy Act of 1867. By tracing filing patterns geographically and analyzing filers' personal data, chapter 5 sets forth certain common characteristics of voluntary filers in the southern areas studied. Chapter 6 explores the less common but often more involved involuntary bankruptcy filings in the three districts. Chapter 7 examines how the terms of the Act and its deference to federalism and a conservative, status quo approach to economic rights resulted in a failure to address the economic position of African Americans and white married women. Chapter 8 illustrates how, like voluntary filings generally, corporation and partnership filing patterns indicate how southerners employed the bankruptcy legislation as an instrument for resuscitation.

The closing chapter concerns the 1878 repeal of the Bankruptcy Act of 1867, exploring the rise of sentiments faulting the law during the 1870s, southern congressmen's role in condemning the law as inefficient and injurious, and how repeal served southerners' interests.

By 1878, both northerners' and southerners' sentiments had traveled a long way from where they were at the time of the Act's passage. Lawmakers in 1867 had represented the legislation as a neutral economic measure distinct from the politically charged Reconstruction debates of the time, and southerners welcomed the Act even while vehemently opposing other Radical Reconstruction measures. Yet the legislation was indeed intimately tied to postwar political Reconstruction, providing economic resuscitation for thousands of southerners (most of them male, white, and propertied).

CHAPTER ONE

An Act of Transcendent Importance

May it be the honor of the next Congress to lay aside minor questions, and, meeting on a common ground of mercy to the unfortunate and justice to the active business man of this country, pass with unanimity "a measure so fraught with beneficence to all, and for which they will receive the blessings of thousands." —J.F.B., *American Law Register*, 1865

March 2, 1867, was a busy and varied day at the U.S. Capitol. Frustrated by the intransigence of the erstwhile Confederate states in not accepting less extreme measures for post–Civil War reconstruction and by reports of abuses of newly legislated federal civil rights in the South, congressmen overrode President Andrew Johnson's veto of the Military Reconstruction Act. The Act represented the pinnacle of corrective postwar legislation directed at the South, dividing the former Confederate states (with the exception of Tennessee, which had already complied with Congress's Reconstruction directives) into five military districts under the control of the army and declaring that no state government existed in these areas. Each of the ten states could gain readmission to the United States by fulfilling various requirements, including ratification of the pending Fourteenth Amendment and passage of a new state constitution that conformed to the U.S. Constitution and granted African Americans the right to vote.[1]

The Military Reconstruction Act also reflected legislators' determination to inhibit President Johnson's efforts to obstruct congressional plans for southern reconstruction. With a similar goal of curbing Johnson's power, Congress on the same day adopted the Tenure of Office Act, which prohibited the president from removing certain federal officers until their replacements received Senate confirmation. Johnson's subsequent violations of this legislation formed the principal grounds for his impeachment in 1868.[2]

Also on March 2, 1867, legislators passed the Local Prejudice Act, which was integrally related to the goals of reining in white southerners' resistance to federal measures and their mistreatment of newly freed slaves, federal officers, and Unionists. This measure enabled out-of-state defendants or plaintiffs to remove their cases to federal court on grounds that they would be unable to receive fair trials in state courts because of local influence or prejudice. In enacting this law, Congress was responding to mounting evidence that southern state courts were denying out-of-state parties and government officers evenhanded trials. Although the law applied nationally, a previous version submitted by the Senate Judiciary Committee had applied only to tribunals in the South.[3]

On the same day, Congress passed what Senator Jacob Howard of Michigan termed "an act of indulgence and mercy and kindness and humanity on the part of the Government": the Bankruptcy Act of 1867. The congressmen recognized that southerners would be among those most benefited by the Bankruptcy Act, given the postwar South's impoverished condition and general insolvency. Yet the legislators, sitting without representatives of the ex-Confederate states (except a few from Tennessee), enacted the beneficent legislation.[4]

The issue of whether to allow former rebels to profit from the bankruptcy law did come up for debate, but the bill's sponsor, Senator Luke Poland of Vermont, retorted, "The subject of the rebellion and the rebels is connected with almost everything that we have here in the Senate; but I thought we had at last got upon a bill that would steer clear entirely of that." Like many other congressmen who voted for passage, Poland distinguished between political and economic measures, maintaining that "when we come to apply [the disqualifying requirement of a loyalty oath] to the ordinary transactions of life, and to say that a man shall not do business, a man shall not work out by the month unless he is able to take the test oath, I cannot agree to it."[5]

Southerners drew a similar distinction between the bankruptcy law and other Reconstruction measures. The region's newspapers reflected this two-sided stance even in areas that had been fervently secessionist. Five days after the legislation passed, the *Jackson (Mississippi) Weekly Clarion* classified the Reconstruction Act as "repugnant to the Constitution of the United States" and compared Republicans in Washington to rulers during the Spanish Inquisition, "veil[ing] under a similar pretence [of benevolence] schemes of cruelty and outrage against the people of the South." But on the first page of the same issue, the *Clarion*'s Democratic editors proclaimed, "We must congratulate the public on the passage of the Bankrupt Bill" and characterized the law as a "just and humane measure" that would "lift a heavy load from the shoulders of many who otherwise never would have thrown it off." The day after the passage of the bankruptcy legislation, the *Charleston Daily Courier,* another Democratic organ, characterized "the very important Bankrupt Bill" as a law in which "every one engaged in any of the departments of business l[i]fe is vitally interest[ed]." According to the *Courier*'s editors, "Probably at no time in the history of the country has such a measure been more desirable and necessary to general and individual welfare."[6]

Such rave reviews of the Bankruptcy Act appeared during an era of entrenched southern opposition to Radical Republican policies. Further, the legislation provided that federal courts were to have exclusive jurisdiction over bankruptcy filings. These federal tribunals served as the Republicans' preferred tools for enforcing Reconstruction policies, such as protecting citizens' civil rights and federal officers from harassment.[7] Historians who have studied lower federal court operations in the South during Reconstruction have portrayed southerners' intense opposition to the handling of civil rights and other Reconstruction measures by federal tribunals. As Robert Kaczorowski concludes, "Both a dislike of the racial and political interests served by federal courts and a desire to preserve local autonomy aroused local opposition to federal involvement in the administration of justice." This opposition reached its zenith in the late 1860s and early 1870s, when federal courts most aggressively applied Radical Reconstruction legislation.[8] But during these years—in particular the late 1860s—southerners (primarily white, propertied males) flocked to the federal courts to employ the Bankruptcy Act. Economic destitution in the former Confederate states made this resort to bankruptcy a practical necessity for thousands of people.

"Change is written upon the face of almost everything in this country," wrote Francis W. Henry in April 1865 from Mississippi. Henry, an agent for an out-of-state merchant, concluded, "Men who were wealthy at the commencement of the terrible War we have passed through are now bankrupt." Much economic turmoil and disruption of commercial transactions had resulted from the Civil War, and destitution was endemic in the South. Worthless Confederate currency and bonds, destruction of property through wartime hostilities, a loss of family laborers as a result of war casualties, and depreciated property values resulted in a population that sought relief. Particularly devastating to white owners was the uncompensated emancipation of slaves worth more than $2 billion prior to the Civil War. The war resulted in the destruction of two-thirds of the value of southerners' assessed property. During the 1860s, while northerners' wealth swelled by 50 percent, southerners' wealth decreased by 60 percent, half of which resulted from slaves' emancipation. As a *New York Times* correspondent reported in June 1865, "Extreme poverty rules in almost every household."[9]

Further, the war had interrupted commercial relations between the North and South. Estimates of the value of southerners' indebtedness to northerners in 1861 reached $300 million. Of that amount, New York merchants accounted for $159 million of the receivables, while $24.1 million was owed in Philadelphia, $19 million in Baltimore, and $7.6 million in Boston. The result was extensive insolvency among northern merchants during the first year of the Civil War. In New York, 913 merchant houses collapsed in 1861, and only 16 of 256 dry goods merchants in good standing at the inception of the conflict remained solvent after a year of fighting.[10] As Scott Sandage recognizes, "Clearly, 1861 was a turbulent year in commerce as well as in politics, and many of the ruined did not rebound with the wartime prosperity that followed." In 1862, Senator LaFayette Foster of Connecticut described the critical situation: "For two years past, trade and business have been so embarrassed in this country that failures among mercantile men, indeed, among all men who were engaged in any trade or business, have been greatly more numerous than they ever were before in this country, great as have been the previous shocks to business and credit."[11] Likewise, economic hardship became entrenched and extreme in the South. At the close of the Civil War, southerners were commonly in debt, particularly to northern creditors, and had insufficient assets to pay these liabilities.

The outcome was a flood of debt-collection suits in southern state courts after fighting ceased. Both southern and northern creditors crowded the dockets, filing forty thousand such cases in South Carolina's state tribunals between September 1865 and the close of 1866. During one week in 1866, creditors initiated more than four hundred suits in one Mississippi county. "The dockets groan under the weight of [creditors'] notes and accounts," claimed a Mississippian in 1866. "The sons of a certain character in Shakespeare's *Merchant of Venice* are abroad in the land seeking their pound of flesh." In June of that year, a meeting of citizens from the Upcountry South Carolina counties of Lexington and Edgefield recognized how "the Courts have been thrown open to creditors, and the debtors of the State suddenly placed in a condition of imminent peril." The citizens bemoaned "the prospective wide-spread ruin and desolation which must surely and inevitably result therefrom."[12]

The issue of debt relief, therefore, was at the forefront of public discussion and a primary concern of lawmakers in the South. As Eric Foner concludes, the question of how to handle the issue divided white southerners to a greater extent than any other topic during presidential Reconstruction. Debtors ranging from planters to yeomen supported laws that repudiated or postponed payment of amounts outstanding. Southerners with ideological, conservative opposition to renouncing obligations and both northern and southern creditors voiced strong opposition to debt-relief measures. In the end, southern legislators passed a varied set of laws. As Foner notes, the legislation in some cases sought to protect debtors' interests but in others represented a legislative attempt to avoid more extreme relief laws. Some statutes stayed the collection of debts for a period;

others exempted certain personal property and land from execution; still others postponed state court sessions. State courts eventually held many of these measures, particularly the stay laws, unconstitutional. Charles Warren maintains that debtors largely received the benefit intended by the laws because the measures shielded debtors from court action between the time the laws passed and when courts struck the measures down. But such stay laws—declared unconstitutional, for example, by state courts in Mississippi in 1866 and South Carolina in 1867—and the temporary postponement of court meetings hardly provided an ongoing, dependable system of debt relief for southerners. Exemptions of personal property and real estate remained effective, however, although they afforded protection only up to a certain property value; their presence provided some security and, indeed, eventually formed an important part of federal bankruptcy operations in the South.[13]

State insolvency laws afforded a more permanent system of debt relief. During the debates on the passage of the 1867 federal Bankruptcy Act, Senator Howard noted, "The whole system of bankruptcy and the system for the collection of debts have been under the complete control of the various State Legislatures and are so until now." These laws varied in particulars but commonly excused debtors from debts incurred after the insolvency measure went into effect. Relief under these state laws, however, had two considerable limitations. As Representative Thomas Ewing of Ohio noted in 1878, state insolvency laws "can have no application to debtors or contracts already existing, because of the inhibition in the Federal Constitution against State laws impairing the obligation of contracts." He added, "Moreover, the State bankrupt or insolvent laws cannot discharge the debtor from debts contracted outside of the State." Only a federal bankruptcy law could grant such relief. But the passage of the 1867 Bankruptcy Act did not suspend the operation of state insolvency laws. As Orlando Bump's bankruptcy treatise of 1875 described case holdings on the issue, "The State insolvent laws are not entirely abrogated"; rather, "they exist and operate with full vigor until the bankrupt law attaches upon the person and property of the debtor." Thus, as a contributor to the *American Law Register* described, "The doctrine seems to obtain that Congress has exclusive power to pass bankrupt laws, but that a state may exercise the right under restrictions."[14] These restrictions, however, made the state laws less serviceable than the federal legislation for those desiring broad discharges.

So while the state insolvency laws remained in effect in 1867 and state legislators passed and courts commonly struck down debt-relief measures, legislators in Washington debated and passed the Bankruptcy Act of 1867. Congress thus invoked its constitutional power to establish "uniform Laws on the subject of Bankruptcies throughout the United States," a power it had exercised only sporadically over the nearly eighty years since the ratification of the Constitution. William Harris observes the seeming incongruity of the enactment of the federal bankruptcy measure in 1867 in his study of Mississippi's presidential Reconstruction: "Ironically, the relief that debtors sought during the restoration period became, to a certain extent, a reality as a result of the policies of the federal government during the early days of the period commonly referred to in the South as Radical Reconstruction."[15] Yet congressmen who voted for passage did not view the Bankruptcy Act as ironic but rather as appropriate, acutely needed legislation to benefit the commercial classes. The congressional debates illustrate the line many representatives drew between political and economic measures and how other congressmen who opposed passage perceived the fallacy of this distinction.

In the summer of 1866, the *Washington News* lamented that "THE BANKRUPT BILL has met the same fate as at the last six sessions." By a three-vote margin, the Senate had held consideration over until the next session, the second session of the Thirty-ninth Congress. "The next session is so limited that the Bill will not be considered at all, and it will die for a resurrection in the fortieth Congress." But the process of passage was quicker than the *Washington News* editors forecast. The House had already passed the bill in March 1866, and the Senate passed the measure in February 1867. After approval of a conference committee's report ironing out differences between the two chambers' versions, legislators approved the final version on March 2, 1867.[16]

The votes reflected deep divisions on the law in both chambers. The Senate approved the bill by a vote of twenty-two to twenty. The House accepted the conference committee's version by a vote of seventy-three to seventy-one, with forty-six representatives not voting. But the "announcement of the vote . . . was received with mingled applause and hisses from members."[17]

While considering the legislation, congressmen were concerned with who would profit from the law. Legislators repeatedly named two groups as primary beneficiaries: northern creditors and southern debtors. State insolvency proceedings in the South were "very poor machinery for the collection of debts," argued Senator William Stewart of Nevada. Because the national statute would allow creditors to force delinquent debtors into bankruptcy proceedings in federal court, creditors could avoid state stay laws and local prejudice thought to exist in state proceedings. Stewart contended that the law was "a measure in favor of creditors, and of northern creditors if you please." Some legislators argued that the bankruptcy legislation would act as a sort of jubilee for southern debtors by discharging debts due to northern creditors since 1861. Senator John

Sherman of Ohio noted that creditors from Cincinnati objected to the law for this reason. But endorsements of the law flooded into Congress from the Boston Board of Trade, the New York Chamber of Commerce, and creditor groups in Cleveland, Detroit, Buffalo, Milwaukee, Chicago, St. Louis, and other urban centers. As Senator Poland concluded, "This class of persons who it is feared are going to be injured by the passage of a bankrupt law, in consequence of their holding debts against the South, are more clamorous for its passage than even the persons who desire to take the advantage of it themselves."[18]

In addition to this interest in how the law would affect northern creditors, discussion during the debates also focused on how the Bankruptcy Act would apply in the former Confederate states. Previous versions of the bill, introduced as early as 1863, had explicitly denied the benefits of the measure to former rebels. As Warren notes, fears that southerners would be the primary beneficiaries resulted in the failure of bankruptcy laws presented in previous sessions. When the bankruptcy bill came before both houses during the Thirty-ninth Congress, the proposed law no longer excluded Confederates. Yet Charles Sumner in the Senate and Thaddeus Stevens in the House attempted either to reincorporate the rebel exclusion or to require a stringent oath of past and future loyalty by all those who desired to use the Act, an oath that would have disqualified most white southerners. Sumner justified the imposition of this stringent "test oath" by asserting the interrelation between motivations for the rebellion and intersectional credit relations. "I have heard it said that certain persons at the South were moved to go into rebellion on the idea that in that way they would wipe out their debts to northern creditors," he maintained. "It seems to me that we ought not to provide them with the means." Others expressed support for a test oath requirement. Senator Samuel Pomeroy of Kansas felt that such a condition excluding rebels should at least apply until the former Confederate states had met prerequisites for reconstruction and been restored to the Union. Senator Howard displayed more extreme motives and a desire for retribution: "An immense proportion of this class at the South have been rendered bankrupt and reduced to poverty by their own criminal conduct," he charged. "Now, sir, can that class of persons, after having done all in their power with fire and sword as well as their money to destroy this Government and overthrow it, come forward consistently and claim at our hands this great act of mercy and indulgence?" Howard concluded in the negative: "Let them meet the fate they have courted."[19]

These arguments—for punishing rebels, for not allowing them any benefits, and for imposing conditions on them before restoration of their states—were familiar and often-repeated positions during congressional debates on Reconstruction measures. Yet what is intriguing is how those who supported extending the benefits of the bankruptcy measure to southerners justified this position. Senator Poland, the bill's sponsor, dismissed efforts to apply the test oath to the bankruptcy measure: "We might just as well apply it to every branch of business, to every vocation in life, it seems to me, as to apply it to this bill." To Poland, the fact that southerners had waged war against the United States did not pertain to whether they should benefit from the law. "If there is any need of a bankrupt bill anywhere there is need of it there; and are we going to exclude that whole southern country and all its people from the benefits of this law because they have been engaged in a causeless rebellion or been led into it by ambitious, unscrupulous leaders?" To him, the answer was clear: "It seems to me this is carrying the thing altogether too far." Poland did mention southern loyalists' support for the bill and how "as a mere measure of reconstruction, as a measure of settlement, as a measure to put things upon a proper basis in the South," the bankruptcy law would benefit them. And others expressed more radical points of view in favor of the law; for example, Wisconsin Senator James Doolittle took the position that sales of property in connection with bankruptcy proceedings would break up large southern landholdings into small farms.[20]

But justification for applying the law to southerners repeatedly relied on the fact that this was an economic measure and that punitive political policies did not apply. Maine Senator William Pitt Fessenden argued that "in legislating upon business affairs, matters merely of every day occurrence, having no connection with the political power of the country, no connection with any question which would tend to create difficulty hereafter, but simply affecting their pecuniary interests, their prosperity as individuals constituting communities, I am shocked at the idea of making a distinction between them and us." Likewise, in response to Stevens's fear that rebels would be undeservedly acquitted, Representative Thomas A. Jenckes of Rhode Island, who sponsored the bill in the House, stressed the economic slavery that southerners would suffer without benefit of the Act: "Will Stevens, who [for] so many years has been known as the champion of the black man, now in his old age, vote for the continued enslavement of the white man?" Jenckes maintained that if a bankruptcy law had been in place before the war "and the relation of debtor and creditor had been established uniformly in every State, would it not have been an element of union strong as the Constitution itself, because it would have bound together the business interests of every man in the country?" Jenckes stated the political/economic distinction most strongly when he described how northern creditors sought to make the same differentiation when dealing with southern creditors: "I say to [Stevens], as this creditor interest says to me, and I will try to use their own language, 'We know our debtors; we wish to meet them as commercial men, mercantile men, business men; we do not care to know whether they have been rebels or not; that is a political question.'" Rather, according to Jenckes, the creditors stated, "We want to meet them upon the ground that business men meet each other upon; and let them meet us before the courts of the country."[21] To Representative Jenckes and other members of Congress, the binds of business interests, the concern of enabling men to engage in industry, and the promotion of economic well-being in the "ordinary transactions of life" trumped and indeed were distinct from the political issues concerning the South that the congressmen considered during the same session. Jenckes and his colleagues reflected themes expressed as early as 1862 by congressmen concerning the prospect of a national bankruptcy law; as Senator John P. Hale of New Hampshire maintained, "If there is any single thing which is desirable to all classes, it is that a bankrupt law should be considered on its purely mercantile and beneficent operations, not brought into the arena of party politics."[22]

Sandage argues that another theme was dominant during the bankruptcy debates: the analogy between emancipation from slavery and freedom from debt bondage. In his study of the cultural dynamics of failure in the nineteenth century, Sandage focuses on the legislative history of the 1867 Bankruptcy Act in the context of Reconstruction and emancipation, concluding that a driving force behind the 1867 legislation was the sentiment associated with freeing slaves. Debtors and congressional supporters of the 1867 measure often analogized the plight of a debtor with that of a slave and referred to "debt slaves." Sandage's arguments are worthwhile and persuasive with respect to the debates and debtor correspondence leading up to passage of the 1867 Bankruptcy Act. Indeed, such analogies were not confined to the halls of and letters to Congress. As one legal commentator noted in the *American Law Register* in 1865, "Thousands of enterprising men of extensive business knowledge are now anxiously waiting to be released from the shackles that bind them." But as Sandage notes, at the time of passage and, indeed, in various instances in previous years, congressmen attempted to divorce the bankruptcy law from political Reconstruction measures. Lawmakers realized that doing so was necessary to achieve passage.[23]

In the end, sentiments in favor of partisan and sectional neutrality and economic stability trumped, at least on paper. Congress required those filing for bankruptcy to swear their present—not their past—loyalty to the United States. As Vermont Senator George Edmunds explained, "The object of this amendment is to apply to these persons who have been rebels and who still ought to be entitled to petition in bankruptcy if they are willing to return to their allegiance."[24]

The Bankruptcy Act of 1867 was the third in the nation's history, following those enacted by Congress in 1800 and 1841. Each passed in response to an economic crisis, and both were short-lived: the 1800 legislation remained in effect for less than three years, while the 1841 Act lasted for just over a year. All three acts (as well as the subsequent 1898 Bankruptcy Act) were adopted when Republicans or their predecessor party controlled both the presidency and Congress. But various conflicts led to the short lives of the early laws. As Peter Coleman notes, the laws were repealed as a result of disputes among parties and sections as well as a lack of agreement concerning the laws' procedures and principles.[25]

The terms of these bankruptcy laws differed. The 1800 Act applied only to merchants, bankers, brokers, traders, and factors and authorized only involuntary bankruptcy proceedings, meaning that creditors could initiate bankruptcy proceedings against a debtor but debtors could not voluntarily file for bankruptcy. The Bankruptcy Act of 1841 allowed for voluntary filings by all debtors and, like the 1800 law, allowed for the filing of involuntary proceedings only against merchants, traders, bankers, and associated commercial occupations. Allowing debtors to initiate cases to declare voluntary bankruptcy was a considerable and controversial expansion of bankruptcy legislation. Opponents argued that voluntary bankruptcy was unconstitutional in that the Constitution's framers had granted Congress only the power to enact bankruptcy legislation as they knew it in 1787, which meant involuntary proceedings. But despite the controversy, the 1841 Act went into effect, resulted in the discharge of thousands of voluntary bankrupts, and was not subject to a Supreme Court ruling concerning its constitutionality before Congress repealed it. Both the 1800 and 1841 laws proved unpopular. Creditors under the 1800 Act complained of small dividends, and critics viewed the legislation as a tool for rich, speculative, and sometimes fraudulent debtors. Under the 1841 law, creditors argued that they did not receive adequate proceeds, while debtors complained that the measure did not shield property exempted by state law.[26] Similar charges of excessive court expenses and incompetent handling by federal court officials would eventually also plague the 1867 Act, but at the time of its passage, the law represented what the members of the New York Chamber of Commerce characterized as "an adequate remedy through the national tribunals" and what the *Jackson Weekly Clarion*'s editors thought would "prove a popular and beneficial law."[27]

The Bankruptcy Act of 1867 represented the first national bankruptcy law enacted, as Warren notes, "with a view to the interest of the Nation and of National commerce and not merely to the interest of individual debtors and creditors." Contemporaries viewed the legislation as a progressive measure. An 1865 contributor to the *American Law Register* praised the terms of what would eventually become the 1867 Act: "The bill before us provides more equitably for the interest of both debtor and creditor than any former law; that of April 4th 1800, which was repealed December 19th 1803, was clearly for the benefit of the creditor, while the law of 1841, in the opposite extreme, favored the debtor." In 1867, a bankruptcy attorney praised the Act because it "for the first time in this country [brought] the failing debtor and his creditors upon a ground of negotiation and adjustment equally beneficial to both." Like the 1841 law, the 1867 Bankruptcy Act authorized both voluntary and involuntary bankruptcy proceedings. Congressional authority to provide for voluntary actions had become so accepted that the matter did not even come up for debate when Congress considered the 1867 measure. In other ways, the 1867 legislation extended beyond the previous laws and generally permitted a wide range of persons to take advantage of its provisions. Both voluntary and involuntary bankruptcy were not limited to merchants and other traders, and laborers and farmers were not exempt from involuntary bankruptcy proceedings, as they had been under previous laws and would be under the Bankruptcy Act of 1898. And any resident of the United States, whether a citizen or not, could file for voluntary bankruptcy or be subject to involuntary bankruptcy.[28]

Detailed procedures governing voluntary and involuntary proceedings crowded most of the fifty sections of the lengthy 1867 statute. But the first matter addressed by the Bankruptcy Act was granting the U.S. district courts original jurisdiction over (that is, the authority to hear and conduct) all bankruptcy proceedings. As Mississippi Federal District Judge Robert A. Hill declared, the Act conferred "upon the district courts, as courts in bankruptcy, full and complete jurisdiction of the bankrupt and his estate, with all parties interested therein." The 1873 revised statutes made explicit the absolute jurisdiction of the federal courts, declaring it "exclusive of the courts of the several states." As such, as Hill noted, federal courts lacked the power to restrain state courts from proceeding with matters that affected bankruptcy proceedings, but federal tribunals did have the authority "to restrain parties litigant in the other courts, when it [became] necessary to give force and effect to the jurisdiction and powers conferred upon it under this law."[29] Likewise, in 1872, a Pennsylvania state court held that when a federal court adjudicated a person a bankrupt, the state's insolvency laws were suspended with regard to that individual.[30]

The 1867 Bankruptcy Act thus shifted the balance of power between the state and federal courts in two ways. First, because federal courts had exclusive jurisdiction over all matters pertaining to bankruptcy cases, the tribunals' authority included issues involving debts contracted by parties residing in two different states as well as obligations involving parties residing in the same state. This was a significant reallocation of power in federal-state spheres of authority. The Constitution and federal statutes had long granted federal courts concurrent power with state courts to hear cases—including debt-collection matters—involving parties who resided in different states. The rationale for granting federal courts jurisdiction over these types of cases was that it allowed out-of-state parties to avoid local prejudice that they might suffer in state courts. But states held exclusive jurisdiction over cases that arose between two resident parties.[31] Second, even if a case involving matters that touched on a bankruptcy case had already begun in a state court, the federal court could restrain the parties to the state action from proceeding further. Thus, the federal courts not only began settling matters of intrastate concern but also gained the power to stop state court activities if they infringed on federal bankruptcy jurisdiction. The result was a sphere of absolute federal judicial authority that had not existed previously (except during the brief periods during which the 1800 and 1841 Bankruptcy Acts were in existence). As South Carolina federal Circuit Judge Hugh Lennox Bond confirmed, "We do not think a state court can, by any process, prevent a party from applying to the district court for the benefit of the provisions of the bankrupt law." In this sense, the Bankruptcy Act was no less threatening to state sovereignty than the other jurisdictional statutes passed by Congress during Reconstruction. White southerners protested the incursions on state authority that resulted from these other jurisdictional statutes, but as mentioned earlier, the initial southern response to the 1867 Act was commonly positive and often enthusiastic. White southerners perceived the law as an economic measure of benefit to them and divorced from abhorred Radical Republican legislation and the harmful effects of extended federal jurisdiction.[32]

The bulk of the Act concerned the logistics of voluntary and involuntary proceedings. To initiate a voluntary bankruptcy, a person residing in the United States who owed more than three hundred dollars and was insolvent (or unable to pay off these debts) could file a petition with the federal district court that had jurisdiction over where the debtor had been living for the previous six months or the greater part of that period. At the same time, the debtor would file schedules of his debts and assets with the court. The filer would ask, as stated in one Mississippi petition, "that he may be adjudged by the Court to be a Bankrupt, within the purview of said Act; and that he may be decreed to have a *Certificate of Discharge from all his Debts* provable under same." When the judge was satisfied that the schedules and petition were correct in form, he referred the case to a register in bankruptcy. If the register confirmed that more than three hundred dollars in debts was outstanding and that the filer was unable to pay, the register issued an adjudication of bankruptcy. After notice by the marshal, the bankrupt's creditors gathered and chose an assignee, who (in Hill's words) acted as "the agent of the law for the benefit of the creditors." As an 1871 article in the *American Law Review* recognized, "The title of the bankrupt's property is in the assignee," yet "he is elected by the unsecured creditors and must not have an interest hostile to theirs." The assignee collected and distributed the bankrupt's assets among the creditors. The bankrupt could apply for a discharge from debts after six months had passed since the adjudication of bankruptcy or, if the bankrupt had had no assets to place in an assignee's hands and no creditor had proved a debt against the bankrupt (by filing, on oath, a writing that verified the amount owed), between sixty days and one year after adjudication. Discharge was not allowed if the filer had engaged in fraudulent conduct or had failed to act as required by the bankruptcy law. Creditors had the opportunity to argue that discharge should not be granted.[33] If the bankrupt had complied with the Bankruptcy Act's requirements, the court ordered the bankrupt "discharged from all Debts and Claims which by said Act are made provable against his estate" that existed on the date the bankrupt filed his petition, unless specifically excluded from discharge by the Act.[34]

In involuntary bankruptcy, a debtor would "be adjudged a bankrupt on the petition of one or more of his creditors" whose aggregate claims against the debtor equaled at least $250, provided that the debtor had engaged in an activity that constituted an "act of bankruptcy" within the past six months. Such activities included, among other acts, concealment of the debtor's property to avoid seizure under court order, a property assignment meant to defraud creditors, or a merchant's suspension of debt payments for fourteen days. The debtor then had the opportunity to have the district court, including a jury if the debtor so chose, determine whether the debtor should be declared an involuntary bankrupt. If bankruptcy was declared, the involuntary bankrupt had to submit schedules of assets and debts similar to those submitted by a voluntary bankrupt. The case then progressed like a voluntary proceeding, with the assignment and distribution of the bankrupt's assets and, if merited, the eventual discharge of the involuntary bankrupt from debts.[35]

The 1867 Bankruptcy Act represented a compromise between debtor and creditor interests. To benefit debtors, the 1867 measure exempted up to $500 of a bankrupt's personal property, including kitchen and household furniture and other articles that the assignee designated "having reference in the amount to the family, condition, and circumstances of the bankrupt." Also exempted were the clothing of the bankrupt and his family and the arms, uniforms, and equipment of those who had served in the U.S. Army or the militia. In addition, all property not included in the federal exemption that was exempt from seizure under state laws in 1864 was likewise exempted from federal bankruptcy proceedings. The aggregate value of property that a bankrupt was allowed to maintain under the federal and state exemptions (particularly in the southern states) could be substantial and could place a bankrupt in a firm economic position after discharge. In addition, a marked decrease in the value of southern farmland between 1860 and 1870 (a drop of 60 percent in South Carolina and 65 percent in Mississippi, for example) benefited debtors, allowing them to shield a greater number of acres if their state property exemption was limited by dollar amount rather than by acreage. Mississippi provides a good example of a state with generous exemptions. Mississippians who filed could exempt as homesteads 160 acres of land (with no limit on its value) or a town lot worth up to $1,500 (not counting the value of the structure on the property). A vast array of personal property was also exempt, particularly types of property that would benefit farmers or professionals. A growing crop, books valued up to $250 for a practicing lawyer or physician, two cows, twenty stock hogs, five hundred pounds of bacon or pork, and a variety of household furniture and kitchen utensils were exempt. Similarly, under Tennessee law, a bankrupt could exempt a homestead worth up to $500 as well as a cow, horse, mule, or yoke of oxen, "twenty-five barrels of corn, ten bushels of wheat, five hundred bundles of oats, five hundred bundles of fodder," "one thousand pounds of pork, slaughtered or on foot, or six hundred pounds of bacon," and an array of household utensils and furniture. In addition, agriculturalists could keep various plows, hoes, and farm implements along with additional sheep and hogs; mechanics could maintain their tools of the trade; and each white man over eighteen years old (or female head of a family) could exempt a gun. Although South Carolina's exempted personal property was less extensive than Tennessee's or Mississippi's, it too benefited those who were established in their occupations: agriculturalists could shield their "farming utensils," and mechanics could exempt their tools of trade. In addition, items including two beds and bedsteads, cooking utensils, a cow and calf, and provisions worth up to ten dollars were protected. South Carolina had repealed its homestead exemption in 1857 in response to the pleas of merchants and farmers who desperately needed to use their land as collateral to obtain credit after that year's panic. Yet, as noted in chapter 5, this repeal did not prevent South Carolinians from emerging from bankruptcy with real property in hand.[36]

In addition to property exemptions, two factors likely allowed bankrupts from South Carolina, Mississippi, and Tennessee to retain property. First, bankrupts likely took advantage of state laws passed before and after the Civil War that allowed married women to own property in their own right (a departure from common-law doctrines that vested married women's property rights in their husbands). Mississippi became the first state to grant property rights to married women when it did so in 1839, Tennessee recognized some rights by 1858, and South Carolina followed suit in its 1868 constitution. As Paul Goodman recognizes, "Planter power, codified in state law, allowed men to save their plantations by signing property over to wives and then declaring bankruptcy" (see chapter 5). Second, as courts construed the Bankruptcy Act, bankrupts who obtained discharge could maintain any assets acquired after the filing of the bankruptcy petition. Creditors had claim only to the property that a bankrupt had at the commencement of the proceedings. A discharged debtor, then, could emerge from bankruptcy with exempt land and personal property, any property that his wife held, and any property acquired since filing. The law, then, favored those who owned property at the time of filing or had ready access to property through family or subsequent business ventures.[37]

Although debtors held these various advantages, creditors received the benefit of restrictive discharge provisions: a majority of a bankrupt's creditors had to agree to discharge if the bankrupt's assets failed to pay at least 50 percent of debts. Yet creditors received only limited profit from this discharge constraint; the requirement for creditor consent did not apply to any bankruptcy cases begun before June 1, 1868.[38]

Moreover, the debtor-creditor compromise proved to be unstable; various amendments to the Bankruptcy Act occurred before it was repealed. The amendments generally benefited debtors more than creditors, and the changes always occurred in response to complaints against what users felt were unfair or cumbersome aspects of the law. An 1868 amendment provided that cases initiated any time prior to January 1, 1869, seven months later than the law had originally provided, were not subject to the requirement of creditor consent for discharge. In 1870, debtors gained another advantage through an amendment providing that the creditor-consent provision would not apply to any debts contracted before 1869. According to bankruptcy scholar Charles Jordan Tabb, the "amendments denuded the provision of what little vitality it still had." Four years later, Congress completely discarded the consent requirement in involuntary cases and eased the approval provisions in voluntary cases to require consent only from a quarter of a bankrupt's creditors who were owed at least one-third of the bankrupt's debts. The result, as the *American Law Review* pointed out, was that discharge requirements were practically void; if a voluntary bankrupt could get friendly creditors to file an involuntary case against him, the discharge conditions did not apply.[39] As discussed in subsequent chapters, southern debtors took full advantage of the relaxation of the creditor-consent requirement, flocking to file for voluntary bankruptcy in 1868.

Southern debtors in particular also benefited from amendments to provisions exempting property from bankruptcy proceedings that left bankrupts with additional property after discharge. The original statute accounted for state exemptions in place in 1864, but an 1872 amendment extended this effective date by providing for the application of state exemptions in effect in 1871.

After the Civil War, all southern and various western states had passed generous exemption laws. As Coleman recognizes, "By 1871 exemptions had grown so large in some states . . . that many creditors recovered nothing." South Carolina, for example, had by 1871 reinstated a homestead exemption including land valued up to one thousand dollars; the state also exempted personal property (including furniture, farm tools and animals, and a family library) worth up to five hundred dollars. Tennessee had increased its homestead exemption from five hundred to one thousand dollars in 1868, and the state's generous personal property exemptions remained in effect. After increasing its exemptions dramatically in 1865, Mississippi decreased its exemptions in 1870, although the state still protected a significant amount of property: in 1871, in addition to the personal property exemptions mentioned earlier, a Mississippian could exempt eighty acres of farmland regardless of value and land worth up to two thousand dollars in a town. An 1873 congressional amendment clarified that the 1872 amendment was intended to apply to debts that existed prior to the passage of the state exemption laws.[40] The result of this generous legislation at the state and national level clearly benefited bankrupts; as a commentator from Georgia noted in the *American Law Register* in 1871, "In most of the Southern States the homesteads and exemptions are so exorbitant and extravagant, that there are but few cases in which any property of the debtor is left, out of which creditors can procure their money."[41]

Although the 1867 Act afforded all persons the opportunity to file for bankruptcy, various provisions of the statute indicated whom the legislators intended to benefit. As was typical in statutory language, the Act referred to the bankrupt using the male pronoun *he*. The language of the 1867 Act thus resembled the 1841 legislation in referring to male bankrupts but varied from the 1800 Bankruptcy Act, which used both female and male pronouns for debtors.[42] In addition, the 1867 law provided that the court could require a bankrupt to appear for examination at any time during the proceedings, and, "for good cause shown, the wife of any bankrupt may be required to attend before the court, to the end that she may be examined as a witness."[43] Legislators thus viewed a bankrupt as a man. Their view is not surprising, for the members of Congress were men of the professional and commercial classes who well knew that the overwhelming majority of people involved in commerce at the time were men. But members of the House and Senate did not contemplate women filers. This measure—put forward as nonpolitical and economic—sustained the traditional view of gender relationships, with the man being involved in business transactions and the woman entering the arena only as an outsider and supporter of her husband's efforts. In that sense, the measure was quite political:

it assumed that women were not part of the realm of commercial dealings at a time when women were vocally advocating their rights to equality and when many state legislatures were passing acts that allowed married women to own property, to trade, and to possess their own wages, rights that had previously belonged solely to their husbands.[44] Yet as chapter 7 discusses, several women in the South did not conform to Congress's point of view and employed the 1867 Act to declare themselves bankrupt or to enforce their rights as creditors.

The language of the 1867 measure also indicated that legislators anticipated that men who were traders (a term also applied to merchants) would use the law to file for bankruptcy: the subjects to which a bankrupt was required to testify included "his trade and dealings with others." In addition, the terms of the statute made it more likely that merchants as opposed to other debtors would commit acts of bankruptcy and thus become subject to involuntary bankruptcy proceedings. A mere fourteen days in suspension of debt payments constituted an act of bankruptcy, but only if the debtor was a merchant, banker, or trader. As a commentator in the *American Law Review* noted in 1870, "Perhaps no single provision of the act has been discussed more frequently, or interpreted more variously, than this." The author concluded, "Courts have differed widely as to its true construction; and the difference is of more importance than might at first be supposed, since it extends to one main purpose of the law." Mississippi's Judge Hill concluded that "the object and purpose of the law-makers" in distinguishing "in the bankrupt act, between merchants, bankers, and traders, in meeting their commercial obligations, and the rest of the community, is to secure promptness and good faith with this useful class of the community." Hill noted that such prompt payment was "deemed a matter of first importance" "for the reason that the failure of one, often occasions the failure of others." Unlike previous federal bankruptcy laws, the 1867 Act allowed for the bankruptcy of corporations and partnerships, as discussed in chapter 8. This inclusion reflected the widespread use of partnerships in commercial and professional pursuits and the increasingly common use of the corporate form in business endeavors. As the predominant parties to these entities, men of trade and of the professions were the intended beneficiaries. That Congress would include provisions that specifically related to merchants and other traders and made their bankruptcy more likely than others' is not unexpected. The 1800 Act had applied only to merchants, and only merchants and other types of traders were subject to involuntary proceedings under the 1841 law.[45] Yet on its face, the 1867 Bankruptcy Act permitted all residents to file for bankruptcy. But the measure favored some parties over others and thus was not a neutral, beneficent measure; rather, the Act promoted the interests of some classes over others and consequently reinforced a certain social and political structure.

In the South, residents who took advantage of these beneficial terms not only found their interests bolstered by the statute but also encountered a federal judiciary sympathetic to their needs. As a result, the Bankruptcy Act of 1867 and its implementation by the federal courts reinforced each other and helped white propertied men experience economic—and, therefore, political and social—resuscitation.

CHAPTER TWO

The Federal District Courts in Bankruptcy Cases

We found that the [southern] people had no courts, and we said to the judges . . . "Go down and hold your courts." —President Andrew Johnson, 1866

In May 1864, almost three years prior to the passage of the 1867 Bankruptcy Act, Judge Connally F. Trigg first presided over the newly reopened federal courts for the Eastern District of Tennessee. President Abraham Lincoln had appointed Trigg, an "ardent, bold uncompromising Union man," as the judge for the three federal districts in Tennessee in July 1862. But unsettled wartime conditions in the eastern part of the state had delayed the reopening of the Eastern District for twenty-two months. Trigg's predecessor, Judge West H. Humphreys, had been an ardent secessionist, described by the *Knoxville Whig* (edited by leading Tennessee Unionist William G. Brownlow) as "an unprincipled man, a corrupt Locofoco, a dirty Disunionist." When Tennessee had seceded in May 1861, Humphreys had not bothered to submit his resignation to authorities in Washington; indeed, he was the only federal judge who went with the Confederate states who failed to officially resign. A displeased Congress had impeached, convicted, and removed Humphreys in 1862, but Humphreys simply continued his judicial duties as Confederate judge for the districts of Tennessee.[1]

When Union victories allowed Judge Trigg to take up the gavel in East Tennessee in 1864, loyalists cheered, anticipating scores of indictments of Confederates for treason. "There will be no less than five hundred indictments here; and the utter ruin of many parties will be the result," the *Knoxville Whig* predicted in November 1863. "They will find to their sorrow, that it is no small matter to engage in an effort to overthrow the Government."[2] As 1865 came to an end, the docket of East Tennessee's U.S. Circuit Court contained more than nineteen hundred indictments for giving the enemy aid and comfort and for treason. Ultimately, not one of these cases resulted in a conviction, as President Andrew Johnson's generous pardon policies enabled the indicted to obtain dismissals.

31

But these treason charges nevertheless dominated the opening terms of the federal circuit court.[3] Similarly, the first postbellum terms of the East Tennessee District Court focused on matters arising from the war, such as forfeitures under the confiscation acts and nonintercourse acts.[4]

By the time Judge George S. Bryan opened the federal courts in South Carolina in the summer of 1866, wartime treason and confiscation were not of central concern. Sixteen months after General Robert E. Lee's surrender at Appomattox and eighteen months after Union troops had occupied Charleston, the South Carolina federal tribunals concentrated on immediate postwar matters. The dockets included habeas corpus petitions by private citizens held in military custody, numerous foreign-born persons' applications for citizenship, criminal cases alleging enticement of U.S. soldiers to desert, and debt-collection cases brought by northerners. Court officials focused on digging out from wartime chaos by finding a suitable court building and prison facility and gathering "the Records and Journals of the Court[, which had] been scattered." The district court's first grand jury gratefully noticed, "When we look around and witness the Civil Courts fully organized, and know that all our wrongs and grievances will be adjudicated before a Jury of our Countrymen, instead of before Military Courts and other Tribunals of a similar character, we have ample cause to be thankful for the peace which we are now enjoying, and should ardently desire, that the sword may ever remain sheathed, and that our country may never know war any more." This sentiment was a far cry from the feelings expressed by former South Carolina Federal District Judge A. G. Magrath on November 7, 1860: in reaction to Lincoln's election as president, Magrath "left the bench divested himself of his judicial robes and declared that the temple of justice is now closed." But even Magrath, who later served as the Confederate judge for South Carolina, could not deny the necessity for making a living and attending to postwar matters; by February 1867, he was practicing before the U.S. federal tribunal.[5]

As in South Carolina, federal tribunals in the Southern District of Mississippi did not reopen until the summer of 1866, more than a year after the surrender at Appomattox, and similar housekeeping matters occupied the Mississippi federal courts. Like Judges Trigg and Bryan, Judge Robert A. Hill was newly appointed and began his tenure rectifying damage and chaos caused by the war and considering the many cases then on the court dockets. Hill ordered the clerk "to demand and receive from any person found in possession of any files or papers, record Book, or furniture belonging to or appertaining to the Clerks Office of this Court or of the District Court of this District, the delivery or possession of the same." The district court considered cases involving former slave property and parties who were now deceased. The tribunal also received the recommendation of a committee of attorneys that the court adopt the same rules of practice used before the war and obtained "specifications, of repairs necessary for the Court Room and Clerks Office and of the Office of the Marshal, and the Jury Rooms attached to this Court, and of the probable cost thereof."[6]

Less than a year after the South Carolina and southern Mississippi federal courts reopened and three years after the opening of federal tribunals in East Tennessee, the Bankruptcy Act went into effect on June 1, 1867. Thereafter, the composition of the dockets significantly shifted to accommodate scores of voluntary and involuntary bankruptcy filings. In 1868, petitioners filed 1,114 bankruptcy petitions in the District of South Carolina and 1,191 in the Southern District of Mississippi, about 500 more than the national average, and 131 filings occurred in the Eastern District of Tennessee.[7] In comparison, the number of law and equity suits filed by private citizens in each of the three districts in 1867 (the first full calendar year of postwar operation of the district courts) was less than one-fourth the number of bankruptcy filings in the districts during 1868 (the first full calendar year during which the Bankruptcy Act was in effect). And the number of 1867 law and equity filings was abnormally high, representing a postwar release of a legal bottleneck: northern and southern creditors poured into federal courts to recover debts incurred before, during, and after the Civil War.[8] Similarly, the number of bankruptcy filings in 1868 was higher than in any other year under the 1867 Bankruptcy Act. As chapters 5 and 6 will discuss, beginning in 1869, far fewer bankruptcy petitions were filed in the three districts and nationally. But cumulatively, the 1,660 bankruptcy cases brought in southern Mississippi, 1,893 filed in South Carolina, and 257 filed in East Tennessee between 1867 and the Act's repeal in 1878 represented a significant portion of the courts' dockets and called for a corresponding amount of labor by court personnel. "For a decade," Felix Frankfurter and James Landis conclude, "the Bankruptcy Act of 1867 added considerably to the business of the district courts and the Supreme Court." Indeed, in 1873, when the U.S. attorney general first began including statistics for private suits in his annual report of the federal courts, only bankruptcy and admiralty received their own categories, with the rest of the private cases (including law and equity matters) broadly classified as "Other."[9]

As the attorney general's classification connotes, bankruptcy played a central role with respect to the influence and operations of the lower federal courts during Reconstruction. This chapter will explore how the functions of and personalities serving the southern federal courts right after the Civil War encouraged southerners to crowd the federal court dockets with bankruptcy filings. The bankruptcy cases provide a means of expanding the limited focus of previous historiography in three ways.

First, historians have commonly oversimplified the role of the southern federal courts during the immediate postbellum years, thereby failing to provide an understanding of the federal courts' multifaceted relationship with litigants and the surrounding community. An appreciation of this varied relationship is vital to grasp what Jacqueline Jones describes as "the rich and complicated history of the relation between the federal government and the South since the Civil War." What Mary K. Tachau recognized in her study concerning the lower federal courts in Kentucky during the early republic applies equally to the federal courts in the South during Reconstruction: "It is doubtful whether any other branch of the federal government acted so directly upon so many people . . . as did this segment of the federal judiciary." Both U.S. troops and Freedmen's Bureau officials largely withdrew from the region within a few years after the war. The principal and permanent remaining arm of the national government was the federal courts.[10] With a diverse caseload and within a fluid political environment, federal tribunals enjoyed both public approbation and denunciation, depending on the circumstances and speaker. Bankruptcy proceedings formed an integral part of this many-sided relationship, both because they constituted a significant part of the courts' business and because they represented a type of federal proceeding that was positive and constructive in southerners' eyes, particularly in the late 1860s.

Second, court personnel—in particular, federal district judges—in Mississippi, South Carolina, and Tennessee favored local interests; this predisposition created an atmosphere that fostered southerners' use of the federal courts to file for bankruptcy. Third, perhaps even more than the varied roles of and public perceptions of the tribunals or the receptiveness of court personnel to southern interests, southerners' utilitarian view of the federal courts for bankruptcy purposes dictated much of the activity in bankruptcy proceedings. Southerners who could strenuously object to federal involvement in the South and extensions of federal jurisdiction could nevertheless employ the courts to attain economic release without seeing any inconsistency in doing so. Bankruptcy proceedings were a necessary resort for many; the federal courts filled this need. Indeed, many southerners felt that the federal government should have provided more financial aid to the region after the war. This attitude likely helped many bankrupts justify their use of the courts to receive the relief offered through the 1867 Bankruptcy Act.

Scholars habitually portray the southern federal tribunals during Reconstruction—particularly during Radical Reconstruction in the late 1860s and early 1870s—monolithically as arms of the Republican Party stationed in the former Confederate states to impose postwar congressional legislation and ensure order. Historians also stress southerners' very negative view of the federal courts. These studies' arguments are important and fundamental to understanding federal justice in the postwar South. Congress repeatedly expanded the jurisdiction and the roles of the federal judiciary during the 1860s and 1870s. Congress extended the subject matter that federal courts could consider through legislation including the Civil Rights Acts, the Enforcement Acts, and the Jurisdiction and Removal Act of 1875, which for the first time granted federal courts the full subject-matter jurisdiction allowed under the Constitution. Congress also repeatedly included provisions in statutes allowing litigants to avoid prejudice in state court proceedings by removing their cases to federal court. Federal officials, former slaves, and Unionists in the South benefited from removal allowances in legislation such as the Habeas Corpus Acts of 1863 and 1867 and Local Prejudice Law of 1867. Thus, Congress decidedly turned to the federal courts to enforce Reconstruction measures and instill northern views of law and order in the South.[11] Historians have given spicy topics such as enforcement of the Civil Rights Acts of 1866 and 1875 and the anti–Ku Klux Klan laws of the early 1870s repeated, thorough, and often quality attention.[12] These works stress southerners' vehement opposition to the enforcement of these laws and, indeed, to federal judicial operations generally. In describing federal judicial officials' efforts to implement civil rights legislation in the late 1860s and early 1870s, Robert Kaczorowski notes "the ubiquitous resistance of southern whites to federal law." He also states that the class and racial qualities of Enforcement Act prosecutions "called into question the very legitimacy of the federal court in the South." Charles Warren explains how the passage of federal habeas corpus legislation "caused great friction and intense opposition to the federal courts, particularly in southern and western states." Kermit Hall and Eric Rise note how Floridians "widely regarded the federal court as a political instrument of Republican administrations."[13]

Although such vehement opposition to federal tribunals occurred, it did not encompass the full range of southerners' feelings about the federal courts during Reconstruction. As political currents shifted during the 1860s and 1870s, so did Democratic and Republican white and black southerners' relationships to these national tribunals. Further, even during such a politically charged era, the varied components of the federal docket meant that southern attitudes toward the courts differed depending on what sort of law was at issue.

An investigation of the types of federal cases pending in 1873, the first year for which figures are available for criminal, U.S. civil, and private suits, portrays the diverse dockets of the southern federal courts and of the nation's federal courts generally. On June 30, 1873, an average of 184 civil cases between private litigants were pending in each federal district in the states of the former Confederacy.

On average, 107 of these cases were bankruptcy matters. This southern average of pending civil cases was just under two-thirds of the national average of 289 per district, but the number of bankruptcy cases in southern courts was virtually identical to the national average of 106. Thus, bankruptcy cases, on average, formed a larger proportion of the cases on southern federal dockets than of the cases on the dockets of federal courts nationally. Actions under the Enforcement Acts and revenue laws dominated the criminal docket. An average of 197 criminal cases were pending in southern federal courts in June 1873, about 80 more than the national average. An average of 90 of these criminal cases in the southern courts had been brought under the Enforcement Acts. The number of pending Enforcement Act cases reached its height in 1872 and 1873. Thus, the fact that other cases formed significant portions of the docket in 1873 reinforces the contention that throughout Reconstruction, the federal caseload was diverse. An average of 71 cases in the southern courts were prosecutions for violations of the revenue acts. The third component of the federal court caseload comprised civil cases initiated by the United States, including, among other types, customs and revenue cases as well as occasional civil cases under the Enforcement Acts (less than one per southern district). These civil suits by the government represented a significantly smaller proportion of the southern courts' dockets than criminal and private suits did: an average of 59 government-initiated civil cases per southern district were pending in June 1873. Most of these were revenue cases or classified as "miscellaneous." Although the national average of civil cases in which the United States was a party was much higher (an average of 141 per district), the countrywide average was 62 (close to the southern court average) when the Southern District of New York is omitted from the equation.[14] In sum, the federal docket in the lower federal courts in the South and nationwide dealt to a degree with controversial postwar legislation such as the Enforcement Acts as well as locally unpopular matters such as revenue law enforcement. But private suits between individuals also formed more than 40 percent of the pending docket, and bankruptcy filings represented close to 60 percent of these pending private claims in the South, even five years after 1868, when the bulk of bankruptcy filings occurred (see chapter 3).

Thus, the southern federal courts juggled various roles, enforcing unpopular laws and empowering individuals. The tribunals, for example, enabled southern (and northern) creditors to file for debt collection in federal court against southerners in other states and allowed desperate debtors and impatient creditors to initiate bankruptcy proceedings.

So it is no surprise that public attitudes toward the southern federal courts were mixed. A memorial to Judge Emory Spear, who sat on Georgia's federal district court during Reconstruction, typified negative views: "From the great mass of the people the [federal District] Court was entirely removed." As a result, "they feared it; they hated it, they kept away from it unless forced into it by its processes." Prosecutions under the revenue laws and Enforcement Acts received particular condemnation. David Corbin, the U.S. attorney in South Carolina, informed Congress, "In 1867 and 1868 the sense of the community was very much opposed to the execution of the revenue laws, very much indeed; and I had great difficulty in conducting the prosecutions there, owing to the combinations effected to evade them." By 1873, a South Carolina federal court grand jury—to Judge Bryan's vexation—had come to the conclusion that a "mass of corruption, having for its object the plunder of the treasury, ha[d] been brought to light" with respect to the revenue cases before the court. According to the grand jury, "The object in all of these cases seem[ed] to be the private gain of the prosecutors and their friends in making their per diem as witnesses in these cases out of the treasury." The jurors then warned Judge Bryan that this dishonesty "may account for the lack of respect and co-operation into which [his] court ha[d] fallen in the community."[15] Two years earlier, the *Jackson Weekly Clarion* had bemoaned the effects of Enforcement Act prosecutions, describing how defendants "had been kidnapped from their quiet homes, leaving their crops to the mercy of the grass, and their wives and little ones unprotected." In South Carolina in 1874, the editors of the *Charleston News and Courier* lamented, "It seems that the November elections have taught neither moderation nor wisdom to the subordinate officers of the Federal Court in this State." The paper published affidavits involved in an Enforcement Act prosecution "to show how the authority of the United States Government is misused and abused in order to serve the partisan purpose of those who are entrusted with its administration."[16] For these white southerners, then, federal court officials conducted Enforcement Act prosecutions not to punish those who had violently attacked and violated the civil rights of African Americans but rather to promote a Republican political agenda and unjustly victimize defenseless whites.

But more general criticisms also plagued the courts: they were inaccessible to most litigants; they met too infrequently; and their dockets were overcrowded. Even federal officers commented on these deficiencies. In 1866, a Freedmen's Bureau officer in Alabama complained to Senator Charles Sumner that the use of federal courts to enforce the Civil Rights Act was "too cumbersome for the effect," comparing it to using the world's largest ship as a ferryboat. The federal tribunals were "remote and infrequent, and homeless complainants [who were] compelled to get a livelihood where they [could], often drift[ed] out of reach and knowledge." Indeed, complaints arose throughout the country regarding the slow, burdened federal courts that had resulted from their expanded jurisdiction after the Civil War. "The dockets of all the courts are crowded," a correspondent for the *Central Law Journal* maintained in an 1875 essay on "Our Federal Judiciary." "The available judicial force is everywhere inadequate to the demands upon it," the reporter asserted. "Cases involving large amounts are delayed, until the delay becomes absolutely ruinous to suitors."[17]

Loyalty oath requirements imposed during and after the Civil War for federal judges, court officers, lawyers, and jury members hampered both the timely reopening of courts and the tribunals' ability to efficiently conduct judicial business. No federal officer could receive compensation without taking the "ironclad" oath, which included a profession that he had not supported the Confederacy. This requirement, of course, disqualified almost all white southerners. Texas Provisional Governor A. J. Hamilton complained to President Johnson in August 1865 that the oath obligations resulted in the "want of influence of the Federal courts." Johnson had a difficult task: he was not able to fill the vacant district judgeships in South Carolina and Mississippi with the appointments of Judges Bryan and Hill until the spring of 1866. Likewise, qualified court officers were also hard to locate. U.S. Attorney General James Speed could not fill the post of district attorney for South Carolina until April 1866; a Union Army veteran from the North assumed the position "as there [was] said to be no competent member of the Charleston bar willing to take the office who [could] subscribe to the oath required by law."[18] Beginning in 1865, lawyers desiring to practice in federal courts also had to profess their past loyalty to the United States. Although, as chapter 4 discusses in greater detail, the U.S. Supreme Court declared this attorney oath requirement unconstitutional in 1867, its stringent terms did not enhance the courts' standing with the local bar or among influential whites in the community, who were often the same people.

At least as damaging to southerners' perceptions of the legitimacy and efficiency of federal court operations was an oath requirement for jurors. Between 1862 and 1879, only jurors who had not voluntarily assisted the Confederate States could serve on a federal tribunal. Court personnel became frustrated because they were unable to empanel a sufficient number of jurors who could meet the oath requirements. As Drew Kershen notes, "Communication after communication poured into the office of the attorney general complaining about the practical difficulties of conducting federal judicial business when juries could not be impaneled because of the stringent requirements." Meanwhile, southern Democrats asserted that the situation resulted in biased juries packed with Republicans.[19]

But critical assessments of the federal courts represent only one side of southerners' views of the federal tribunals during Reconstruction. As Michael Perman describes, white southerners, led by Mississippi's former provisional governor, William L. Sharkey, turned to the U.S. Supreme Court in an effort to prevent implementation of the 1867 Reconstruction Act. The effort failed; the Supreme Court refused to consider the case, concluding that it was a political question outside of the Court's jurisdiction. After this dismissal in 1867, Perman maintains, former Confederates gave up hope of using the federal courts as a means to check what they viewed as unconstitutional Reconstruction measures. But political tides shifted. In his study of the enforcement of civil rights legislation, Kaczorowski notes that southern criticism of federal tribunals as partisan tools of a Republican Congress waned after 1873, when the courts stopped aggressively enforcing civil rights laws. The Supreme Court's narrow readings of the laws allowed the lower federal courts to avoid executing laws strongly opposed by influential groups of southern whites. As a result, Kaczorowski argues, whites increasingly accepted the judicial authority of the less politicized courts.[20]

Yet despite the merit of Perman's and Kaczorowski's conclusions, evidence shows that white southerners' positive views of the federal courts did not completely abate in 1867 and resurface in 1873. Rather, various sources indicate that during Reconstruction, southerners saw federal tribunals as preferable to state courts. Suppliers of this evidence were often associated with the federal courts, and their perspective thus cannot conclusively establish the proposition. But the sentiment that the federal courts were a preferred venue was common enough to be repeated. And the thousands of bankruptcy filings filed by white southerners in federal tribunals at the height of Radical Reconstruction in the late 1860s buttress this position. "Since I last wrote you I have been very much pressed with my judicial duties, arising in part from the large amount of Bankrupt causes in this State," Hill wrote from Mississippi to Chief Justice of the U.S. Supreme Court Salmon P. Chase in August 1868. "In addition to this[,] the uncertainty of the State Courts in our [present?] disorganized condition, induces almost every suit that can be brought in, or transferred into, the U.S. Court to be so done, besides the consequences of the war have greatly increased the business on the U.S[.] Docket." U.S. Attorney General Amos Akerman stated a similar sentiment in 1871: "On general grounds, I should like an increase of the judicial force of the United States in all parts of the country; especially in the South." Akerman maintained, "The State Judiciaries are not as much trusted as formerly; and all litigants, who can, will go into the United States courts, if there is accommodation for them." In 1870, the editor of the *New Orleans Picayune* wondered at the phenomenon of Louisiana conservatives turning to the federal tribunals to make claims against Radical state laws: "What reasonable man would have thought ten years ago that any of our citizens whose rights were threatened, could have gone before a federal court and solemnly sworn that he could not obtain justice in the state courts?" Five years later, South Carolina attorney Edward McCrady echoed a similar opinion in the *Central Law Journal:* "For reasons not necessary to be mentioned, the bar in this section of the country are much inclined to take their cases into the United States courts, and the dispatch of business in those courts is perhaps a matter of greater concern to us than to our brethern [sic] of those communities which have been less affected by the recent political convulsions."[21]

Although the extent of southerners' preference for the federal courts remains unclear, its existence to some degree is unmistakable. Three principal reasons likely lay behind the preference and, of particular importance here, help explain why the federal courts served as a promising venue in which southerners could file for bankruptcy.

First, various southerners' negative attitudes toward state courts during Reconstruction likely made the federal tribunals appear to be attractive alternatives for pursuing legal remedies, such as filing for bankruptcy. Although state and local courts traditionally had a reputation for representing community interests and favoring locals to the prejudice of outsiders, Reconstruction was no ordinary time in terms of court sympathies. Adopting the viewpoint of the white southern man, Wilbur J. Cash concludes, "For ten years the courts of the South were in such hands that no loyal white man could hope to find justice in them as against any Negro or any white creature of Yankee policy; for twenty years and longer they continued, in many quarters, to be in such hands that such justice was at the least doubtful." Yet as states came under Democratic control during the postwar years, the opposite tide dominated: blacks and Unionists were prosecuted and received little protection in state courts.[22] In sum, during Reconstruction, the local interests that state courts served changed as political control fluctuated. The *Vicksburg Daily Herald,* a Democratic paper, condemned Republican state judges in 1868: "HENRY WARD BEECHER said in a recent sermon that the very 'name of Judge stinks.' Wonder, which Radical Judge he had a smell of! Has he been down this way?" About two years later, the *Jackson Weekly Clarion* complained that the state judiciary's expenses showed "an excess of $81,825 in the carpet-bag era of 1870, over the year 1861, in the cost of supporting a Judiciary which, with some worthy exceptions, [was] made up chiefly of . . . charlatans and humbugs." The *Clarion* then noted, "No wonder the burthened people are clamoring for reform; and in their distress and outraged feelings are carried to the verge of desperation." In January 1876, when the state legislature first met after the Democrats had "redeemed" Mississippi, editors from Aberdeen called for the legislators "to dispose of the scum that now cumbers the bench."[23]

Similar complaints issued from South Carolina. "The Judges of olden time were distinguished alike by rare ability and spotless purity; upon them not the shadow of suspicion ever rested," assessed the *Charleston News and Courier* in 1876. "Since Reconstruction, it is needless to say, the Judiciary has not maintained its pristine reputation." Five years earlier, South Carolinian James Chesnut, who described himself to Congress as "an unpardoned rebel" and "unrepentant," negatively characterized the personnel of the state court in Kershaw County: "A more vicious and worthless body of men I have never known, with one exception." During an 1871 conservative taxpayers' convention that decried what participants viewed as the waste of the Republican state administration, Richard Lathers of Charleston depicted how "trial justices, State constables, and herd of expensive and useless officials are rapidly corrupting the people and eating out their substance."[24]

In Tennessee, prior to the Republicans' loss of political control of the state to Democrats in 1870, Governor Brownlow packed the judiciary with Republican appointees. As Thomas Alexander notes, among conservatives, "confidence in decisions was not high." Indeed, after 1870, the conservative state supreme court reversed many of the Republican judges' decisions. Consequently, prior to 1870, former Confederates felt alienated from the state courts; after 1870, Unionists believed they were unable to achieve redress through the state tribunals.[25]

Thus, during the late 1860s and early 1870s, when Republicans' power was at its height in the South, the conservative federal tribunals must have appeared comparatively welcoming to former Confederates. When the federal government offered these southerners the opportunity to relieve themselves of burdensome debt by filing under the Bankruptcy Act of 1867, the mass of white southern men who responded as voluntary bankrupts also perhaps reflects this comfort with turning to the federal courts during a time when Republicans often ruled the state courts, the other venue for legal redress and insolvency proceedings. Likewise, Unionists in areas such as East Tennessee probably saw the federal courts as a welcoming venue, particularly as the state courts became controlled by Democrats after 1870, although, as discussed subsequently, the political persuasions of the federal court judge meant that the area's Unionists were often disappointed.

The second reason that southerners found federal courts attractive was that their rulings stressed continuity in legal relations and transactions by recognizing prior legal actions—even those of Confederate courts—as valid and thus provided an element of stability in an environment of postwar chaos. In contrast to the positions of state lawmakers and courts, which shifted regarding the enforceability of wartime legal actions, federal decisions in the late 1860s and early 1870s supported the continuing validity of indebtedness, property transfers, and insurance coverage within the former Confederate states.[26] According to the circuit reporter for Chief Justice Chase, the federal decisions meant that the "acts of all the officers, agents, and employees . . . of each one of the late Confederate States, would be recognized as valid by the Federal tribunals, provided those acts were not in aid of [secession, slavery, or] the war against the Federal Government." The reporter praised Chase for his contributions to this smooth transition: "With a contrary course of decisions we should have been plunged in endless confusion." The reporter noted, "All contracts made during the war and acts done, all judicial proceedings, would have been considered void, and years of turmoil and exasperating controversy would have been before us." But Chase had "saved us all this."[27]

The Bankruptcy Act likewise contributed to this stability by recognizing the continuing validity of prior indebtedness and allowing creditors to jointly divvy up a debtor's assets. The bankruptcy legislation also granted the opportunity for debtor discharge, meaning that commercial business in the South was less likely to come to a standstill because fewer southerners would be incapacitated by debt. In addition, the continuity that the federal courts stressed in legal relations generally also likely contributed to bankruptcy claimants' eagerness to file. Creditors who initiated involuntary proceedings could be confident that the courts would recognize prior valid debts. For debtors, the federal tribunals' recognition of the breadth of debts—incurred before, during, and after the war—granted the opportunity for an extensive discharge. If the federal tribunals had left uncertain the status of commercial relations, a federal bankruptcy discharge would have been less attractive.

A third likely reason that southern filers of bankruptcy claims would have found the federal courts a welcoming venue was that the court personnel—including, in particular, the district judges—were inclined to support local interests. Bankruptcy registers handled the day-to-day administrative duties in bankruptcy cases. As federal officers, these registers were required to take the ironclad oath to affirm that they had remained loyal to the Union during the war. Evidence indicates that both northerners who moved to the former Confederate states after the Civil War and southern natives served as registers and that they were often Republicans.[28] Yet although the registers handled many aspects of cases, the district judges ruled the court and dictated certain principal decisions, such as whether a bankrupt was entitled to discharge (see chapter 1). Thus, a judge's political attitude was of concern to those who filed, since his reaction to their plight could dictate whether their experience as a bankrupt was rough or smooth.

Political scientists and historians have recognized how a judge's personal history and relationship with the surrounding community influence the judge's behavior. As Kaczorowski concludes, the studies "suggest that the longer and the more involved the connection between the judge and the community the more likely and the more strongly will he conform to and reflect local values, attitudes, interests, and objectives in his decisions."[29] In the 1867 Senate debates regarding the Bankruptcy Act, the issue of district judges' familiarity with their communities arose in the context of whether district or circuit judges would appoint bankruptcy registers. At that time, Supreme Court justices presided over circuit courts when they traveled "circuits" in various regions of the country. Senator Luke Poland of Vermont argued that district judges would be better able to appoint the registers because "the district judge, who is a resident of the State and always has been, knows the entire bar of the State [and] who would be suitable and proper men." Senator William Pitt Fessenden of Maine recognized the underlying political motives of the debate: Republican congressmen hesitated to give patronage opportunities to district judges, many of whom were Democratic appointees. But Fessenden attempted to calm such fears: "I have noticed, however, as a general rule, that judges, after they get safely on the bench in a position which they hold for life, do not trouble themselves much about these small matters." He continued, "They are very apt rather to be disposed to make friends with the bar, and make such appointments as will be satisfactory to the bar in the different parts of their district." In sum, "they become in a measure conservative."[30]

Fessenden's conclusion concerning the "conservative" disposition of district court judges after appointment was fitting for the three district judges studied in depth here. Tennessee's Judge Connally Trigg had been appointed by President Lincoln based on Trigg's reputation as an uncompromising Unionist; both George Bryan of South Carolina and Robert Hill of Mississippi had received their appointments from President Johnson after swearing that they had not voluntarily supported the Confederacy. But all three ultimately gained a reputation for serving the white conservative elements of their communities, which were often composed of former Confederates.

In December 1868, Gordon Adam, a Mississippi lawyer formerly of Massachusetts, proposed to Senator Charles Sumner the transfer of the federal court for southern Mississippi from Jackson to Vicksburg; Adam contended that the "influence of old political hacks . . . makes it positively impossible to convict at Jackson any offender against the Revenue Laws."[31] Hill, the district's judge, was a native southerner, born in North Carolina and raised in Tennessee. He had moved to Mississippi in 1855. Hill admitted to Senator Lyman Trumbull and

Chief Justice Chase that he often had to bend to local predilections, especially to gain attorneys' support in the sensitive task of enforcing Reconstruction legislation. Indeed, Hill acknowledged the influence of the community on a judge's decisions in an 1871 opinion: "Judges, no matter how learned they may be, and honest of purpose, are subject to like influences with other men, and it would be strange if under such excitement and pressure of public opinion, they would not sometimes come to conclusions to which they would not come under other circumstances."[32] After lenient sentencing by Judge Hill in Enforcement Act cases in the Northern District of Mississippi during the 1870s, a deputy marshal included a plea in a list to Attorney General Akerman requesting "necessities" for the district: "We need a judge but that I suppose we cannot have." Akerman recognized Hill's leniency and responded to a frustrated district attorney, "Yours is not the only district where the judiciary succumbs to the pressure of a local sentiment." Akerman admitted, "There is no remedy but the harsh and difficult one of impeachment."[33] Sentiments such as these led historian Everette Swinney to conclude that Hill "enforced United States laws with as much leniency as possible" and thus "won the confidence, respect, and gratitude of the Southern people."[34] This leniency, of course, often meant a lack of justice for African Americans and other southern Unionists.

Yet Judge Hill, who had been a Whig before the war and subsequently became a Republican, was not universally loved by white Mississippians, especially when he was enforcing controversial national laws. In a letter to the editor of the *Jackson Weekly Clarion* in May 1872, William from eastern Mississippi lashed out at Hill for his involvement in Enforcement Act cases: "Surely old man Hill's bowels will gush out if he does not stop the infamy of these persecutions. Poor old man! Poor old man! To live in a land from childhood, and then to be cursed by every decent man and woman and child in that land when one is old, must be bitter." Three months later, the *Weekly Clarion* characterized Hill as sitting "in all the mock majesty of civil law in harmony with the bayonet."[35] Kaczorowski points out that of the eleven federal district judges who presided over Enforcement Act trials, Hill was one of only three who supported the goals behind congressional Reconstruction. Kermit Hall portrays Hill as "a source of strength for the federal government."[36]

How can these contradictory views of Hill be harmonized? How could his constituents have esteemed him for upholding local interests and abhorred him for doing the opposite? The explanation stems from the sensitive nature of his job, southerners' fears that he would be severe in his imposition of nationalistic laws that were anathema to many white southerners, and the diverse nature of the federal court docket, which called for him to consider matters ranging from private contract disputes to Ku Klux Klan prosecutions. Yet although these conflicting assessments of Hill exist, the public perceived him by and large as having sympathy for local concerns. Harsh criticism occurred primarily at the time of the Enforcement Act cases and on similar occasions when the populace felt threatened by uncharted national laws. Once his leniency became clear, white southerners generally received Hill positively. White Mississippians achieved a comfort level with Hill, a security that they likely also felt when they filed their bankruptcy petitions in his court.

Judge Trigg's position in Tennessee was more complex. Like Hill, Trigg felt the wrath of his neighbors, particularly in East Tennessee. But censure of Trigg came increasingly from Unionists after the war as he ruled in favor of conservative former Confederates. During the early years of the war, Trigg had been, in the words of his former law partner, Oliver Temple, "an ardent, bold, uncompromising Union man, with the courage to proclaim his opinions in terms sometimes startling." Yet Temple noted how just a few months after ascending to the bench, "it became evident that [Trigg's] sympathies and feelings were all on the side of those to whom he had been lately so hostile." Unionist leader William Brownlow grumbled in November 1864 to Governor Andrew Johnson, "Our Federal Court is in Session, and I think I am not saying any thing more than the loyal people say, when I state that it is a complete farce." Brownlow was appalled that treason convictions were not being handed down: "The worst rebels and traitors, against whom indictments have been found, are all turned loose upon taking the amnesty oath." Indeed, "to go to into this rebel court is to be acquitted." By February 1865, a Memphis correspondent of Johnson's noted that East Tennessee Unionists sought to replace Trigg. In response, Trigg had traveled to Washington with a letter from the area's former Confederates, "the object being to strengthen Trigg against the terrible denunciations of Union men in East Tennessee, on account of his alleged kindness and consideration for outrageous rebels." Complaints against Trigg were wide ranging: he was charged with failing to regularly hold his court, declining to hear cases under the Enforcement Acts, neglecting to enforce federal revenue laws, showing too much partiality to defendants, and being inclined to release prisoners. As a result, in 1871, the U.S. attorney in Nashville concluded, "the Federal Courts in his hands in this State amount to very little." Two years later, George Anders, the U.S. attorney in the Eastern District, explained to the attorney general that he hesitated to present pension fraud cases to the district court: "Judge Trigg's sympathies and associations are such that I very much dislike to try such cases before him."[37]

Why did Trigg make such a switch? One late-nineteenth-century commentator concluded that Trigg curtailed punitive treason cases against former Confederates because "resentment and malice had no place in his heart." Likewise, *Goodspeed's History of Tennessee of 1887* explained how "Judge Trigg, with the same undaunted courage that he displayed in turning his back on secession, now calmly and serenely opposed and drove from the temple of justice the spirit of hate and revenge." Yet in his recent history of the Civil War era in East Tennessee, Noel Fisher contends that Trigg's conservatism led him to oppose the extremes of both secession and postwar radicalism. Whether or not these supposed sympathies governed Trigg's actions, other motivations may have also contributed. Temple admitted that no one—perhaps including Trigg—knew the real reason for his newfound loyalties, but Temple surmised, "Possibly the subtle influence of social recognition and position, then as now, so strong in the State, silently and even unconsciously, touched his ambition, or his pride, and did its potent work." Temple then tried to excuse his friend: "It is not ungrateful even to a judge to receive the flattering attention of the powerful and the rich, and to find the doors of elegant and hospitable homes at all times open to him."[38] Such flattery likely did flow to Trigg, particularly as he presided over the Middle and Western Districts of Tennessee, where the populace was more prosperous and the proportion of Confederate sympathizers was higher than in the eastern part of the state. In the bankruptcy context, it is unclear how his support for former rebels affected the number of filings in East Tennessee. The amount of federal judicial business in the Eastern District was perennially light when compared to other southern federal districts, such as southern Mississippi and South Carolina. Yet more generally, Trigg's political leanings while on the bench portray the extent to which Senator Fessenden's point applied: federal judges often became more conservative after assuming their positions. For southern filers for bankruptcy, who were usually white males of the merchant, professional, and planter classes (see chapter 5), this conservatism must have been comforting.

Judge Bryan in South Carolina resembled Trigg in two ways: both men catered to former Confederates after the war and both were, as Kaczorowski notes, "notoriously derelict" and commonly absent from their courts. But Bryan's support for white, conservative southern interests in his district did not represent a change in attitude. Rather, Bryan was tied to those interests in multiple ways. Formerly a Whig, Bryan became a Democrat after the war. He was a slaveholder and was related to or friends with numerous influential South Carolina families. Thus, his ties to local interests were strong. In trying Enforcement Act cases in the early 1870s, Circuit Judge Hugh Bond complained of Bryan's incompetence and susceptibility to local pressures: "I am in a peck of trouble with old Bryan," Bond wrote to his wife. "The democrats have got hold of him—visit him in crowds & persuade him to be a stick between our legs at every step." Bond concluded, "They have stuffed him full of the idea that the Democrats will make him Gov if he differ with me" in the Enforcement Act judgments. Three years earlier, Treasury Secretary Hugh McCulloch had complained to Attorney General William Evarts that Bryan enforced revenue laws too leniently.[39]

Indeed, Democrats endorsed Bryan's judicial actions as early as the summer of 1866, the end of his first term as district judge, when the *Charleston Daily Courier* enthused, "His Honor Judge BRYAN has given perfect satisfaction to the members of the Bar, and parties coming before him, by the patience, care and urbanity with which he has heard all cases that have been before the Court." Similarly, almost thirty years later, when Bryan died, southern writers with implicit sympathies for states' rights and the Democratic Party praised Bryan's record. An article in the 1895 *City of Charleston Year Book* claimed, "For long, long years there was no law in South Carolina, no pure administration of justice outside of the District Court of the United States." Quoting the benediction from Bryan's funeral, the article proclaimed, "He was the strong tower of the people's defence in the years when military despotism prevailed, and when the United State-Courts [*sic*] were organized to aid the political powers." The *Charleston News and Courier* gave Bryan partial credit for South Carolina's return to Democratic control in 1877: "Had the United States Court been prejudiced and partisan or corrupt, it would have been difficult, indeed, to arouse the people as they were aroused." The paper contended that the people had "achieved their deliverance," and "the good gray head, which all men know, was bowed in thankfulness."[40]

These three judges' reputations allow for reassessment of the scholarly debate regarding whether lower federal tribunals have predominantly served local or national interests. And, of particular concern in this volume, a study of these men allows for contemplation of how southern judges' consideration of thousands of bankruptcy cases under the 1867 Act influences this debate. Historians have taken various positions on the role of federal courts. Kermit Hall stresses the "persistent localism" served by nineteenth-century federal courts. Focusing on the insufficient institutional structure of the post–Civil War national courts, Hall notes how Congress expanded the tribunals' jurisdiction but did not expand the number of courts or grant sufficient funding. Flooded with cases, the courts suffered in their nationalistic mission from inadequate fiscal and structural support and, instead, catered to local concerns. As evidence, Hall points to the example of South Carolina. Congressional Republicans passed the Judiciary Act of 1869, which created nine circuit judges, to help relieve Supreme Court justices of some labors and to help enforce national laws, especially in the South, where Reconstruction measures met with resistance. According to Hall, "The two-headed circuit court system created by the Judiciary Act of 1869 did bring greater national authority into the [South Carolina federal] court through the presence of Judge Bond, but it still remained anchored to local interests, as the role of Judge Bryan fully displayed."[41] Other historians, including Mary K. Tachau in her history of federal courts in Kentucky from 1789 to 1816 and Howard Gillman in his characterization of the federal courts up to 1869, have concluded that the federal tribunals were essentially local institutions. Indeed, Gillman notes that "federal courts played an important role precisely because they were structured to be accommodating of local concerns and relatively weak carriers of national authority," buttressing the sense of an unintrusive national state in the young American republic. Tachau argues that Kentuckians approved of the district court because it supported "the perceptions and priorities of those who lived in the West" more than of "those who worked in the nation's capital."[42]

In contrast, Tony Freyer stresses how the late-nineteenth- and early-twentieth-century federal courts favored national business concerns over local business and thus spurred economic development. When business-related matters involved residents of two different states, out-of-state petitioners would file suits in federal rather than state courts because the petitioners believed that the federal tribunal was less subject to local bias and would rule in ways that supported interstate business.[43]

Scholars have sought to rectify these seemingly conflicting historiographical positions, particularly the contentions of Hall and Freyer, both of whom address late-nineteenth-century courts. Charles Zelden proposes that the tribunals attempted to enforce nationalist principles as well as to support local norms and that the seeming complexity of the courts' role arose from a variety of factors, including federalism and whether the docket included primarily cases involving public or private law.[44]

Zelden's position highlights the fact that the lower federal courts played a variety of roles during Reconstruction. The same southern federal courts that handled Enforcement Act and revenue law prosecutions also handled private debt-collection suits and bankruptcy filings. As a result, southerners had varied responses to the federal tribunals. But while handling bulging dockets and applying legislation passed at the height of the Radical Republican nationalist vision, the southern federal courts remained wedded to local interests. In South Carolina, Mississippi, and Tennessee, federal district judges consistently ruled in favor of former Confederates and often failed to aggressively implement federal laws.

Yet the courts' handling of bankruptcy proceedings under the 1867 Act adds a new wrinkle to the debate. Bankruptcy proceedings resemble private debt-collection cases in that they both involve the settlement of obligations between debtors and creditors. In this sense, they are of the same ilk as the private suits that Freyer maintains formed the core of the federal courts' nationalist role; because federal courts had jurisdiction only over private suits involving parties in different states, these private cases were initiated by a citizen of one state against a citizen of another. According to Freyer, the interests of local businesses and national firms often conflicted, and federal courts resolved these conflicts in ways that "not only favored national rather than local businesses, but economic development as well."[45] Bankruptcy proceedings, although private and based on economic matters, did not simply advance national interests. Rather, cases under the 1867 Bankruptcy Act primarily served local concerns by granting the thousands of southerners who filed for voluntary bankruptcy the opportunity to attain discharges from their debts. Yet the Bankruptcy Act served national interests as well, primarily through involuntary proceedings by which creditors (who often came from different states than the debtors against whom the creditors filed) sought to collect at least a portion of the amounts owed. So in carrying out the 1867 Act, the southern federal courts acted both as local and national tribunals simply because the terms of the Act required both roles. But in the aggregate, residents of the districts took advantage of the bankruptcy legislation more often than distant creditors. As chapter 3 discusses, the three districts studied in detail here witnessed more than eight times more voluntary filings than involuntary filings. And Judges Bryan, Hill, and Trigg's inclination to hold in favor of their white neighbors generally is reflected in the outcome of bankruptcy cases: as chapter 5 shows, voluntary bankrupts in the southern districts studied received discharges from their debts more frequently than did filers nationally.

Yet although federal court officers' sympathy for local interests likely made the prospect of filing for bankruptcy more attractive to various southerners, this arguably was not the primary factor that determined who took advantage of the 1867 Bankruptcy Act in the South. As chapter 3 will illustrate, southerners viewed the bankruptcy legislation (and thus the courts when they handled these proceedings) largely from a utilitarian perspective: southerners resisted the courts' intrusion yet simultaneously were willing to take advantage of benefits available through the courts, an attitude that southerners extended to the national government more broadly even during Radical Reconstruction in the late 1860s. An understanding of this complex dance is essential to comprehend fully the dynamics of reunion and Reconstruction. Bankruptcy filings offer insight into these intricate relations.

The economic chaos wrought by the Civil War in the South left many residents without financial means. Despite common and continuing feelings of resentment toward the conquering forces, scores of southerners applied to the federal government for aid, as an 1878 description of the work of Mississippi Senator Lucius Q. C. Lamar attests: "Scarce a mail that does not bring one or more letters from old citizens of Mississippi, (Democrats) asking favors to be done at the Patent Office, Pension Office, Land Office, Interior Department, War Department in the Treasury, before the Southern Claims Commission, information as to cotton claims, etc., etc., all of which are promptly attended to with pleasure, and of course, gratuitously." In her dissertation exploring southerners' identity from 1863 to 1868, Anne Rubin notes both many southerners' need for federal economic assistance and some southerners' difficulty in asking Yankees for help. Some people accepted employment with the federal government but "struggled to balance the economic necessity with loyalty to the cause." One reaction was to accept employment but complain about "Yankee character." A Virginia engineer "found no contradiction in hating Yankees even as he worked for them," seeing them as "a means to an end." As Rubin concludes, southerners generally appear to have excused their neighbors who sought jobs from northerners, seeing such actions as a practical necessity.[46]

Another common perspective among postwar southerners was that the federal government owed such assistance to them. Elite families in South Carolina and Richmond, Virginia, explained to journalist Whitelaw Reid in 1865 that they accepted government handouts not only for subsistence purposes but also because "they preferred to make 'the Washington government' support them." They reasoned that it "had robbed them of all they had, and now the very least it could do was to pay their expenses."[47] But federal economic assistance in the South after the war was minimal. The Freedmen's Bureau, established primarily to help former slaves, distributed basic necessities to many thousands of needy southerners. The federal government reconditioned southern railroads, primarily in its own interest, and often contributed to local economies by purchasing goods. Union soldiers also spent money in the region and sometimes gave directly to southerners. But as Samuel Ezell points out, "Southern whites in the main were left to work out their own economic destinies."[48] In the 1870s, southerners continually sought federal aid for internal improvements. In 1870, Senator Willard Warner of Alabama pleaded to his fellow legislators, "The South now needs your aid." He asked, "Dig out her harbors; give her the share of bank circulation which belongs to her; aid to build her railroads, and in every way by your practical legislation aid to upbuild her material interests . . . and . . . you will have done a wise work in the matter of the reconstruction of these states." Mississippians, for example, sought federal dollars to help rebuild the levee system along the Mississippi River, to build a transcontinental railroad that would benefit the state, and for flood damage relief. But aid to the South was not forthcoming. During the war, enterprise in the Union states had received numerous grants, appropriations, and bonds; residents in the former Confederate states now requested what they perceived as their fair share. Southerners thus presented bills requesting funds for internal improvements after the Panic of

1873. But, as C. Vann Woodward well expresses, the southerners "were informed that the Great Barbeque was over and they were too late." Rather, "it was now time for reform," and northerners provided southerners only with "lectures on economy." It was remarkable, the *New Orleans Times* noted, how "an excessive fit of economy should have seized the country when the North was gorged and the hungry South was begging a modicum of the same fostering generosity."[49]

Arguably, the most far-reaching economic assistance that the federal government provided to the postwar South was the Bankruptcy Act of 1867. Some southerners may have viewed the government as acting beneficently; others may have felt that they deserved this assistance from the federal authorities. But particularly in the late 1860s, when the number of bankruptcy filings was at its height, southerners clearly looked to the Bankruptcy Act of 1867—and likely to the federal courts when they sat as bankruptcy tribunals—as useful tools for relief. As a result, necessity and self-interest dictated southerners' use of the federal courts for bankruptcy filings. These filers quelled any ideological objections, viewed their actions as not conflicting with their adherence to states' rights principles, or adjusted their beliefs concerning the federal government and states' rights to accommodate their actions.

CHAPTER THREE

Southerners' Use of the 1867 Act

Though stripped of property, and almost a people of bankrupts, yet our race have still the advantage of property. —South Carolina Federal District Judge George A. Bryan, 1866

"It was a great boon, a great blessing, to the southern people." So Senator Augustus Merrimon of North Carolina characterized the 1867 Bankruptcy Act when he argued against its repeal in 1878. Merrimon maintained that the Act "relieved thousands of people [in the South] who otherwise would have been practically slaves to their debts and debtors for life." He lamented that thousands more southerners had not taken advantage of the Act but believed that false pride and feelings that filing would be dishonorable had kept many from initiating cases. Whether or not many more white southerners could have filed for bankruptcy, however, a considerable number did so, pouring into federal courts to file voluntary cases and often initiating involuntary cases against fellow southerners. Mississippi's *Jackson Weekly Clarion* recognized the legislation as of "transcendant importance" and praised the law for allowing people to make "a new start in the struggle of life." In testament to the prevalent use of the bankrupt law in the region, the Democratic *Vicksburg Daily Herald* proclaimed in 1868 that bankruptcy was "popular and . . . fashionable." Also during 1868, Mississippi Federal District Judge Robert A. Hill informed Chief Justice of the U.S. Supreme Court Salmon P. Chase, "This law has given great relief to those laboring under pecuniary embarrassment in this State, and is regarded[?] as an act of clemency upon the part of the North, where the largest debts are held against our Merchants and business men."[1] Throughout the late 1860s and the 1870s, the southern press advised readers of amendments to the law and significant bankruptcy rulings, coverage reflecting the law's relevance to those in the region.[2] In addition, notices of bankruptcy consistently appeared in the papers. Such notices—a legal requirement under the Bankruptcy Act—also portrayed how often people were filing in the federal courts. The first two columns of the first page of one 1869 edition of the *Jackson Weekly Mississippi Pilot* contained fourteen notices of bankruptcy (each indicating an adjudication of bankruptcy), while forty-five additional notices of bankruptcy or of sales of bankrupts' property appeared on page 3. These bankruptcy announcements took up a large portion of the four-page newspaper.³

Soon after the Act passed in March 1867, the publishers of the *Charleston Daily Courier* began offering sixteen-page pamphlets that spelled out the legislation's terms, while publishers of the *Jackson Weekly Clarion* in the early 1870s sold "bankrupt blanks" (forms for use in filing for bankruptcy) at prices that favored buyers in bulk: "75 cents per set; six sets for $4; or $7 per dozen setts." By the 1870s, bankruptcy had apparently become so familiar that advertisers used it to sell their products. In 1872, readers of the *Jackson Weekly Clarion* were asked,

> **Are you a Bankrupt?**—Do not resent this question, reader.
> It is not an impertinence. We have no right to inquire into your
> business affairs, and don't intend to. But are you Bankrupt in Health?
> If so, recruit, regulate and renovate your insolvent system with
> **Tarrant's Effervescent Seltzer Aperient**

Four years later, a large advertisement in the *Clarion* boasted of "the GREAT BANKRUPT SALES." The purveyors bragged, "People when pressed by hard times and dearth of money WILL FIND OUT where they can get the MOST GOODS FOR THEIR MONEY" and stressed "the TREMENDOUS INDUCEMENTS" being offered.⁴ These commercial statements surely reflected the economic stress of the times. As historian Eric Foner has recognized, while the whole nation endured a disastrous economic depression during the 1870s, the South suffered more acutely than other regions did: "The effects rippled through the entire economy, plunging farmers into poverty and drying up the region's already inadequate sources of credit."⁵ But the expressions also portray the common practice of referring to and employing bankruptcy during the era. Even federal officials charged with administering the 1867 Bankruptcy Act did not evade filing: South Carolina bankruptcy register Richard Carpenter submitted his voluntary petition in 1868 and listed among his assets "Fees due Petitioner in the Cases in Bankruptcy referred to him as Register by the Dist: Court of the United States."⁶ Bankruptcy and knowledge of its effects were pervasive.

Of the more than 86,000 voluntary and involuntary bankruptcy cases filed nationwide between June 1, 1867, when the Act took effect, and September 1, 1878, the effective date of the measure's repeal, more than 31,000, or 36 percent, were filed in the eleven states that had previously formed the Confederacy.⁷ These southern states composed less than 30 percent of all states and accounted for only a quarter of the nation's 1870 population.⁸ Thus, southerners filed for bankruptcy at higher rates than would be expected based on the percentage of states that they represented and their population. The vast majority of these

Chart 1. Bankruptcy cases commenced each year nationwide versus southern states

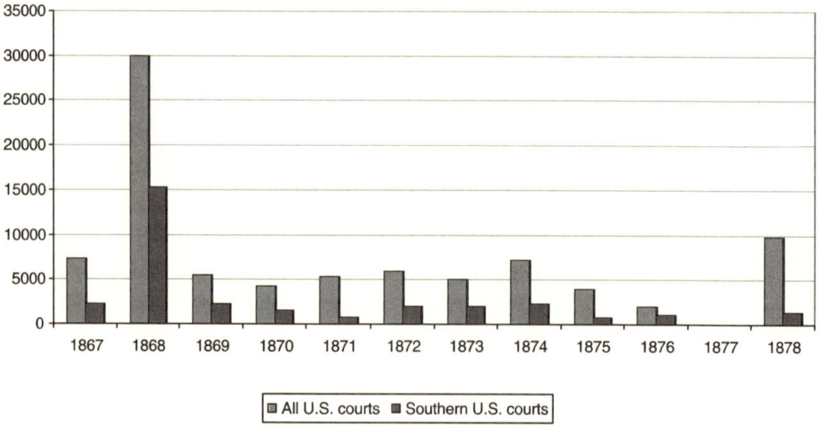

■ All U.S. courts ■ Southern U.S. courts

Sources: U.S. Senate, *Letter*; U.S. House, *Annual Report* (1873–78); Bankruptcy Case Files and Dockets (see appendix on methodology).

filings were voluntary. Between 1867 and 1871, parties nationwide initiated sixteen times more voluntary cases than involuntary cases—approximately 53,000 versus 3,300.[9] The Act, therefore, much more commonly freed debtors from their obligations than it enabled creditors to collect money owed to them. The three southern districts studied in depth follow a similar pattern: between 1867 and 1878, debtors initiated 3,406 voluntary cases, a number more than eight times greater than the 404 involuntary filings initiated by creditors.[10] Consequently, the volume of filings largely indicates the number of U.S. residents who went to the courts to try to obtain discharges from their debts.

Charts 1 and 2 illustrate two significant trends in the volume of filings under the 1867 Bankruptcy Act. First, the pattern of filings in the South largely mirrors that of the nation as a whole, with a noticeable peak in 1868 settling to substantially lower numbers of filings in subsequent years.[11] Southerners—and U.S. residents generally—thronged the federal courts in 1867 and particularly 1868 to be discharged of their debts before the requirement took effect that a majority of their creditors had to agree to the discharge if bankrupts' assets did not pay at least 50 percent of debts. The huge numbers of cases filed during 1868 indicate the extent that the 1867 Bankruptcy Act was used as a sort of jubilee for debtors.

Second, the Act was used more frequently in the southern districts than in districts nationally during the first year and a half of the Act's existence. Those in the South took advantage of the less stringent discharge provisions more frequently than filers nationwide did: cases filed in 1868 represented almost half of

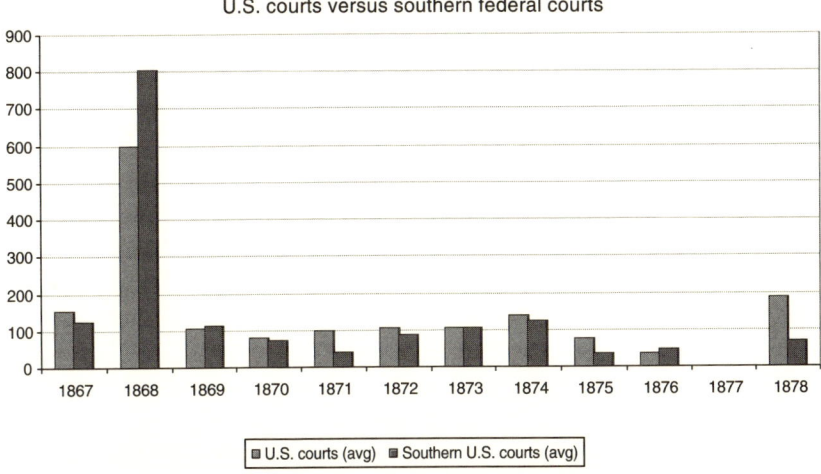

Chart 2. Average bankruptcy cases filed by district: U.S. courts versus southern federal courts

Sources: U.S. Senate, *Letter;* U.S. House, *Annual Report* (1873–78); Bankruptcy Case Files and Dockets (see appendix on methodology).

those filed in the southern federal courts under the 1867 Bankruptcy Act, while 1868 filings equaled approximately 35 percent of the cases filed under the Act nationwide. Further, a comparison of the average number of cases commenced in 1868 per U.S. federal district with the average number filed in the southern federal districts shows that the southern districts averaged roughly 800 cases, a third more than the average of about 600 cases in districts throughout the country. In contrast, however, during most of the 1870s, the average number of filings (both voluntary and involuntary) in the southern districts lagged behind that filed in the country as a whole. The average number of filings was slightly lower in the South in 1870 and was considerably lower in 1871, 1872, 1874, 1875, and 1878. Given the economic distress felt in the South during the 1870s—conditions more extreme than those faced in other regions during the economically turbulent decade—the relatively infrequent use of the Act by residents of the South and their creditors attests to the legislation's immediate postwar role.[12] Southerners used the law largely to relieve immediate needs growing out of postwar insolvency rather than as a permanent bankruptcy regime; they sought to remove debts—many of them to northern merchants—in the easiest way possible.

Yet usage of the Bankruptcy Act varied in different areas of the South. Chart 3 shows a much higher number of bankruptcy filings in the Deep South areas of southern Mississippi and South Carolina, where residents commonly held Confederate, anti-federal-government sympathies, than in Unionist eastern

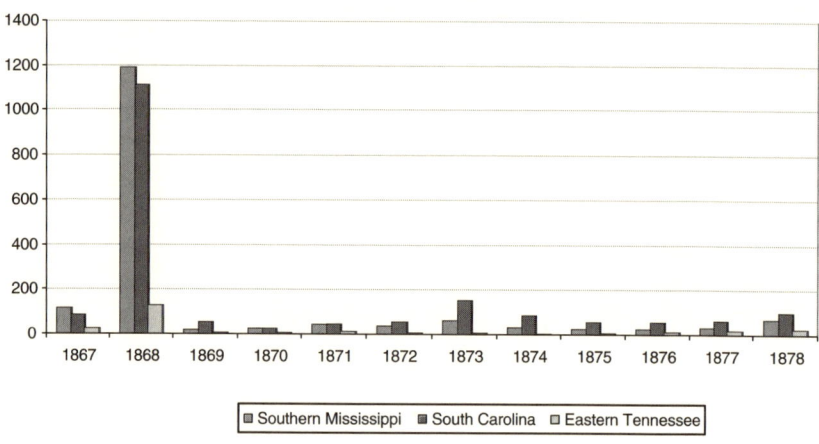

Chart 3. Bankruptcy cases filed: Districts of Southern Mississippi, South Carolina, and Eastern Tennessee

Sources: U.S. Senate, *Letter;* U.S. House, *Annual Report* (1873–78); Bankruptcy Case Files and Dockets (see appendix on methodology).

Tennessee. Indeed, by 1873, a bankruptcy register for East Tennessee remarked how "the office [of register] ha[d] almost expired for want of proper food."[13] This difference largely reflects how South Carolina and Mississippi were more economically developed and prosperous—at least before the war—than eastern Tennessee. But as the introduction and chapter 2 have discussed, Mississippians and South Carolinians did not shrink from using the federal courts despite strong sentiments from those areas against federal intrusion in southern affairs. As chart 4 shows, the number of 1868 filings in these two states was much higher than the southern or national averages.

As in the nation as a whole, voluntary cases crowded the dockets in all three districts and particularly in southern Mississippi and South Carolina, while involuntary cases were relatively scarce, as charts 5 and 6 illustrate. However, changes in the number of involuntary filings suggest another reason why no southern uproar opposing repeal of the 1867 Bankruptcy Act occurred during the 1870s. Chart 6 illustrates that although involuntary filings in the three districts fail to follow a consistent pattern, a comparatively substantial increase in the number of these creditor-initiated bankruptcy cases occurred during certain years in the 1870s, possibly as a result of creditors' reactions to the decade's financial woes, including the 1873 panic. The increased incidence of these involuntary bankruptcy cases, combined with southerners' decreasing penchant for filing voluntary bankruptcy cases, meant that the 1867 Act played a different role in the 1870s than it had in the late 1860s in the South.

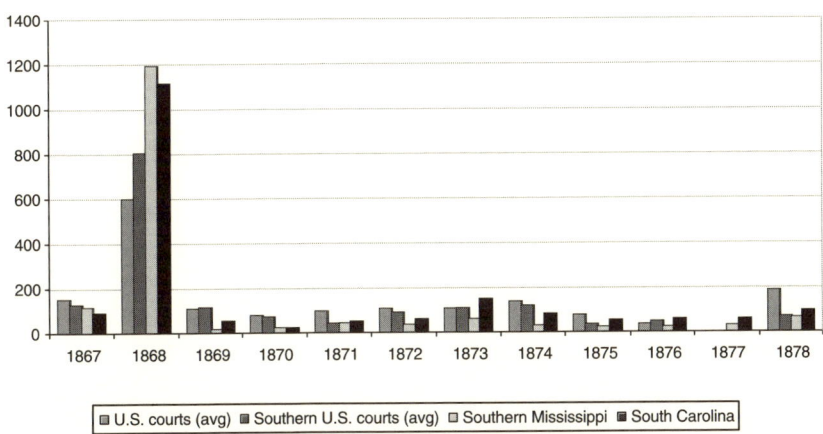

Chart 4. Bankruptcy cases filed: All U.S. courts, southern federal courts, and Districts of Southern Mississippi and South Carolina

Sources: U.S. Senate, *Letter;* U.S. House, *Annual Report* (1873–78); Bankruptcy Case Files and Dockets (see appendix on methodology).

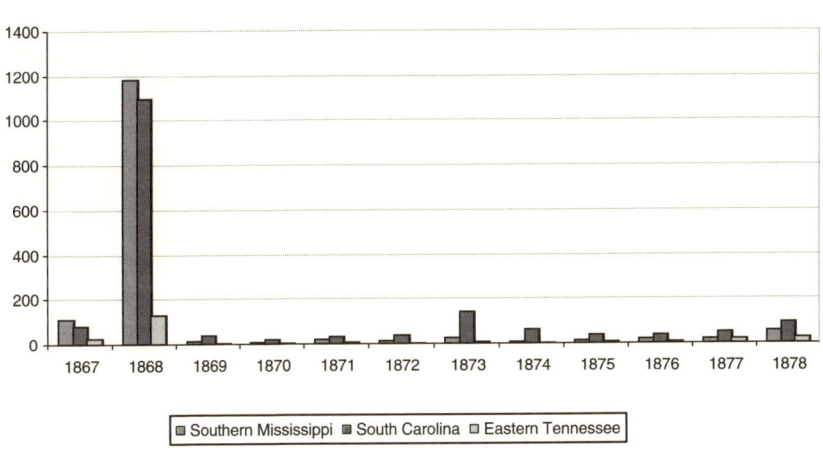

Chart 5. Voluntary bankruptcy filings: Districts of Southern Mississippi, South Carolina, and Eastern Tennessee

Sources: Bankruptcy Case Files and Dockets (see appendix on methodology).

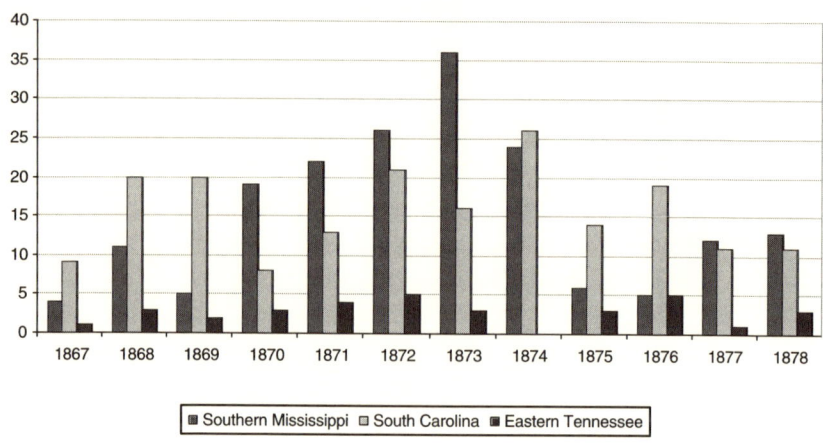

Chart 6. Involuntary bankruptcy filings: Districts of Southern Mississippi, South Carolina, and Eastern Tennessee

Sources: Bankruptcy Case Files and Dockets (see appendix on methodology).

Thus, thousands of southern debtors did not perceive the 1867 Bankruptcy Act as a failure (despite the assessment of contemporaries and later scholars) but rather saw it as serving their needs, particularly as they employed the legislation most actively in the late 1860s to relieve their economic burdens. The decrease in southern voluntary filings during the 1870s may have resulted from more stringent requirements for discharge or because southerners felt that the statute had already served their needs, but the Bankruptcy Act unquestionably benefited many in the former Confederacy.

Southerners who desired to benefit from the Act almost without exception sought the services of attorneys. An investigation of these attorneys, their practices, and their role in determining who filed for bankruptcy is necessary to fully understand the dynamics of the Act's operation. Did attorneys churn bankruptcy claims—and thus attorney's fees—by encouraging mass filings? Or did the bankrupts frequently initiate the filing of voluntary bankruptcy petitions? As the following chapter explains, the answer appears to be the latter, which again reinforces the idea that southerners in economic straits welcomed the 1867 Bankruptcy Act.

CHAPTER FOUR

Southern Attorneys as Bankruptcy Counsel

The staid and sober man of the law must wait till a return of peace shall bring with it the blessings of lawsuits. —Harvard Law School Closing Lecture by Bussey Professor, 1864

"As a body, I believe, the members of the Bar have fared better here than in other parts of the State, but the most fortunate of us have hardly done more than make a living." So prominent Charleston attorney M. P. O'Connor assessed the lot of his fellow lawyers in September 1868. "Things are very little better here than in the interior," O'Connor gauged. "Our merchants are gloomy, trade is stagnant, and every interest is suffering." O'Connor knew of this economic stress from his clients; he represented the second Charlestonian to file for bankruptcy under the 1867 Bankruptcy Act and a dozen who filed thereafter. Across the South, poverty was rampant. Creditors scurried to collect on debts incurred prior to, during, and after the Civil War. Lawyers in southern states represented clients in the scores of debtor-creditor cases that crowded state and federal court dockets, but Mississippi attorneys, for example, found such business less than lucrative, since some clients could not pay their fees. Yet creative advocates found new sources of revenue: a Florida attorney and other lawyers began serving as collection agents and investigators for northern creditors. Competition among attorneys in such places as Warren County, Mississippi, intensified, with the bar growing from twenty-one in 1860 to forty-eight in 1870. "If we do not have an abundance of lawyers," the *Vicksburg Daily Herald* commented ironically in 1865, "it will not be for want of lawyers." Similarly, by the mid-1870s, the *Charleston News and Courier* lamented the large number of new attorneys that had resulted from "the loose manner in which admissions to the Bar [were] conducted" and pleaded that the examination of candidates serve as "a true safeguard to the profession."[1] Yet postwar attorneys did not suffer solely from competition and economic stress; that many of them were associated with the Confederate cause also proved a hindrance. As Supreme Court Justice Samuel F. Miller recognized in 1867, "if all the members of the legal profession in the States lately in insurrection had possessed the qualification of a loyal and faithful allegiance to the government, we should have been spared the horrors of the Rebellion." Attorneys who had been disloyal could not practice in federal courts between 1865 and 1867. Other attorneys suffered more extreme penalties: a leading East Tennessee lawyer and former member of Congress, William H. Sneed, was one of the thousands of southerners indicted for treason in 1865.[2]

Although postwar southern attorneys felt the effects of the region's economic doldrums, experienced increased competition, and contended with the effects of past loyalty to the Confederacy, one primary factor governed their activities during Reconstruction: the need to make a living. Even if these attorneys were not pleased with the war's outcome, they needed to move forward and acquire sources of revenue, and serving as counsel in bankruptcy cases offered one such opportunity. Parties were allowed to represent themselves in federal court, but, as Tennessee Federal District Judge Connally Trigg noted in 1865, "In practice, . . . causes in those courts [were] generally, if not universally, managed by the assistance of the attorneys at law." Indeed, of the 864 bankruptcy cases studied in depth from East Tennessee and counties in South Carolina and southern Mississippi, in only 6 claims did filers elect to represent themselves.[3] Thus, the more than 30,000 bankruptcy cases filed in southern federal courts served as promising avenues through which attorneys could generate revenue.

In an attempt to acquire legal work, Vicksburg attorneys McGarr and Smedes pledged in 1868 that they would "attend to all business entrusted to their care." In their law card (or advertisement) in the *Vicksburg Daily Herald,* the two lawyers first mentioned that "they practice in all the Courts of the Third Judicial District of the State and in the High Court of Errors and Appeals," making clear that their primary practice was before the state courts. But the advertisement then noted that McGarr and Smedes "have all the necessary forms to suit cases of Bankruptcy, and are prepared to attend to all cases of that nature."[4] McGarr and Smedes did not mention the fact that they practiced in the federal courts or that the bankruptcy cases were federal proceedings. In fact, the advertisement implies that the bankruptcy cases were not connected with a certain tribunal. Yet McGarr and Smedes, either together or separately, represented parties in sixteen cases involving bankrupts from Warren County under the 1867 Bankruptcy Act in the Federal District Court for the Southern District of Mississippi.

McGarr and Smedes's advertisement indicates that like their lay neighbors, southern lawyers did not necessarily connect bankruptcy proceedings with the judicial arm of the conquering national government, or if they did, they may have tried to obscure the fact from potential clients. Rather, the two attorneys focused more on the practical economic needs of those around them and sought to capitalize on those needs. However, as McGarr and Smedes's law card also makes clear, they were not purely bankruptcy specialists. Rather, they had a general practice before the courts in the state; bankruptcy was a component—indeed, an appendage—to their overall workload. Evidence from bankruptcy filings in South Carolina, East Tennessee, and southern Mississippi indicates that other lawyers who served as bankruptcy counsel followed the same approach as McGarr and Smedes, with bankruptcy as but one element of a broader practice. In the three districts, many different lawyers filed a few bankruptcy filings. As a result, bankruptcy representation under the 1867 Bankruptcy Act was neither highly concentrated nor specialized. There were relatively few leading bankruptcy attorneys, defined as solo practitioners or firms that served as counsel in ten or more voluntary or involuntary claims. Five out of the fifty-five law firms or solo practitioners that served Charleston County voluntary bankrupts were leading attorneys. Similarly, only about one of every ten lawyers representing voluntary bankrupts in Warren or Lauderdale Counties, Mississippi, and Anderson County, South Carolina, represented more than ten filings, while only 4 percent of the seventy-five attorneys for voluntary filers in East Tennessee were leading bankruptcy attorneys. The same pattern held true in the representation of initiating creditors in involuntary filings, where only one firm in each of Charleston, Lauderdale, and Warren Counties provided counsel to initiating creditors in more than ten involuntary bankruptcy cases. In Anderson County, South Carolina, and East Tennessee, there were no leading firms in involuntary cases. Thus, concentration of bankruptcy filings in a particular legal practice was rare, and no attorneys or firms dominated.

This conclusion of widespread representation leads to the two principal arguments set forth in this chapter. First, the fact that representation of parties in bankruptcy cases was spread among many lawyers and that no attorneys filed many cases at one time indicates that attorneys were not churning bankruptcy claims (drumming up business and then filing claims in bulk). The distribution of legal representation implies that lawyers were not gathering potential bankruptcy filers in masse through printed or personal solicitation but rather that bankrupts or creditors were instigating the process.[5]

Second, southern attorneys during Reconstruction, including prominent secessionists, eagerly sought to practice before the federal courts; as part of this effort, the lawyers had a federal statute that restricted former Confederates from practicing before federal courts deemed unconstitutional. Furthermore, federal court personnel proved welcoming to attorneys who had recently advocated secession from the United States, adopting lenient policies that permitted such lawyers to practice. A primary reason for southern attorneys' attraction to practicing before the federal tribunals was economic: representation in federal cases provided a welcome source of income, particularly during the financially tight post–Civil War years. Thus, ideological opposition to federal policies, which dictated southern attorneys' aggressive resistance to federal law in Ku Klux Klan trials, for example, was not at issue in bankruptcy representation.[6] As O'Connor noted in 1868, lawyers, like other southerners, strove to make ends meet in an economically depressed region after the Civil War. In this sense, lawyers from South Carolina to southern Mississippi to East Tennessee resembled the nineteenth-century North Carolina attorneys described by historian Gail Williams O'Brien: they "were neither economists nor philosophers; they were practical men concerned with making a living."[7]

The nineteenth-century bankruptcy bar was inchoate. As David Skeel notes in his valuable study of bankruptcy in U.S. history, not until the twentieth century did a permanent bankruptcy bar come into existence; the long life of the Bankruptcy Act of 1898 allowed attorneys to develop specialized practices. In contrast, the short-lived nineteenth-century Bankruptcy Acts of 1800, 1841, and 1867 did not permit such entrenchment. Most nineteenth-century attorneys practiced alone and represented clients in a broad variety of matters. This model was particularly dominant in the South, where lawyers continued to serve as solo practitioners engaged in general practice after the Civil War even while legal elites in the Northeast and Midwest began gathering into firms of five or more attorneys. At the core of many attorneys' practices was collecting debts for their creditor clients. As a result, when federal bankruptcy acts went into effect sporadically throughout the nineteenth century, lawyers' representation in bankruptcy matters was, as historian Edward Balleisen puts it in his work on the 1841 Act, just "an extension of their most basic stock in trade—debt collection and the handling of matters related to real estate." When the Bankruptcy Acts were repealed, as Skeel notes, lawyers simply continued to tend to their accustomed workload of collection efforts and other cases.[8]

But while the bankruptcy laws were operative, attorneys performed many tasks in bankruptcy proceedings. Lawyers who represented voluntary bankrupts often assisted in preparing and filing petitions and schedules of assets and debts and represented their clients in matters related to the petitions—for example, disputes with creditors or matters related to discharge. Lawyers also served creditors who initiated involuntary proceedings, objected to discharges in voluntary proceedings, or filed proofs that bankrupts owed money to the creditors. Defendants in involuntary cases also turned to legal counsel to fend off suits and represent their rights.[9]

Yet attorney representation patterns in East Tennessee, southern Mississippi, and South Carolina indicate that these attractive opportunities for representation (and thus fees) did not result in a few southern attorneys dominating bankruptcy practice under the 1867 Act. Rather, the representation of voluntary bankrupts in these three southern districts was widespread. What Skeel concludes concerning nineteenth-century bankruptcy practice in general applies to southern attorneys after the Civil War: "Specialization was relatively unusual," and "for thousands of attorneys, the bankruptcy acts provided one or a small number of cases." Skeel maintains that this finding also holds true for the 1867 Act, as "bankruptcy remained a limited, peripheral practice for all but a few attorneys."[10] The court cases culled for this study establish that his statement is correct to a certain extent: many attorneys participated in a small number of claims. But a close investigation of two classes of attorneys, those who represented voluntary bankrupts and those who served creditors who initiated involuntary proceedings, reveals two more specific conclusions. These findings grant insight into the dynamics between southern attorneys (and southerners generally) and the federal tribunals during Reconstruction. First, attorneys who served in bankruptcy matters had fluid professional affiliations. Thus, different lawyers and firms appeared on federal bankruptcy dockets over time as new lawyers moved to the area and as those already practicing formed new partnerships or dissolved firms and went into solo practice.[11] Second, the characteristics of the leading bankruptcy attorneys differed depending on whether they were counsel in voluntary or involuntary cases. Many leading attorneys for voluntary bankrupts had been practicing law in the same southern locale prior to the Civil War, whereas no leading counsel for initiating creditors in involuntary claims had been. This profile indicates what the different clients sought in their lawyers. In particular, and in line with the general theme of this chapter, this finding highlights how both southerners and southern attorneys turned to the federal courts to gain practical benefits from filing voluntary petitions in the late 1860s.

Because the number of voluntary cases vastly outnumbered the number of involuntary filings in the three districts, the number of attorneys who represented voluntary bankrupts was similarly more numerous than counsel representing initiating creditors in involuntary suits. Fifty-five attorneys or firms represented claimants in 237 voluntary bankruptcy filings by Charleston County residents. Of the sixty-eight firms or solo practitioners identified in John Livingston's *1868 Law Register* as practicing in Charleston County, 57 percent served as counsel to voluntary bankrupts. Similarly, in Anderson County, South Carolina, ten firms or single attorneys served in thirty-four voluntary filings. Four of the eight firms or attorneys listed for Anderson County in 1868 served as voluntary bankrupts' counsel. Voluntary filers in Mississippi also used a broad cross-section of the bar. In Warren County, thirty-four attorneys or firms acted as attorneys in 122 voluntary claims. Of the twenty-five firms and attorneys Livingston listed in Warren County in 1868, seventeen (68 percent) represented at least one voluntary bankrupt. Voluntary bankrupts from Lauderdale County also called on a variety of attorneys. Roughly ten different groupings of lawyers provided representation in sixty-six voluntary bankruptcy cases involving Lauderdale County residents. Although the varying partnerships among attorneys in the county between 1867 and 1878 make a precise comparison with Livingston's 1868 listing difficult, bankruptcy attorneys accounted for a large percentage of the twelve firms or solo attorneys in Lauderdale County in 1868.[12] East Tennessee showed similar patterns of representation: approximately seventy-five different attorneys and groups of attorneys represented debtors in the district's 224 voluntary bankruptcy filings.[13]

Studying the order in which claims were filed establishes that there was no period during which one attorney or firm submitted voluntary filings to the courts in bulk. This differs from attorney representation in other types of cases during this era, such as the property claims that southerners filed with the Court of Claims under the Captured and Abandoned Property Act. In those cases, a few lawyers filed scores of cases representing claimants from certain jurisdictions, such as Mississippi, South Carolina, or Tennessee. Washington, D.C., attorney Joseph Casey, for example, filed 98 of the 372 such claims involving Mississippians or Mississippi cotton, all on the same day, July 3, 1874. Casey or his agents appear to have sought out potential claimants and convinced them to file claims. The July 1874 petitioners came primarily from a few counties in eastern Mississippi. All of the claims were weak and ultimately were dismissed. In other words, Casey or those acting under him, not the claimants, likely generated those federal cases.[14] Such churning, at least to such an extreme extent, did not take place in bankruptcy claims, although some attorneys served as bankruptcy counsel more frequently than others. Since most attorneys or firms represented just a few bankrupts, it appears that bankrupts sought out attorneys, usually ones who practiced nearby, to initiate voluntary proceedings. Advertisements such as McGarr and Smedes's law card surely caught the eye of many people who were contemplating bankruptcy, but bankruptcy representation was a pot shared by many minor players who were likely approached individually by debtors.

Certain firms and solo practitioners in each studied jurisdiction represented more voluntary bankrupts than did other attorneys. Two characteristics were common to these leading bankruptcy counsel in South Carolina, East Tennessee, and southern Mississippi. First, there were few such lawyers, again pointing out the widespread nature of voluntary bankruptcy representation. Second, many of these counsel, particularly in the Deep South states of South Carolina and Mississippi, had been practicing in the same location prior to the war. In South Carolina's Charleston County, three of the five leading firms or attorneys had been practicing in Charleston in 1860; in Anderson County, the one leading firm had been counseling clients prior to the war. In Warren County, Mississippi, three of the four leading bankruptcy firms (or individual members of those firms) were already practicing in the county seat, Vicksburg, in 1860. This persistence in practice is higher than would be expected given the high turnover of attorneys. Fewer than half of all lawyers listed in Livingston's *1868 Law Register* as practicing in Charleston had been in law practice prior to the Civil War; similarly, only 38 percent of all Warren County attorneys practicing in 1868 had been representing clients in the county in 1860. The same pattern of a high incidence of pre–Civil War attorneys acting as leading voluntary bankruptcy counsel did not hold true in Lauderdale County, Mississippi, or in East Tennessee.[15]

But as table 1 shows, leading voluntary bankruptcy counsel in all the studied jurisdictions shared a separate characteristic: many were native to the states that had comprised the Confederacy. Using the 1870 manuscript census and other nineteenth-century publications, birthplaces were located for fourteen of the twenty-five attorneys who composed the fourteen leading voluntary bankruptcy practices in East Tennessee and the studied counties in South Carolina and southern Mississippi: nine of these men were born in the South, and an additional two were native to Kentucky, which had stayed with the Union but maintained geographic and cultural ties to the former Confederate states. (The three other counsel whose birthplaces were identified had been born in the East Indies, New York, and Ohio, respectively.) Furthermore, of these twenty-five attorneys, eleven were not practicing in the same county and district in both 1860 and 1868. Birthplaces were identified for eight of these men, of whom four were native to the South and another one was born in Kentucky.

Thus, most of the leading voluntary bankruptcy attorneys in these areas, and particularly in such urban centers as Charleston, Vicksburg, Chattanooga, and Knoxville, were not northerners coming to the South to take advantage of a new source of fees from southern debtors under the 1867 Bankruptcy Act. Rather, these leading counsel were often well-established southern firms or solo practitioners who clearly garnered business from their recognized positions. Some became prominent (and prominently linked with the federal government): leading voluntary bankruptcy attorney Charles H. Simonton followed George S. Bryan as federal district court judge for South Carolina in 1886 and subsequently became federal circuit judge after Hugh L. Bond's death in 1893.[16]

In addition, review of the leading voluntary bankruptcy attorneys in East Tennessee reveals two factors that likely contributed to attorneys' participation in bankruptcy cases. First, as in South Carolina and Mississippi, the three leading East Tennessee bankruptcy attorneys resided in the district's population and business centers, with two located in Knoxville and the third in Chattanooga.

Table 1 Leading debtor attorneys in voluntary cases

Attorney or firm	No. of cases	Notes regarding representation	Birthplace
South Carolina			
Charleston Co.			
Asher D. Cohen	14		S.C.
J. N. Nathans	10		n/l
M. P. O'Connor*	12		S.C.
Simons & Siegling*	11	Listed individually in 1860	Thomas Y. Simons: n/l; Rudolph Siegling: S.C.
Simonton & Barker*	21	Listed individually in 1860	Charles H. Simonton: S.C.; Theodore G. Barker: n/l
Anderson Co.			
Harrison & Whitner*	12	Includes 10 by individual firm members, 1 by firm, and 1 by firm members Whitner & Whitner	James W. Harrison: n/l; J. H. Whitner: n/l; B. F. Whitner: S.C.
Eastern Tennessee			
H. M. Aiken (Knoxville)	16		Ohio
A. Caldwell (Knoxville)	15		Tenn.
Key, Eakin & Key (Chattanooga)	13	12 by firm (3 shared with S. M. Burkett), 1 by S. A. Key individually	D. M. Key: Tenn.; W. L. Eakin: n/l; S. A. Key: n/l

continued

This pattern surely resulted because densely populated areas produced both more legal business in general and more debtors who were insolvent as a result of commercial dealings. But perhaps even more determinative were the close relationships that two of the three leading East Tennessee attorneys had with bankruptcy registers. In at least fourteen of the sixteen bankruptcy cases in which Knoxville attorney H. M. Aiken served as counsel, William Aiken was the register. Another Knoxville attorney, A. Caldwell, appeared individually on many voluntary petitions but was in partnership with bankruptcy register L. S. Trowbridge.[17] For both H. M. Aiken and Caldwell, access to information from the registers likely contributed to success in acquiring business. In addition, this teamwork depicts the interaction of federal officials with the local bar and the business rewards that attorneys gained as a result.

Table 1, continued

Attorney or firm	No. of cases	Notes regarding representation	Birthplace
Southern Mississippi			
Warren Co.			
Adam & Speed	19	Includes 10 cases by Adam individually	G. Gordon Adam: East Indies (U.S. citizen in 1870) Frederick Speed: N.Y.
Brooke & Cook[e]*	10	Listed in separate firms in 1860	Walker Brooke: n/l H. F. Cooke: n/l
Marshall & Miller*	14	13 by firm, 1 by Miller individually	Thomas A. Marshall: n/l H. H. Miller: Ky.
McGarr & Smedes*	10	Listed individually in 1860; cases include 8 by firm, 2 by Smedes; cases involving McGarr in another partnership not counted	McGarr: listing unclear A. K. Smedes: Miss.
Lauderdale Co.			
Shannon & Gallagher	19	9 by firm, 8 by Shannon and 2 by Gallagher individually; cases involving firm members in other partnerships not counted	J. J. Shannon: Miss. C. W. Gallagher: Ky.

Notes: * = practicing in county in 1860; n/l = not located

Sources: Bankruptcy Case Files and Dockets; Livingston, *United States Law Register;* Livingston, *1868;* Census Records (see appendix on methodology); Caldwell, *Sketches.*

Some of these same trends occurred in involuntary cases, but some telling differences from voluntary representation also existed. In-state and out-of-state creditors seeking representation to initiate involuntary suits similarly turned to numerous local attorneys. As with voluntary suits, most attorneys handled only a few suits on behalf of initiating creditors in involuntary cases. One leading attorney or firm existed in Charleston County, South Carolina, and in both Warren and Lauderdale Counties, Mississippi. Table 2 provides some information about these attorneys. Neither Anderson County, South Carolina, nor East Tennessee had any leading attorneys. Unlike the leading attorneys in voluntary claims, none of these leading involuntary counsel had been practicing in the same jurisdiction prior to the war. Several of these leading creditor attorneys

Table 2 Leading attorneys for initiating creditors in involuntary cases

Attorney or firm	No. of involuntary cases	Notes regarding representation	Birthplace
South Carolina			
Charleston County			
J. N. Nathans	11 of 53 cases	In Charleston in 1868	Not located
Mississippi			
Warren County			
Adam & Speed	23 of 62 cases	Adam, not Speed, listed as practicing in Warren Co. in 1868; cases include 16 by firm (with 2 shared with other firms) and 7 by Adam individually	G. Gordon Adam: East Indies (U.S. citizen in 1870) Frederick Speed: New York
Lauderdale County			
Ramsey & Shannon	10 of 26 cases	7 by firm, 3 by Shannon individually; cases involving firm members in partnership with others not counted	B. Y. Ramsey: North Carolina J. J. Shannon: Mississippi

Sources: Bankruptcy Case Files and Dockets; Livingston, *United States Law Register;* Livingston, *1868* (see appendix on methodology).

did not establish their practices until after 1868; some did not even arrive in the locality until after that year.[18]

No one firm dominated filings by creditors from a particular state. For example, in the twenty involuntary cases where New Yorkers were among the initiating creditors against Charleston debtors, the New York creditors employed eleven different Charleston counsel. One attorney, J. N. Nathans, provided representation in seven of these cases, but the other attorneys generally served only in one case each. In addition, the fact that no leading creditor attorneys from the studied jurisdictions had been practicing there prior to the Civil War hints at the type of attorney that creditors found attractive as well as which attorneys sought creditors' business. The background of the attorneys in the dominant Warren County firm, Adam and Speed, suggests what characterized leading involuntary bankruptcy lawyers. G. Gordon Adam was born in the East Indies and began practicing law in 1860. He came from Massachusetts to Mississippi, in his words, "with the Federal army in 1863." He served as a legal adviser to the Freedmen's Bureau and later as a U.S. district attorney for almost a year, resigning in the summer of 1869. He had begun his Vicksburg practice by 1868. New York–born Frederick Speed served as assistant adjutant general for the Union forces in western Mississippi, settled in Vicksburg after the war, studied law, and became a member of the bar in 1868. Both Adam and Speed were well-off, with Adam owning fifteen thousand dollars in personal property in 1870 and Speed owning twenty-five thousand dollars' worth.[19] Part of their good fortune likely flowed from their representation in various types of cases for a wide range of clients. During the 1860s and 1870s, while they represented both debtors in voluntary filings and creditors in involuntary suits, Adam and Speed also served as counsel on both sides of the docket (to both southern claimants and the government) in property claims before the U.S. Court of Claims.[20] Adam and Speed thus were well positioned to handle claims by northern creditors as well as by southern debtors in bankruptcy.

Handsome returns from bankruptcy representation, however, were not assured. In voluntary cases, one hundred dollars was not an uncommon fee "for professional services in preparing & prosecuting [a] petition."[21] But counsel were not certain to get this full amount. Orlando Bump explained in the 1877 edition of his respected treatise on bankruptcy that under bankruptcy rule 30, attorneys were not treated like court officials, who drew their fees from the bankrupt's estate. Rather, in both voluntary and involuntary cases, "no allowance [could] be made against the estate of the bankrupt for fees of attorneys, solicitors, or counsel." As a result, in voluntary cases, fees for services in preparing a bankrupt's petition and schedules did not receive priority over other debts. Various court rulings established that "no matter how meritorious or necessary the services may have been, the claim [of a voluntary bankrupt's counsel] stands on the same footing as the claim of any other creditor." However, the attorney could receive payment for his services before the debtor filed for voluntary bankruptcy or might even try to gain priority over other debts by securing his claim with the debtors' property (although there was some doubt about the propriety of this practice). Without taking such actions, attorneys received no more than other unsecured creditors, which could range from full payment to no payment.[22] Courts had discretion in awarding fees in involuntary cases to counsel for the creditors' trustee. As South Carolina District Judge Bryan explained, the judge "does not allow the fee unless satisfied that full value has been given in the services rendered." Bryan reasoned, "The estate of the creditors is thus protected against any possible sinister speculations of client and counsel, or any innocent fanciful valuations that counsel might attach to their services, and clients might be disposed to allow, if permitted without restraint to tax the estates of bankrupts."[23] Yet these restrictions on collecting fees did not inhibit a large percentage of the bar in the localities studied from acting as counsel in bankruptcy filings; indeed, many of the repeat players were well-established firms, which would likely have been in a stronger position to turn away business.

The group of southern bankruptcy attorneys also included some of the most prominent states' rights proponents and former secessionists in the districts. Judge A. G. Magrath had closed the South Carolina federal courts in disgust following President Lincoln's election in November 1860 and subsequently served as a prominent Confederate official, yet by May 1868 his firm served as counsel in a voluntary bankruptcy claim before the U.S. District Court of South Carolina, and during the 1870s he represented several other voluntary filers and initiating creditors. By 1873, Magrath had no compunctions about associating with Republicans and federal officers: Republican U.S. Circuit Judge Hugh Bond dined with the Magraths while attending to judicial duties in Charleston in the spring of that year.[24]

Other bankruptcy attorneys also were prominent former Confederates and principal proponents of southern redemption from post–Civil War federal involvement in state affairs. James Conner, of the Charleston firm Porter and Conner, had served as a Confederate brigadier general and lost his leg in the effort. In 1876, the state's Democrats nominated him for attorney general, and he became a leader of the paramilitary Rifle Clubs, which, as historian Richard Zuczek explains, "made up the Democratic army, and it was their mission to destroy the Republican voting base."[25] Yet while Conner worked to redeem South Carolina and thus rid the state of what he viewed as federal intrusion, he also employed the federal tribunals in the state to gain advantages for his clients and fees for himself by providing counsel to both debtors and creditors in bankruptcy cases. Conner's political aversion to national interference apparently did not extend to bankruptcy proceedings.

East Tennessee attorney John M. Baxter was a leading moderate Unionist before the war but was unable to meet the strict loyalty requirements under Governor William G. Brownlow's administration and was disfranchised in Tennessee in the late 1860s. Yet even while he was unable to vote, his firm, Baxter, Champion, and Ricks, served as attorneys in some of the earliest bankruptcy claims in the Eastern District, filing several petitions on behalf of voluntary bankrupts and in one involuntary case in the Federal District Court at Knoxville in 1867 and 1868. According to Brownlow's *Knoxville Whig*, in June 1868, Baxter felt comfortable enough in the federal tribunal to use it to deliver "a political harangue." He "assailed the State Government as oppressive, and said, in substance, that justice could not be had in the State Courts, because of the prejudice of officers and jurors." Brownlow's paper maintained that most people in East Tennessee did not have good feelings for Baxter, but the editors concluded, "We can't see that this is cause for Baxter occupying the time of a Federal Court in denunciation of the State Courts." To what extent other attorneys shared Baxter's views is unknown; an 1898 sketch characterized him as "positive, often extreme; sometimes arbitrary, always combative." Further, his affiliation with the federal courts became stronger after Reconstruction: he became a U.S. circuit court judge in 1877. Yet even during the immediate postwar years, when Brownlow's Republican contingent controlled Tennessee, Baxter, a Unionist, could not hold back his denunciation of the prejudice of and lack of justice in state courts as he stood before the federal tribunal.[26] Thus, like their clients, the southern attorneys who acted as counsel in bankruptcy cases came from throughout the spectrum of political beliefs, embracing the 1867 Bankruptcy Act regardless of their views.

Indeed, southern advocates' widespread involvement in bankruptcy filings represented a more general trend: counsel who had supported the Confederate cause were eager to resume their practices in the federal tribunals after the Civil War and successfully fought congressional legislation that barred former Confederates from doing so. The attorneys at the forefront of this challenge to the test oath included those who would subsequently serve as bankruptcy counsel. In January 1865, Congress passed an act that required all attorneys who practiced in federal courts—even those who had previously practiced before those courts or had obtained presidential pardons—to subscribe to an ironclad oath that they had remained loyal to the Union.[27]

Yet just five months later, Connally Trigg of Tennessee became the first federal judge to declare the oath unconstitutional. In response to a constitutional challenge initiated by Baxter, Trigg concluded that the law was ex post facto, punishing attorneys for past acts in a way that was not prescribed at the time the acts were committed. He also declared that the law deprived lawyers of their property without due process of law. By May 1866, district judges in Alabama and Georgia also ruled the Act unconstitutional. One month later, during the summer when the federal courts in South Carolina first reopened, Judge Bryan heard attorney William Whaley's challenge to the law. Whaley was not just standing on principle: his firm represented numerous bankruptcy filers before the federal tribunal during the following two years. Former Confederates such as Whaley surely anticipated the mass of litigation that would flow to the courts after the war and fought exclusion from this source of revenue. Bryan's action with respect to Whaley and others who could not subscribe to the oath had the same practical effect as Trigg's ruling: Bryan "decided at once that the test oath in question was unnecessary and from the first opening of the Court all the members of the Bar could practice in the United States and State Courts without let or hindrance."[28] Similarly, Judge Robert Hill allowed Mississippi counsel who had practiced in federal tribunals before the war and had obtained presidential pardons to continue appearing before his court. Hill wrote to Chief Justice Salmon Chase in November 1866 that "the objection to the law as an ex post facto law and as requiring the party indirectly to testify against himself, may apply to those previously admitted."[29] By the time the U.S. Supreme Court declared the attorney test oath unconstitutional in January 1867 in *Ex parte Garland*, former Confederates in East Tennessee, South Carolina, and Mississippi had been practicing before the federal tribunals for some time.[30]

The successful challenges to the test oath—often led by counsel who would later serve as bankruptcy attorneys—and the lenient positions of the federal district judges in the three districts demonstrate both southern attorneys' eagerness to practice before the federal courts and the federal tribunals' receptivity to counsel who had recently rebelled against the United States. Although opposition to Radical Republican legislation likely played a part in the southern effort to overturn the test oath, practical considerations also contributed to federal judicial officials' and southern attorneys' opposition to the law. The *Charleston Daily Courier* concluded, "Not one lawyer in a hundred of those who had been called to the Bar in South Carolina before 1861 could have taken the test oath." By allowing former Confederates to practice essentially from the time the courts reopened, the federal tribunals in East Tennessee, South Carolina, and southern Mississippi (as well as other southern districts) averted the unfortunate predicament of having a particularly sparse bar during an era when caseloads were heavy. The courts also avoided alienating southern counsel. In addition, the *Garland* case and the district judges' lenient position prior to *Garland* "made possible the financial recuperation of great numbers of former Confederates," as William Russ concludes.[31] This economic resuscitation of southern attorneys was tied, at least in part, to the financial recuperation of fellow southerners through bankruptcy filings.

CHAPTER FIVE

Voluntary Bankruptcy Proceedings in the South

I have been very much pressed with my judicial duties, arising in part from the large amount of Bankrupt cases in this state. —Mississippi Federal District Judge Robert A. Hill to Chief Justice Salmon P. Chase, 1868

"I hope the day is near when we may be able to sell our land, the only property we now have, and that we may realize sufficient from it to enable us to turn our back on this accursed government and people." William Heyward, a member of what had been the wealthiest family of rice plantation owners in South Carolina, expressed this denunciation of his country and its inhabitants in 1865. Five years later, apparently forgetting his previous wish to turn his back on the government, he filed a petition for voluntary bankruptcy with the federal district court. Against approximately twenty-four debts, primarily contracted before or during the war and all but one with South Carolina creditors (the exception was a North Carolina obligation), Heyward claimed three plantations as assets worth collectively more than thirty-eight thousand dollars. Eight months later, he benefited from the Bankruptcy Act, obtaining a discharge from his debts.[1]

In 1868, the South Carolinian who according to a U.S. army officer was "the most objectionable man to the [federal] Govt in the State" submitted his bankruptcy application to a federal tribunal. General and later South Carolina Governor Wade Hampton sought discharge of his debts in the District Court for the Southern District of Mississippi. This filing indicated a severe shift in fortunes for a man who had been perhaps the richest southern planter before the Civil War. Hampton owned full or partial interest in nine tracts of land— six of them large plantations in southern Mississippi—worth approximately $235,000 at the time he filed. But Hampton's obligations were far greater than his assets. His secured debts (or those guaranteed by collateral, often mortgages on his land) totaled about $490,000, while a listing of Hampton's unsecured debts (not guaranteed by collateral) covered two pages. Some of these debts had originated before the war—for example, for purchases of slaves or land—and others were postbellum obligations. His secured creditors resided primarily in South Carolina and New Orleans; many of the unsecured creditors also hailed from southern cities, including Vicksburg, St. Louis, Columbia, and Charleston.[2] Described by one historian as "the most prominent of South Carolinians," Hampton was elected the state's governor in 1876 on a platform that stressed the necessity of redeeming the state from federal influence. In the race, his postwar destitution became a political asset. The *Charleston News and Courier* proclaimed, "Wade Hampton suffered with the state, and grew poor when she was made desolate." As a result, the editors exclaimed, "So has he become her foremost citizen, and, as such, is worthy to be her Governor." Neither the newspaper's editors nor Hampton (as he promoted the virtues of home rule and scaling back federal involvement) appears to have focused on the fact that Hampton had applied to the federal government for debt relief.[3]

Heyward's and Hampton's voluntary bankruptcy filings illustrate how even the southerners most critical of federal policies employed the 1867 Bankruptcy Act. These filers apparently viewed filing either simply as a practical economic necessity that did not affect their political critique of Republican federal policies or perhaps as a right that southerners had earned as a result of the hardships suffered at the hands of federal authorities. Either way, use of the statute granting economic reprieve did not politically disadvantage a filer, at least in Hampton's case, even in the cradle of the Confederacy.

In addition, the two cases portray how often southern bankrupts owed debts to southern creditors and not just to northern creditors, as the congressional debates regarding the 1867 Act might indicate. Third, Heyward's and Hampton's filings indicate how the postbellum economic depression hammered even the richest antebellum southerners. Economic destitution was widespread among both once well-heeled merchants and planters and those whose fortunes had been modest. As Mississippi District Judge Robert A. Hill acknowledged in 1866, "Debt . . . was almost universal, and was at the present time a common misfortune and calamity." South Carolina voluntary bankrupt Elijah W. Brown noted how his promissory and sealed notes and his books of accounts had amounted "to about Five Thousand Dollars" each, but when he filed for bankruptcy, they were "utterly worthless."[4]

But in significant ways, Hampton and Heyward differ from the mass of voluntary filers in the three districts studied. Filers were not commonly landed elites and well-known politicians; rather, most bankrupts were merchants, professionals, or agriculturalists who had fallen on hard times. South Carolina Federal District Court Clerk Daniel Horlbeck captured the economic straits of bankruptcy filers in an 1873 letter to U.S. Attorney General George H. Williams: "The estates of bankrupts in the State, in consequence of the results of civil convulsion, have been very small, and in the great mass of bankruptcy cases there has been no estates at all, and where there have been estates, after paying liens of judgments and mortgages, but a very small percentage, if any, has ever gone to creditors." Horlbeck described how lack of funds meant that "bankrupts, in very many of the cases, often had to throw themselves on their friends and the clemency of the officers, for fees of attorneys and costs of officers in bankruptcy."[5]

In addition, destruction of records as a result of the war caused difficulties for filers. When he filed his schedules in voluntary bankruptcy, South Carolinian William A. Wardlaw recounted how U.S. General William T. Sherman's army had taken Wardlaw's memorandum book and confessed, "So far as could be done from memory I have made entries, but it is not improbable that some that should be made have been omitted only because they have escaped my memory." Mississippian Robert J. Moseley also testified that "the books & all the papers of petitioner were burned at the time Gen Sherman made his expedition to Meridian in 1864 and for that reason petitioner is unable to render a more accurate schedule, having to rely upon his memory [and] one of the journals of his business for the year 1861." Julius Spring of South Carolina also noted that almost without exception, his notes and account books had been "lost by the Conflagration of Columbia SoCa."[6]

But although filers' records had often been destroyed or were in chaos as a result of the war and the value of their estates was generally small, the volume of bankrupt filings was large. The characteristics of the filers in southern Mississippi, South Carolina, and East Tennessee reveal much about the 1867 Bankruptcy Act's role in the South, how southerners employed the Act, and the lower federal courts' sphere of influence in the region during Reconstruction.

The four maps of each state (maps 1–12) indicate the residence county of all voluntary bankrupts in the three judicial districts and demonstrate the factors that influenced which southerners filed. Maps 1, 5, and 9 depict traffic patterns according to county: the darker the county, the greater the number of voluntary bankrupts from that county. To determine what may have caused residents in some areas to file more frequently than residents of other areas, I considered four factors: the county's total population and white population; the county's aggregate property value according to the 1870 census; the county's proximity to the federal courthouse; and the presence of railroads in a county.

Maps 1, 5, and 9 demonstrate that residents from all regions of all three judicial districts filed for voluntary bankruptcy, despite the demographic, economic, and cultural differences among the three districts and within each district. However, greater numbers of voluntary bankrupts resided in particular areas of each district. Assessment of the incidence of voluntary bankruptcy in

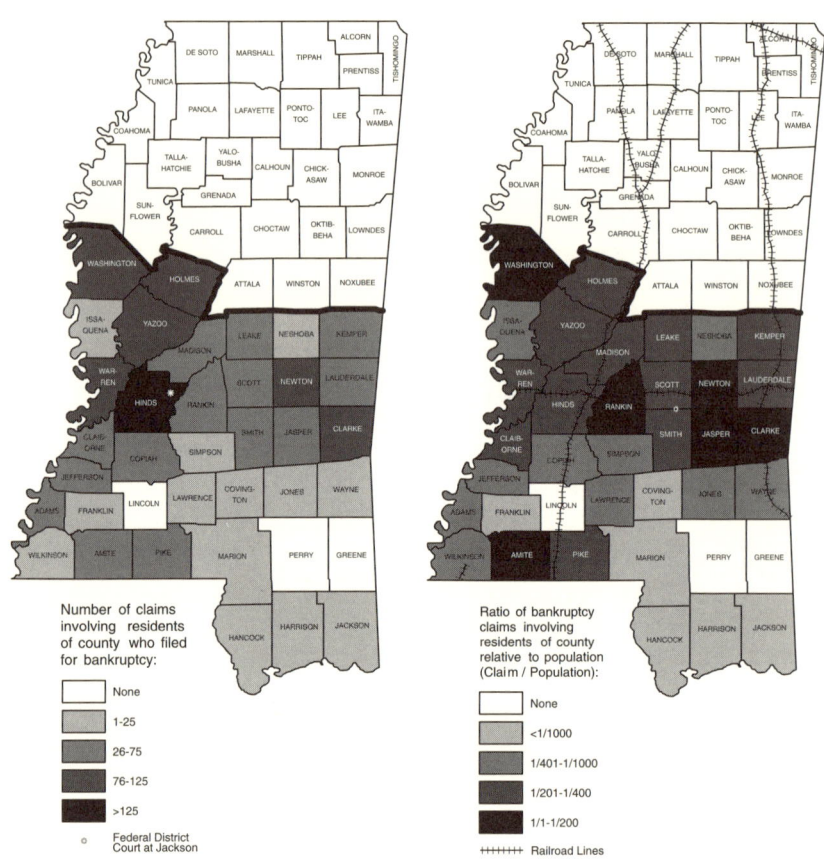

Map 1 Southern District of Mississippi voluntary bankruptcy filings by county

Map 2 Southern District of Mississippi voluntary bankruptcy filings by county relative to population density

Notes: Two filings involved Sharkey County residents; Sharkey County was created in 1876 out of Issaquena and Washington Counties. One filing involved a resident of Sunflower County and one involved a resident of Carroll County, counties in the Northern District of Mississippi.

Sources: Southern District of Mississippi Bankruptcy Case Files and Docket (see appendix on methodology); Thorndale and Dollarhide, *Map Guide*, 186; Inter-university Consortium for Political and Social Research, Census Data for the Year 1870, at http://fisher.lib.virginia.edu/census; Wyld, *Map of the Southern States;* Harris, *Presidential Reconstruction,* 195.

Cartographer: John Huggins.

Map 3 Southern District of Mississippi voluntary bankruptcy filings by county relative to white population density

Map 4 Southern District of Mississippi valuation of property by county (1870 Federal Census)

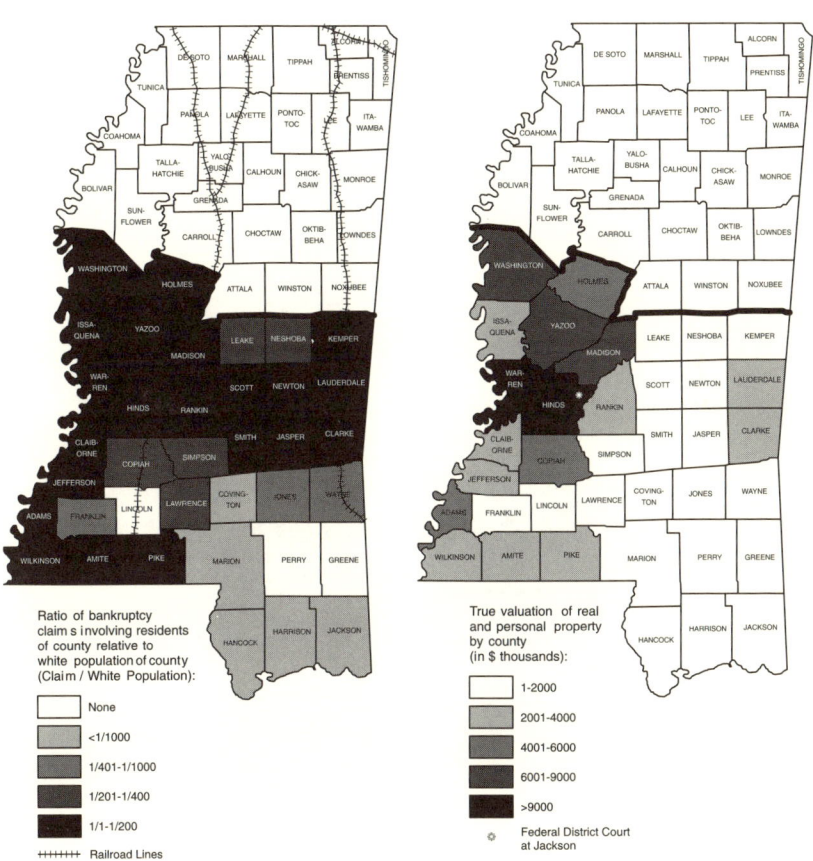

Notes for Map 3: Two filings involved Sharkey County residents; Sharkey County was created in 1876 out of Issaquena and Washington Counties. One filing involved a resident of Sunflower County and one involved a resident of Carroll County, counties in the Northern District of Mississippi.

Sources: Southern District of Mississippi Bankruptcy Case Files and Docket; Inter-university Consortium for Political and Social Research, Census Data for the Year 1870, at http://fisher.lib.virginia.edu/census; Thorndale and Dollarhide, *Map Guide*, 186; Wyld, *Map of the Southern States;* Harris, *Presidential Reconstruction,* 195.

Cartographer: John Huggins.

Map 5   District of South Carolina voluntary bankruptcy filings
         by county

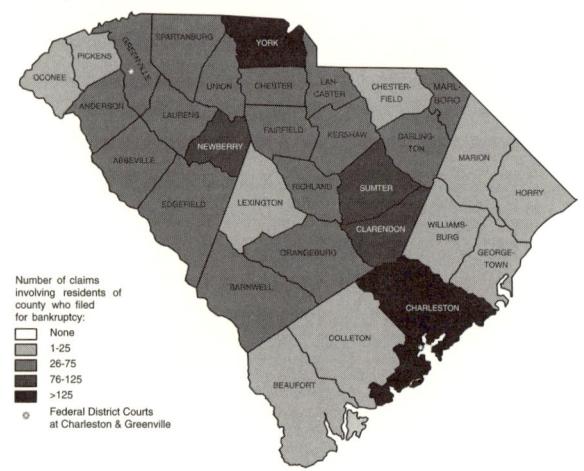

Map 6   District of South Carolina voluntary bankruptcy filings
         by county relative to population density

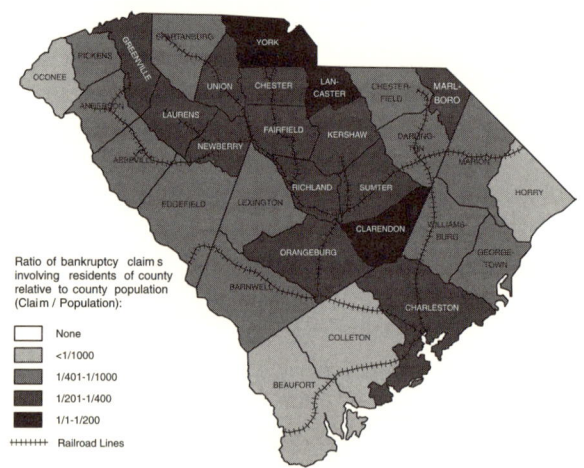

Note: Five filings involved residents of Aiken County, which was formed in 1871 from parts of Orangeburg, Lexington, Edgefield, and Barnwell Counties.

Sources: District of South Carolina Bankruptcy Case Files and Docket (see appendix on methodology); Thorndale and Dollarhide, *Map Guide*, 300; Inter-university Consortium for Political and Social Research, Census Data for the Year 1870, at http://fisher.lib.virginia.edu/census; Wyld, *Map of the Southern States*; Map of the State of South Carolina, from Wagener, *South Carolina*.

Cartographer: John Huggins.

Map 7   District of South Carolina voluntary bankruptcy filings
        by county relative to white population density

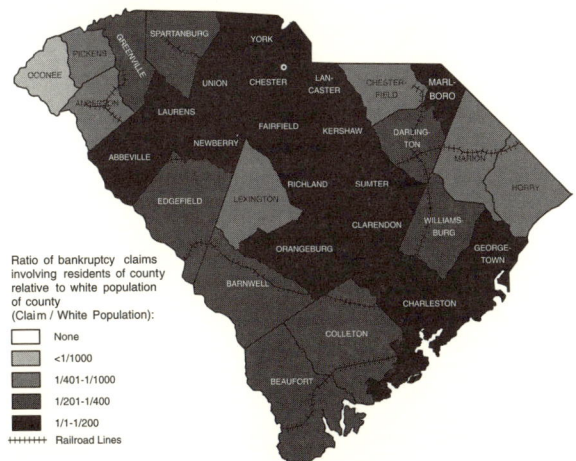

Map 8   District of South Carolina valuation of property
        by county (1870 Federal Census)

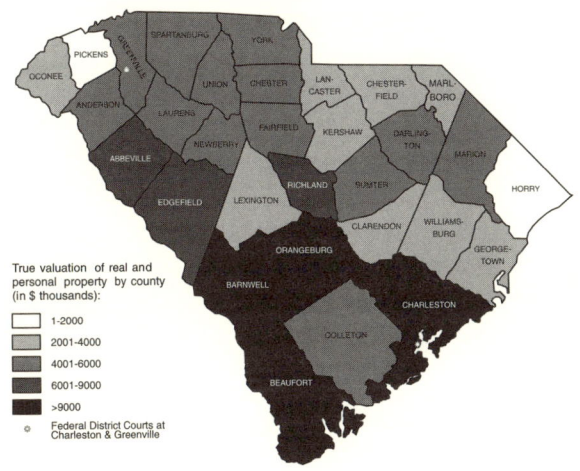

Note for Map 7: Five filings involved residents of Aiken County, which was formed in 1871 from parts of Orangeburg, Lexington, Edgefield, and Barnwell Counties.

Sources: District of South Carolina Bankruptcy Case Files and Docket (see appendix on methodology); Inter-university Consortium for Political and Social Research, Census Data for the Year 1870, at http://fisher.lib.virginia.edu/census; Thorndale and Dollarhide, *Map Guide*, 300; Wyld, *Map of the Southern States;* Map of the State of South Carolina, from Wagener, *South Carolina.*

Cartographer: John Huggins.

Map 9   Eastern District of Tennessee voluntary bankruptcy filings by county

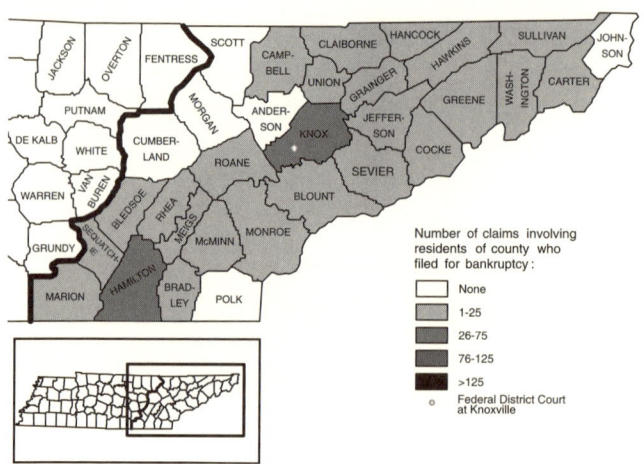

Map 10   Eastern District of Tennessee voluntary bankruptcy filings by county relative to population density

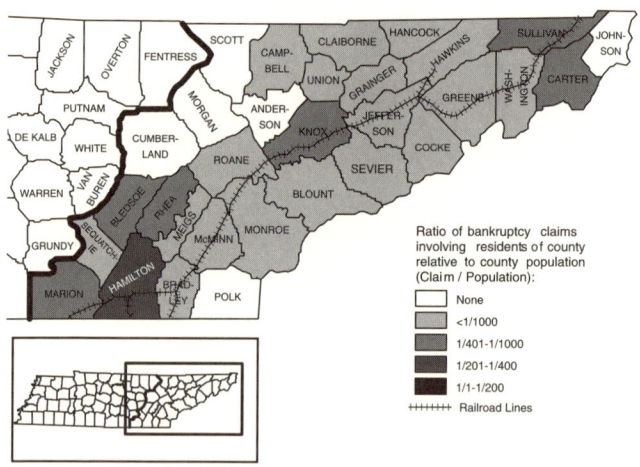

Sources: Eastern District of Tennessee Bankruptcy Case Docket (see appendix on methodology); Thorndale and Dollarhide, Map Guide, 322; Inter-university Consortium for Political and Social Research, Census Data for the Year 1870, at http://fisher.lib.virginia.edu/census; Wyld, Map of the Southern States; Deborah Cahill, Map of East Tennessee in 1861, in Groce, Mountain Rebels, 3.

Cartographer: John Huggins.

Map 11 Eastern District of Tennessee voluntary bankruptcy filings
by county relative to white population density

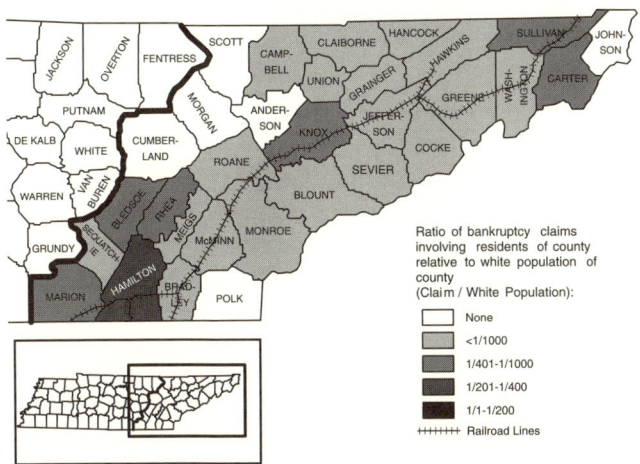

Map 12 Eastern District of Tennessee valuation of property
by county (1870 Federal Census)

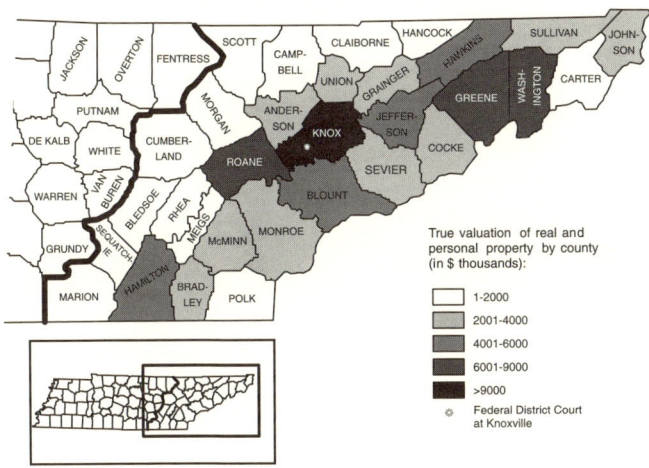

Sources: Eastern District of Tennessee Bankruptcy Case Docket (see appendix on methodology); Inter-university Consortium for Political and Social Research, Census Data for the Year 1870, at http://fisher.lib.virginia.edu/census; Thorndale and Dollarhide, *Map Guide*, 322; Wyld, *Map of the Southern States;* Deborah Cahill, Map of East Tennessee in 1861, in Groce, *Mountain Rebels*, 3.

Cartographer: John Huggins.

a certain county (the per capita rate) shows concentrations of filers in certain areas. (See maps 2, 3, 6, 7, 10, and 11, which illustrate the per capita rate according to total population and white population.)

In southern Mississippi, as map 2 shows, an east-west band of counties across the middle of the state (in the northern part of the Southern District) had the highest frequency of voluntary bankrupts. Because virtually no African Americans employed the Act (see chapter 7), looking solely at the white population reveals even more precisely the incidence of filing per county among the group that used the legislation. Map 3 thus demonstrates that the same band of counties as well as the counties lining the Mississippi River had proportionally high numbers of white residents who filed for voluntary bankruptcy. Map 6 illustrates the filing pattern in South Carolina, where bankruptcies were most likely to occur in a broad strip stretching from the northwest counties of Greenville and York to the southeast county of Charleston on the coast. Map 7 indicates how this same pattern holds when only the white population is considered. Similarly, although the number of bankruptcies in East Tennessee was smaller, map 10 indicates that filing frequency was higher in a discontinuous line of counties stretching from Marion and Hamilton in the southwest to Sullivan and Carter in the northeast. (Because of East Tennessee's relatively small African American population, map 11 shows that accounting solely for white filers does not significantly affect the filing pattern.)

Certain factors influenced whether residents in certain parts of the judicial districts were more likely to file. First, counties containing the district's major metropolitan areas—Vicksburg and Jackson in southern Mississippi, Charleston in South Carolina, and Chattanooga and Knoxville in East Tennessee—consistently had a high number and frequency of voluntary bankrupts. This high incidence of filers reflects a concentration of commercial activity in urban areas and an associated high number of debts and obligations.

Second, property values did not affect filing frequency. According to maps 4, 8, and 12, the counties in all three districts with high concentrations of bankruptcy filers had both high and low aggregate property values in the 1870 census. The maps also indicate that counties where few residents filed had both high and low property values. Thus, it would not be consistently accurate to argue either that areas with low property values (which were likely to have a high number of poor residents) would result in more filings or that areas with high property values (where residents had more assets, agricultural land produced valuable crops, and more commercial activity took place) would have more filings.

Third, a county's proximity to the federal courthouse was not a dependable indicator of whether residents were prone to filing for bankruptcy. Residents of such Mississippi counties as Kemper, Lauderdale, and Clarke, located far to the east of the federal court at Jackson, frequently filed. The same trend holds true in South Carolina and East Tennessee. Further, in all three districts, some counties near or adjacent to the home county of the federal courts (for example, Lincoln County in southern Mississippi, Oconee and Pickens Counties in South Carolina, and Anderson County in East Tennessee) had no or relatively few voluntary bankrupts. These facts cast doubt on the accuracy of the traditional complaint that the federal courts' distance from litigants impeded residents from using them. "You cannot administer any law of this kind in a great State like Pennsylvania, for instance, with the [federal] courts one hundred and fifty miles apart: it is utterly impossible," charged Pennsylvania Senator Edgar Cowan during the 1867 debates on the Bankruptcy Act. "The people cannot get to them." Eleven years later, during debate on the law's repeal, Senator Roscoe Conkling of New York urged overturning the law partially on the grounds that federal tribunals operated "without a judicial staff so numerous as to bring justice or the instrumentalities of justice to every man's door." On the same day in the House, Representative Michael D. White of Indiana argued that the inconvenience of "the United States or bankrupt court . . . located one hundred miles away" contributed to its ineffectiveness. Bankruptcy scholar David Skeel points to the practical obstacles caused by federal district court administration of the nineteenth-century bankruptcy acts: "The federal courts were especially inconvenient for potential debtors, many of whom lived far from the nearest city."[7] Yet although distance from the federal courts likely dissuaded some people from filing for bankruptcy, the frequency of voluntary filings by debtors who resided far from the tribunals casts doubt on the extent to which distance was consistently a determining factor.

A fourth factor, however, does appear to be determinative: residents in counties through which railroad lines passed were more likely to file. In a large number of cases, railroad tracks in all three districts followed the path of counties with the heaviest incidence of filers, although some counties that lacked railways had numerous filers, while some counties with railroads had low filing rates. The overall trend is unquestionable, however. Three elements likely contributed to this connection between railroad thoroughfares and voluntary bankrupts. First, the railroad offered these locales greater access to commercial markets. People who had become overextended through these commercial transactions would have sought relief from the economic stress of the late 1860s and 1870s. Second, the railroads brought residents greater access to information. Word of mouth or newspapers would have conveyed the availability of federal bankruptcy proceedings. Of course, knowledge of the availability of bankruptcy was a necessary prerequisite for filing. Third, the railroads facilitated these filers' and their attorneys' access to federal court, countering the negative effect that distance would have had on filing rates. This recognition of the importance of railroad connections may not entirely contradict the traditional complaint regarding the inaccessibility of federal courts, but railroads shortened the distance between people and the federal tribunals.

Not only did a large number of southerners file for voluntary bankruptcy, but a large percentage of filers also attained the ultimate goal, discharge from their debts. In 1879, the U.S. attorney general reported that only about a third of debtors nationally received discharge from their debts under the 1867 Bankruptcy Act.[8] The rates in southern Mississippi, East Tennessee, and South Carolina were significantly higher, however. As table 3 shows, the Eastern Tennessee District Court issued discharges in more than 70 percent of the voluntary cases filed; a majority of cases filed by residents of Mississippi's Warren and Lauderdale Counties resulted in a discharge; and in South Carolina, the district court issued discharges in almost 60 percent of voluntary cases filed by Charleston and Anderson County residents.

In addition, those southerners who received discharges obtained them relatively promptly. The average time between filing a petition and gaining discharge was about twenty months for East Tennesseans, seventeen months for Mississippi filers in Warren and Lauderdale Counties, and thirteen months for South Carolina residents of Charleston and Anderson Counties. Thus, southern debtors walked away free of their debts within a couple of years of declaring bankruptcy. Because the bulk of voluntary filings occurred prior to 1869, this meant that many of these southerners had garnered the benefits of the bankruptcy system by the early 1870s. However, even if discharge was granted, petitioners still had to suffer through the economic stress of the era, as did other southerners. Nevertheless, successful voluntary bankrupts could approach the future without being hampered by the burdens of past obligations and with property in hand that had been acquired after filing or exempted from bankruptcy proceedings. These southerners capitalized on the federal government's largesse—first offered in the midst of Radical Reconstruction—to escape the effects of past economic dealings, an ironic twist during an era when Congress passed numerous other laws to remind former Confederates that they needed to make amends for their past political actions.

But what sectors of the southern population received these benefits? An analysis of the characteristics of voluntary bankrupts indicates who employed this economic measure for their gain and who thus received social and political benefits from the law.

A telling sign of the Bankruptcy Act's role in the South is whether voluntary filers were native southerners. If the bulk of filers were transplanted northerners,

Table 3 Incidence of voluntary bankrupts receiving discharge

District	% attaining discharge	Notes
Southern Mississippi (2 counties)	56.15	
South Carolina (2 counties)	59.04	In seven cases, some but not all filers were discharged
Eastern Tennessee	72.77	In one case, one of two partners was discharged

Note: In four cases in southern Mississippi and seven cases in South Carolina, the court discharged all filers in cases involving multiple bankrupts.

Sources: Bankruptcy Case Files and Dockets (see appendix on methodology).

this would indicate that southerners were remaining aloof from the federal courts and declining to take advantage of Congress's beneficence. Indeed, if former Confederates had acted in this standoffish way, it would have been entirely consistent with the policy of "masterly inactivity" that white southerners adopted with respect to federal efforts for political Reconstruction of the South, a policy ably explored by historian Michael Perman.[9] But a determination of the birthplace of southern voluntary bankrupts yields the opposite conclusion. Birthplaces were identified for 45 percent of voluntary filers in East Tennessee, 42 percent of filers from Warren and Lauderdale Counties in Mississippi, and 26 percent of filers from Charleston and Anderson Counties in South Carolina.[10] Any conclusions based on the resulting data must be qualified by the fact that the information does not account for all filers; nonetheless, certain trends are notable.

For all three judicial districts, native southerners formed the majority of filers identified: 78 percent in East Tennessee, 50 percent in Mississippi, and 66 percent in South Carolina had been born in one of the eleven former Confederate states. Most of these were indigenous to the state where they filed: 62 percent of the East Tennessee filers were born in Tennessee, and 65 percent of South Carolina filers were born in that state, although only 21 percent of the Mississippi bankrupts had been born there. These findings reflect that the populations of all three states were largely native: in 1870, 81 percent of Tennesseans, 68 percent of Mississippians, and 97 percent of South Carolinians were indigenous to their states.[11] Despite the limitations to these conclusions as a result of the fact that the origins of many filers could not be determined, it is clear that many native southerners took up the opportunity for economic liberation offered by the Bankruptcy Act of 1867.

The regions studied had far fewer voluntary bankrupts born in the United States but outside the South than native southerners, reflecting the origins of the southern population as a whole. Seventeen percent of East Tennessee's voluntary bankrupts who could be located in the census had been born in the United States but outside of the South, while a quarter of Mississippi filers and only 8 percent of South Carolina bankrupts from the counties studied fit this description. Only 17 percent of the non-southern-born Tennesseans were from the slave states that had remained with the Union—Delaware, Kentucky, Maryland, and Missouri—and a third of the nonnative South Carolinians came from those four states. In Mississippi, 57 percent of those born outside of the South were native to those border states. Most of the relatively few filers from outside of the South were from northern and western states without strong ties to the South, but these findings do not support the hypothesis that the Bankruptcy Act was a tool employed predominantly by those who had moved to the South after the war. Rather, the high percentage of southern natives among filers located in the census leads to the inference that most voluntary bankrupts had roots in the region and lived in the Confederacy during its rise and fall.

Table 4 provides some information about the remaining voluntary bankruptcy filers, those who were born in countries other than the United States. This group included 26 percent of the South Carolina and Mississippi filers and 4 percent of the East Tennessee voluntary bankrupts whose birthplaces could be identified. All were from Europe, and none were from countries that allowed slavery, a factor that may have contributed to an absence of planters from the group. Because foreign-born residents comprised only 1–2 percent of the 1870 populations of Mississippi, South Carolina, and Tennessee, it is likely that the percentage of foreign-born bankrupts who were identified is higher than the percentage of foreign-born persons in the full group of voluntary filers in these districts. Many of the foreign-born had uncommon names, which might have made them easier to track in the manuscript census schedules. Although the 1867 Bankruptcy Act allowed noncitizens to file for bankruptcy, more than 90 percent of the located foreign-born voluntary bankrupts from the three judicial districts were U.S. citizens. These foreign-born voluntary bankrupts were predominately city-dwelling merchants: about 80 percent resided in the districts' major urban areas—Vicksburg and Meridian, Mississippi; Charleston, South Carolina; and Knoxville and Chattanooga, Tennessee—and about 80 percent were merchants; none were planters.[12]

As with the foreign-born, the dominant occupation for all filers was merchant, as charts 7–8 show. Whether one looks only at occupation information

Table 4 Foreign-born voluntary bankrupts

Eastern Tennessee	Southern Mississippi (2 counties)	South Carolina (2 counties)
Baden (U.S. citizen): 1 filer	Bavaria (U.S. citizen): 4 filers	Hamburg, Germany (U.S. citizen): 1 filer
Germany (not U.S. citizen): 1 filer	France (citizenship unclear): 1 filer	Hesse-Darmstadt, Germany (U.S. citizen): 1 filer
Germany (U.S. citizen): 1 filer	Hamburg, Germany (U.S. citizen): 1 filer	Ireland (U.S. citizen): 4 filers
Hungary (U.S. citizen): 1 filer	Hesse, Germany (U.S. citizen): 1 filer	Poland (U.S. citizen): 3 filers
	Ireland (U.S. citizen): 3 filers	Prussia (U.S. citizen): 10 filers
	Poland (U.S. citizen): 2 filers	
	Prussia (not U.S. citizen): 1 filer	
	Prussia (U.S. citizen): 7 filers	
	Switzerland (U.S. citizen): 2 filers	

Sources: Bankruptcy Case Files and Dockets; Census Records (see appendix on methodology).

discernable in the bankruptcy case files or uses a broader set of sources, including the 1870 manuscript census schedules and city directories (which are less accurate in reflecting the occupation of the bankrupt at the time of filing), merchants consistently and substantially outnumbered other occupations among filers from East Tennessee and from the two Mississippi and South Carolina counties studied in depth. Planters and farmers followed as the next most common occupation and indeed formed the most common vocation identified among East Tennesseans. Professionals and skilled workers were the next most likely to file; voluntary bankruptcy filings by laborers were virtually nonexistent.

The data thus support Representative White's contention during debates in 1878 concerning the repeal of the Bankruptcy Act: "Away, then, with the pretense that this law is for the benefit of the laborer!" He asked, "Will gentlemen refer to the records of the bankrupt courts and tell me how many laboring-men have resorted to the bankrupt law to relieve their misfortunes?" White concluded that "there are none."[13] Bankruptcy records from these three southern jurisdictions demonstrate the essential truth of this statement. In contrast, people who

Chart 7. Occupation of voluntary bankrupts at time of filing

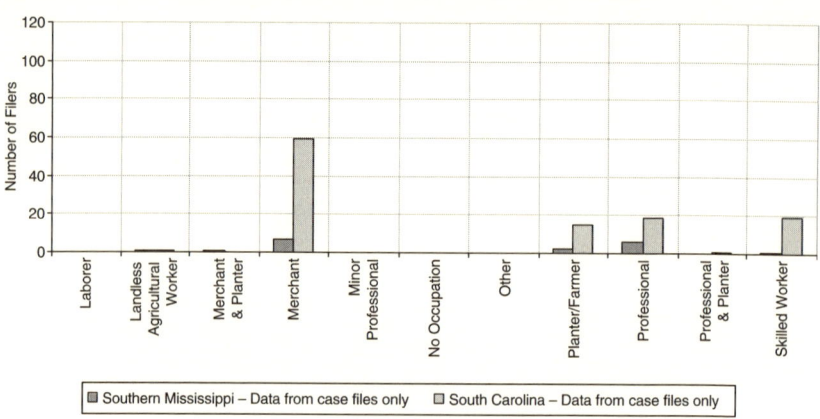

Chart 8. Occupation of voluntary bankrupts at or near time of filing

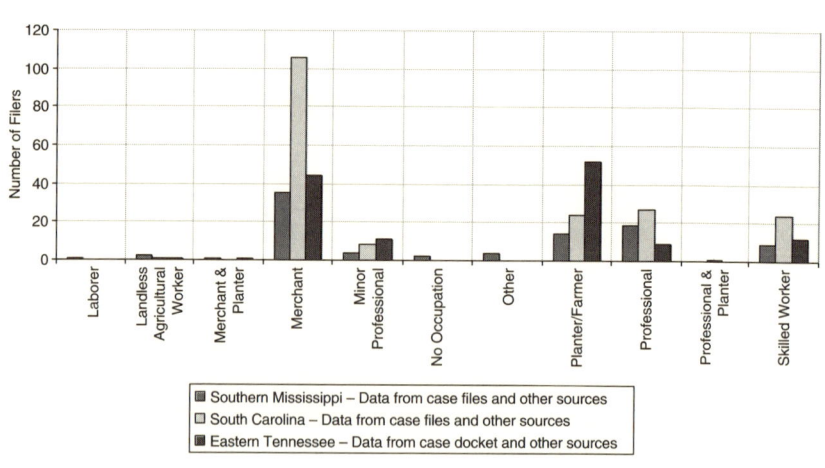

held greater amounts of property and incurred more expansive obligations than did laborers—merchants, farmers and planters, and professionals—commonly filed for voluntary bankruptcy. This finding is not unexpected, but it leads to three conclusions. First, the Act's beneficiaries were precisely those groups that Congress had intended to benefit—those of the trading class. Second, the three occupational groups that most used the proceedings were also those with the greatest political power in the South: professionals, landed agriculturalists, and merchants. Members of these groups sat in state legislatures, edited newspapers, and influenced court decisions. Third, identifying the groups that profited from voluntary bankruptcy proceedings makes clear how the Bankruptcy Act reinforced the status quo in southern class structure. During an era when Radicals in Congress were proposing a redistribution of southern planters' lands to freedpeople, former slaves were asserting claims to the property that their labor had developed, and women were clamoring for recognition of their conventionally circumscribed political and economic rights, a Republican-dominated Congress passed an act that helped members of the propertied southern class gain economic equilibrium, regardless of their past disloyalty to the United States. Through the Bankruptcy Act, these white men may have had to give up many of their assets, but as discussed in chapter 1, they also retained a substantial amount of property. Thus, a high percentage of those who achieved discharge were able to proceed with their economic pursuits free from burdensome past obligations.

The economic liberation allowed many people to quickly rebuild their assets. An examination of the property reported by voluntary bankrupts in the 1870 federal census indicates the extent that this was the case. Table 5 contains information on all bankrupts who had filed and obtained discharges prior to June 1, 1870 (the effective date of the 1870 census returns), and who could be located in the 1870 manuscript census.[14] If a filer met these criteria, it was possible to determine how much property the bankrupt possessed reasonably soon after filing for bankruptcy and obtaining discharge. Fourteen percent of East Tennessee voluntary bankrupts, 23 percent of southern Mississippi voluntary bankrupts, and 15 percent of South Carolina voluntary bankrupts studied in depth met these criteria.[15]

Because of the relatively low number of voluntary filers who satisfied these criteria, conclusions based on the property ownership of this group must be considered guardedly. Yet certain patterns are evident—most notably that these bankrupts, on average, held a significant amount of property soon after filing for bankruptcy and obtaining discharges. The average conceals a wide range of property ownership, with some voluntary bankrupts owning much more than the average and others owning much less: barely half of the Mississippi

Table 5 Property ownership by voluntary bankrupts after discharge

District	% of filers meeting criteria	Avg. property ownership	
		Real	Personal
Southern Mississippi (2 counties)	23	$3,981.52	$1,762.61
South Carolina (2 counties)	15	$894.05	$1,102.38
Eastern Tennessee	14	$2,546.97	$1,430.33

Sources: Bankruptcy Case Files and Dockets; Census Records (see appendix on methodology).

and South Carolina filers owned any property at all, while about 90 percent of those in East Tennessee held property. Yet the average amount of property held by these voluntary bankrupts might actually have been much higher. Scholars have noted southerners' common underreporting of property ownership to 1870 census enumerators, particularly in areas where whites feared that Republican governments would use the property data to assess greater taxes.[16]

Nevertheless, many bankrupts reported owning substantial property. South Carolina native George Von Kolnitz submitted his voluntary bankruptcy petition in January 1868 and received his discharge eleven months later. In the 1870 census, taken a year and a half later, Von Kolnitz, a merchant, reported assets worth seventeen thousand dollars. Grainger County, Tennessee, farmer William H. Taylor obtained a discharge in March 1870, almost twenty months after filing his petition. Yet just a few months after discharge, the Tennessee native possessed ten thousand dollars worth of real property and six thousand dollars worth of personal property. Mississippian Andrew D. Banks experienced similar favorable circumstances after filing for bankruptcy in December 1868. At his Freeland Plantation in Warren County, Banks, who was originally from Virginia, could proceed with his agricultural operations with land worth forty thousand dollars and personal effects valued at ten thousand dollars just a few months after he had obtained his discharge in March 1870.[17]

In addition, the wives and mothers of various male voluntary bankrupts held property in their own right. The number of such cases discovered through investigation of the manuscript census is relatively few, but the fact that they ex-

Table 6 Property ownership by wives and mothers of male voluntary bankrupts

District	Name (wife or mother)	Property owned by wife/mother		Property owned by husband/son	
		Real	Personal	Real	Personal
Southern Mississippi (2 counties)	Sallie E. Hamberlin (wife)	$3,000	0	0	0
	E.[?] H. Crutcher (wife)	$8,000	$2,000	0	0
	Rebecca Billingsly (wife)	$2,000	$1,223	0	0
South Carolina (2 counties)	M. M. Dawson (wife)	$750	0	0	$300
Eastern Tennessee	Martha M. Coffin (wife)	$3,000	0	0	$1,200
	Sallie A. Palmer (wife)	$1,000	0	0	$400
	Harriet Hart (mother)	$4,500	$500	$525	$5,000
	A. C. McReynolds (wife)	$4,000	$1,000	0	0
	Lizzie E. McReynolds (wife)	$6,000	$300	0	$150
	Sarah M. Whiteside (wife)	$2,000	$500	0	0
	Eliza Epperson (wife)	$1,200	$400	0	0

Sources: Bankruptcy Case Files and Dockets; Census Records (see appendix on methodology).

isted at all is notable. According to the 1870 census, of all voluntary filers studied in depth from the three districts, the wife of one South Carolina voluntary bankrupt, the wives of six East Tennessee voluntary filers and the mother of another, and the wives of three filers from Mississippi owned real or personal property or both. In such cases, as noted in table 6, the voluntary bankruptcy filers usually did not list any property ownership. As discussed in more detail in chapters 1 and 7, liberalized state laws during this era increasingly permitted married women to hold property in their own right. A primary impetus behind such married women's property acts was to enable men to shield their property from creditors. Whether this was the case in the instances considered here is unknown; however, property possessed by these women surely benefited the bankrupts, providing them with an additional tool with which to reconstruct their lives after declaring bankruptcy.

Like the voluntary proceedings discussed in this chapter, involuntary bankruptcies also served as means to advance southerners' interests. Almost as often as northern creditors, southern creditors initiated involuntary filings, while southern debtors strove to defeat such efforts. The next chapter will examine how involuntary proceedings constituted both a negotiating device and a collection tool as debtors and creditors sorted out their economic affairs.

CHAPTER SIX

Involuntary Bankruptcy in Southern Tribunals

The enforcement of this side of the bankrupt law is decidedly unpleasant . . . but few have come to the final hearing. —Mississippi Federal District Judge Robert A. Hill, 1869

By April 1875, the Vicksburg, Mississippi, dry goods firm of Henry Bodenheim and Company had become insolvent. Company debts topped $150,000, including more than $100,000 bought on credit from New Yorkers and others that spring. As the assignee of these creditors later alleged, principals of Bodenheim and Company knew that bankruptcy was imminent and "for the purpose of defrauding their creditors, they caused a large number of their confidential friends and customers to be secretly notified to come to their store for the express purpose of disposing of their goods and stock in trade, under the pretence of trading with them in the usual and ordinary course of business." The firm's intention to sell its goods "at any sacrifice for money in fraud of their creditors and of the bankrupt law became quite generally know[n] in the city of Vicksburg and its vacinity among the merchants who were customers" of the company. On Thursday, April 22, and Friday, April 23, according to the assignee, confidential friends and small dealers selected and removed a large share of the $75,000 worth of goods in the company's storehouse. By Saturday, April 24, creditors had secured a writ of attachment (a court order to seize the firm's property as security for creditors' claims). But the firm regained possession of the goods by giving a bond with the promise that it would keep the goods in their present condition pending settlement of the creditors' cases. Yet later that night, the "fraudulent disposition" continued. "Their doings had become notorious through out the City of Vicksburg, and their storehouse was invaded by hundreds of persons, in large crowds seekings bargains for cash." So many people came that they could not fit into the structure. Policemen arrived to monitor the doors and ensure that the storehouse did not become unsafe from overcrowding. The assignee charged "that the most costly goods were thrown from the shelves and delivered to persons for sums of money which were mere trifles compared with the value of the goods and indeed, the pretended sales were made without reference to the cost or value of the goods." Salesmen did not abide by their normal practice of completing sales tickets, which would then be delivered to the bookkeeper or cashier. Rather, employees "received the money without making any sort of memorandum of sales, and litterly cramed the money which they received into their pockets." Such chaotic transactions continued until after midnight on Saturday, and further "reckless and illegal disposition of goods" took place until creditors closed the store by legal attachment on Monday, April 26. Even that morning, the assignee contended, "numerous drays were crowding around the door of Bankrupts house, to deliver in hot haste the goods selected and purchased by their various confidential friends" on Sunday.[1]

Five years earlier, in June 1870, two St. Louis creditors had filed an involuntary bankruptcy petition against Mississippian W. W. Jefferson, a grocery merchant in Lauderdale County. Some confusion apparently occurred in getting the petition and an order to the court clerk—the judge in Jackson instead sent them to the creditors' attorneys, Shannon and Grace, in Meridian, Mississippi. By the time the documents reached Shannon and Grace, Jefferson's property "had been run into Alabama." The attorneys noted, "When we prepared the petition on the 18th there were about $3000.00 worth of goods." But the remaining assets were worth about $200. When Shannon and Grace realized the court's mistake, they prepared a document requesting the sequestration of the remaining property (its seizure pending a decision in the bankruptcy case). "Excuse us for not fastening the sheets in the petition for writ of sequestration together," they implored the federal court clerk. "The thing was fixed up in great haste." But the writ would not cure the damage that had been done, and the attorneys conceded, "After waiting a reasonable time if we can not find more goods we will pay the Costs and dismiss the case."[2]

In May 1875, a Charleston merchant firm, G. A. Trenholm and Son, alleged that fellow Charlestonian A. F. Chevereux had attempted to swindle his creditors by leaving South Carolina with the intent of evading debt payments. Chevereux had owed George A. and William Trenholm more than sixteen hundred dollars since August 1874. George Trenholm, a principal actor in the Charleston Chamber of Commerce and Board of Trade, had also served as the Confederate secretary of the treasury. This high-ranking rebel official thus appealed to the government against which he had recently revolted to collect payment from a fellow southerner. The Trenholm firm discontinued the case about two and a half years later, perhaps having either settled with Chevereux or decided that the claim was not worth pursuing.[3]

These three case studies display the complex interactions among parties to involuntary bankruptcy proceedings. Both debtors and creditors jockeyed for advantage. Anticipating creditors' filings, debtors at times attempted to disappoint claimants by disposing of their assets or by fleeing to another state. Creditors likewise maneuvered for position, sometimes discontinuing cases shortly after filing them, thus indicating that settlement had likely occurred and that the involuntary filing had perhaps served as a bargaining chip. Filing involuntary proceedings likely formed a forceful action in a complex array of otherwise out-of-court settlement negotiations between creditors and debtors. The terms of the Bankruptcy Act limited when creditors could employ it, but creditors stretched the statute's involuntary provisions to serve another goal: settlement. The Bankruptcy Act anticipated and encouraged such out-of-court resolutions; creditors, however, applied the Act beyond what the statute anticipated.

Further, almost as many southern creditors as northerners initiated involuntary proceedings in the areas of the three districts studied in depth. Congressmen who passed the Bankruptcy Act of 1867 had anticipated that it would enable northern creditors to collect prewar debts from southerners. In practice, however, southern creditors, like those from other regions, employed this federal mechanism. And, as reflected in the debtor's alleged actions in the Trenholm case, southern debtors were not averse to trying to defeat claims by creditors of their own region. Thus, involuntary bankruptcy proceedings in southern federal courts did not involve a simple North-versus-South dynamic (as might have been expected from the congressional debates leading to the Act's passage). Rather, they involved complex interactions between southern debtors and creditors resident in the North as well as the South.

In 1869, Mississippi Federal Judge Robert A. Hill acknowledged that he found the enforcement of involuntary cases to be an unpleasant task. Yet the number of involuntary filings before the Mississippi court had been small: "Fortunately, so far, out of nearly five hundred cases, not more than twenty have been on the involuntary side of the docket, and not more than half that number have been contested; and of the remaining number but few have come to the final hearing." Consequently, Hill maintained, "this portion of the law has received but little consideration from either the court or the bar."[4] But although the Act's involuntary bankruptcy provisions had received little attention from formal judicial rulings, the law apparently received consideration in that it shaped the actions of parties—or potential parties—to involuntary suits. Like Bodenheim and Company and Jefferson, debtors took action to defeat creditors when involuntary filings were imminent. Creditors similarly worked outside of the Bankruptcy Act's provisions by filing to force debtors to pay through out-of-court settlements.

In these senses, the terms of the 1867 Bankruptcy Act structured but did not entirely circumscribe the actions and reactions of creditors and debtors. Thus, the Act passed to relieve southern debtors from burdensome economic obligations became an offensive instrument employed by both southern and northern creditors as well as southern debtors. As a result, southerners benefited from this federal law in ways that the Republican-dominated 1867 Congress had not anticipated.

Two factors shape this discussion of involuntary bankruptcy. First, a much smaller number of involuntary cases than voluntary cases was filed. Only 404 of the 3,810 cases filed in the districts of eastern Tennessee, southern Mississippi, and South Carolina were involuntary. As a result, the number of southern debtors and likely the number of northern and southern creditors affected by involuntary cases were smaller than the number touched by voluntary proceedings. Conclusions about the impact of the involuntary provisions of the Bankruptcy Act thus must be qualified accordingly. Nonetheless, the involuntary filings were not inconsequential. Unlike current bankruptcy law, which has liberal provisions for debtors, "in the nineteenth century, . . . involuntary bankruptcy figured quite prominently," David Skeel recognizes. Creditors believed that nineteenth-century state laws afforded debtors too many advantages and "saw a uniform, federal bankruptcy law as the best way to assure that everyone to whom a debtor owed money would be treated equally."[5] Which parties were involved in these adversarial proceedings indicates how southerners viewed the role of this federal bankruptcy law—and, more generally, the role of the federal courts—during Reconstruction.

Second, conclusions regarding creditors involved in involuntary proceedings concentrate on the creditors who initiated the actions. The involuntary bankrupt likely also owed debts to other creditors, but the initiating creditors turned to the federal court to enforce their claims and constituted the most aggressive users of the Bankruptcy Act. Other creditors joined later in the proceedings. The filing creditors also are consistently identifiable from the court documents and thus comprise a verifiable group for purposes of forming conclusions.

Under the original terms of the 1867 Act, a single creditor could commence involuntary proceedings against a debtor. This remained the case until Congress amended the statute in 1874. The Panic of 1873 and the fact that many people blamed involuntary bankruptcy proceedings against a major Philadelphia mercantile firm, Jay Cooke and Company, for precipitating the crisis resulted in calls for revamping the bankruptcy law. In late 1873, President Ulysses S. Grant expressed his belief that the Act was "productive of more evil than good at this time." In particular, he charged that the involuntary bankruptcy provisions "operate[d] to increase the financial embarrassments of the country" because a single unfriendly creditor "oftimes accomplish[ed] the financial ruin of a responsible business man." Grant requested the repeal of the provision that made suspension of debt payments an act of bankruptcy. Instead, Congress made the requirements for instigating involuntary proceedings more rigorous by requiring a greater number and percentage of creditors to begin such an action. After December 1, 1873, a single creditor could no longer submit a petition; instead, at least a quarter of a debtor's creditors holding at least one-third of the debtor's obligations had to act as initiating creditors.[6] As a result, the group of creditors who filed involuntary proceedings after the beginning of December 1873 in the three judicial districts investigated represented a much greater number of a debtor's obligees. But those who filed both pre- and post-December 1873 cases shared the characteristic of turning to the federal courts and specifically the Bankruptcy Act of 1867 to obtain redress. The fact that many of these creditors were residents of the South illustrates that involuntary proceedings often acted as an offensive, empowering instrument for southerners rather than merely a device that oppressed southern debtors.

Maps 13 through 15 consider the state residences of creditors who commenced involuntary proceedings against residents of East Tennessee; of Warren and Lauderdale Counties, Mississippi; and of Charleston and Anderson Counties, South Carolina.[7] The maps elucidate two principal trends. First, those residing outside of the South were somewhat more likely than southern creditors to file involuntary bankruptcy cases against residents of the districts and counties considered. But the number of initiating southern creditors was not appreciably smaller. Table 7 compares the number of filing creditors residing in the former Confederate states with those residing in other areas.

Second, southern creditors tended to initiate cases against fellow state residents. And many filing creditors who resided outside of the former Confederate states lived in the previously slaveholding Union states of Kentucky, Maryland, and Missouri, demonstrating these border states' ties to their southern neighbors. Ten Tennesseans initiated involuntary cases against fellow Tennesseans. The next most common residence state of filing creditors in East Tennessee cases was Maryland, with six creditors. Similarly, the eighty-four Mississippi residents who filed against residents of Warren and Lauderdale Counties comprised a plurality of the petitioners, followed by New Yorkers, with fifty-eight. Fifty-four of the nonsouthern creditors filing against Mississippians resided in Kentucky, Maryland, and Missouri. In South Carolina, 120 New York creditors initiated cases, as did 114 South Carolinians. A sharp drop occurred between these two groups and the next-most-common group of filers of South Carolina involuntary cases, eight creditors from Maryland.

Map 13 Southern District of Mississippi involuntary bankruptcy filings: Residence of creditors filing against Mississippi debtors

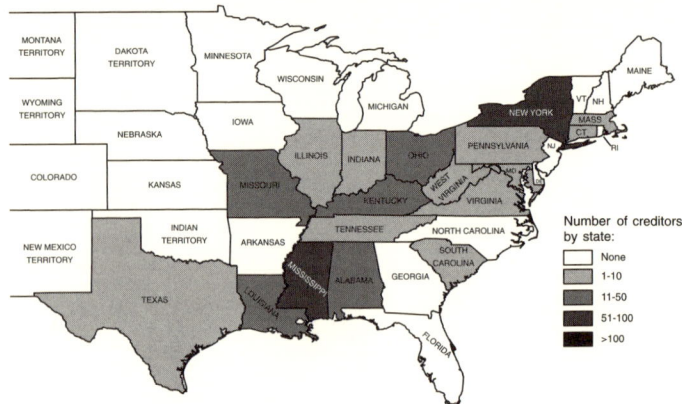

Notes: One creditor's residence is either Massachusetts or Missouri; the record is unclear. The state of residence of eleven other creditors is unclear.

Sources: Southern District of Mississippi Bankruptcy Case Files and Docket (see appendix on methodology); Thorndale and Dollarhide, *Map Guide*, 9.

Cartographer: John Huggins.

Map 14 District of South Carolina involuntary bankruptcy filings: Residence of creditors filing against South Carolina debtors

Notes: The state of residence of three creditors is unclear.

Sources: District of South Carolina Bankruptcy Case Files and Docket (see appendix on methodology); Thorndale and Dollarhide, *Map Guide*, 9.

Cartographer: John Huggins.

Map 15 Eastern District of Tennessee involuntary bankruptcy filings: Residence of creditors filing against Tennessee debtors

Number of creditors by state:
- None
- 1–10
- 11–50
- 51–100
- >100

Notes: The state of residence of eleven creditors is unclear, including the records for one creditor that indicate "out of state."

Sources: Eastern District of Tennessee Bankruptcy Case Docket (see appendix on methodology); Thorndale and Dollarhide, *Map Guide*, 9.

Cartographer: John Huggins.

Yet filing patterns differed among the three districts. East Tennessee had the fewest number of involuntary cases and thus filing creditors—thirty-three and thirty-seven, respectively. As is apparent in map 15, although numerous Tennessee creditors filed in the district, the few creditors who resided outside of the state largely resided in the North, including the border Union state of Maryland. Creditors from the states immediately surrounding Tennessee were virtually absent from the court dockets. This filing configuration likely represented the relative geographic isolation of the East Tennessee region. The pattern also hints at why large numbers of East Tennessee residents remained loyal to the Union during the Civil War, unlike people in other parts of the state. According to the measure of out-of-state filing creditors, the region had little commercial contact with residents of the South. This pattern thus confirms what other historians have recognized: slight ties with other Tennesseans and the South generally (including a lower incidence of slavery than that found in other Confederate regions) contributed to East Tennesseans' lack of desire to join the Confederacy.[8]

In contrast, involuntary filings involving debtors from Warren and Lauderdale Counties, Mississippi, indicate a great deal of cross-border commercial ties between Mississippians and their neighbors in Louisiana and Alabama. The largest concentration of out-of-state creditors was from Louisiana, with twenty-

Table 7 Residence of filing creditors in involuntary bankruptcy cases

District	Residing in the South	Residing outside the South	Residence unclear
Southern Mississippi (2 counties)	131	162	11
South Carolina (2 counties)	115	139	3
Eastern Tennessee	11	16	10
Total	257	317	24

Sources: Bankruptcy Case Files and Dockets (see appendix on methodology).

five residents of that state, all from New Orleans, initiating cases. Eighty-two of the ninety debtors in Mississippi involuntary cases were from Vicksburg or Meridian, Mississippi (and the residences for seven of the other eight debtors were unclear). Likewise, almost all of the initiating creditors in the Mississippi filings lived in major urban centers, both northern and southern. Thus, creditors from Missouri, New York, and Ohio almost without exception resided in St. Louis, New York City, and Cincinnati.[9]

Involuntary filings in South Carolina most closely resembled the caseload that the congressmen who passed the 1867 Bankruptcy Act thought would result from the legislation. The large number of New York creditors who initiated involuntary cases against debtors from Charleston County in particular as well as Anderson County dwarfed that of any other state except South Carolina. The commercial ties between Charleston and New York are strongly evident. Yet legislators did not foresee the substantial number of South Carolina creditors who filed against their neighbors. Indeed, twenty-nine of the fifty-one involuntary proceedings (57 percent) against residents of the city of Charleston involved a Charleston creditor.[10]

Across all three judicial districts, more than two-thirds of the 598 filing creditors in the cases studied were partnerships or companies. Most of these entities for which line of work could be determined were merchants: case files provided occupation information for 108 creditors, of which 93 (86 percent) were merchants, 14 were professionals, and 1 was a planter. Similarly, most defendants in involuntary suits were merchants. Case records identify the occupations of 121 of the 186 defendants in the cases studied: 103 (85 percent) were merchants.[11]

Most of these findings are not surprising but rather confirm that the 1867 Bankruptcy Act had the effect that Congress had intended, allowing northern creditors to collect on claims against southern debtors. Yet southern creditors also comprised a substantial portion of those who filed. That the law served as an empowering and a constraining device is indicated by the ways in which creditors from both sections employed the involuntary provisions of the Bankruptcy Act to obtain payment and by the ways in which southern debtors similarly stretched the law to fit their needs.

On November 25, 1870, the New York merchant firm of Evans, Gardner, and Company filed an involuntary bankruptcy petition against Vicksburg merchants Herman and Moss to collect a debt of more than two thousand dollars. Three days later, the defendant's attorney, H. H. Miller, wrote to the federal bankruptcy register, George C. McKee, "I will take it as a favor if you will see Judge Hill *this evening*, & explain that the case against Herman & Moss has been settled; & the particular[s], as stated to us by Moss, of the manner in which he was treated by the Agent of the N.Y. House." Miller concluded, "I think H & M have been treated very shabbily." This shabby treatment occurred despite the fact that both Joseph Herman and Lewis Moss were New York natives. Further, the short time between filing and settlement suggests that this creditor did not use the involuntary bankruptcy proceedings as an end in themselves or as a self-contained procedure for debt collection. Rather, filing an involuntary petition likely served as a tool—perhaps the most forceful tool available—to achieve an advantageous settlement of debts.[12]

Various factors contributed to creditors' desire to settle out of court, including the logistics of bankruptcy proceedings and the economic situation of southern debtors. In July 1873, a writer in the *American Law Review* referred to creditors' frustration with the fees and expenses in bankruptcy proceedings, which swallowed the bankrupts' assets and thus decreased the amount that creditors ultimately received: "From the beginning to the end, there is one continuous, increasing plucking at the estate," the writer concluded. As a result, "merchants have come to believe it best to settle with their debtors out of the Bankrupt Court." In addition, postwar economic conditions promoted compromise. As historian Dan T. Carter recognizes, "Most creditors, whether in New York or Charleston, were well aware of the precarious financial situation of most southern planters and were willing to adjust antebellum and war debts downward, forgiving interest accrued during the war and often reducing the outstanding principal from 10 to 60 percent." The value of southerners' assets, especially their land, had plummeted. Creditors realized, as Carter points out, that "it was often more advantageous in the long run to readjust old debts, arrange for a gradual repayment, and hope for the best." In the give-and-take dynamic that accompanied settlement negotiations, debtors gained some advantage because they were so numerous. But while "each side sought a solution that would allow recovery without forcing bankruptcy," the gloomy prospect of bankruptcy proceedings hovered over debtors' shoulders since they knew that their obstinacy or an ungenerous creditor could result in an involuntary filing.[13]

Lawmakers eventually formally recognized what had been occurring informally. Amendments to the Bankruptcy Act passed in 1874 allowed composition, the predecessor to modern reorganization procedures in bankruptcy, which enabled a debtor in either voluntary or involuntary proceedings to enter into an agreement with creditors to pay a percentage of the debtor's obligations over time; the debtor could retain property (rather than turning it over to an assignee) and receive a complete discharge of the debts. To be effective, at least two-thirds of the debtor's creditors holding at least half in value of debts had to approve the debtor's proposal. Creditors who approved the composition proposal were bound to its terms; those who did not approve were protected by the guarantee that they would receive as much as they would have been paid had the debtor liquidated. As nineteenth-century bankruptcy scholar Orlando Bump explained, the composition provision "was passed for the purpose of remedying [the] wrong" of the power of "an obstinate creditor [to] defeat an advantageous composition." As Bump maintained, "Such a power in the hands of an exacting and unscrupulous creditor, although legal, was inequitable, for it enabled him to violate that principle of equality which is equity." Yet even though composition might have addressed the problem of holdout creditors, some observers maintained that such an agreement was unconstitutional. As Maryland Senator William Pinkney Whyte argued four years after the composition provisions went into effect, "Providing for a compromise whereby a certain number of creditors could release a man upon paying a certain amount of debt, and leaving the minority to take it or not as it might be agreeable to them" was "a clause which I never could bring my mind to believe was within the constitutional power of Congress." Creditors leveled other criticisms: in 1877, the National Board of Trade protested that the Bankruptcy Act operated "as a premium upon fraud, by making it in the interests of debtors to offer low terms of composition, thereby making to themselves more money, or rather retaining money not belonging to them."[14]

Despite these complaints, bankrupts employed the composition procedures. Voluntary bankrupts often submitted proposals for composition at the same time that they filed petitions for bankruptcy. By 1877 in South Carolina, a preprinted "Form of Supplementary Petition" accompanied petitions, with blanks to fill in the terms of the proposed composition with creditors. When South Carolinian Robert White filed a voluntary bankruptcy petition in November 1876, he also submitted his composition proposition to creditors for "Thirty Cents Cash [on the dollar], in full settlement and satisfaction of the debts due by said Robert White."[15]

Yet even after the allowance of composition under the 1874 amendments, parties in both voluntary and involuntary proceedings continued to employ less formal settlement procedures. In May 1877, T. L. Brown of Danville, Virginia, wrote to G. Fallin and Sons of Charleston, which had filed for voluntary bankruptcy a month earlier. Brown, one of the firm's creditors, had opposed the discharge of the Fallin firm's debts but later informed the U.S. district court clerk that he would withdraw his opposition if he received thirty cents on the dollar for the approximately $765 he was owed. The clerk informed Brown that he would need to hire a lawyer to effect this deal. Frustrated by the thought of hiring an attorney, Brown wrote to Fallin and Sons, "Now I do not want to incur this expense & Certainly will not get 30 pc of My debt. therefore if you will instruct me I will for[war]d through bank the original acceptance. with the 30 pc Dft & you can pay the 30 pc Dft & End the Matter." Economic conditions were apparently as constraining to this southern creditor as the southern debtor: "I have a widow Sister & five Children to support & no money to throw away on bankrupt Courts." By filing for voluntary bankruptcy, the debtor had forced the creditor's hand, leaving him no choice but to consent to the debtor's discharge and a 70 percent reduction in the amount of money owed. Similarly, three months after East Tennessee natives and residents T. J. and H. T. Jarnagin filed for voluntary bankruptcy in June 1876, their "case was compromised and the case stricken from the Docket the Bankrupts and the Court consenting thereto, evidences of debt withdrawn by leave of the Court." The Jarnagins had apparently settled with their creditors out of court. By employing the Bankruptcy Act, these southerners apparently reaped the benefits of using the voluntary provisions not simply to gain discharge but also to encourage settlement.[16]

But the most prevalent evidence of the use of bankruptcy filings as a negotiating tool is in the context of involuntary filings. Creditors often initiated involuntary proceedings but withdrew the filings shortly thereafter. Many case files either explicitly or implicitly indicate that after creditors filed, debtors and creditors had reached swift settlements.

Yet even while northern and southern creditors often forced a quick settlement after filing involuntary bankruptcy cases, debtors were not without their weapons, including claiming mental infirmity and wasting their assets. Alonzo

Murphy presented the U.S. District Court of Middle Tennessee with "a petition supported by affidavits, showing that he was non compos mentis at the time the debts of petitioning creditors were created, as well as the time of the institution of proceedings, and the adjudication of bankruptcy, and until a very recent period." District Judge Connally Trigg granted Murphy's petition to present to a jury his case that an adjudication of bankruptcy would be improper under these circumstances, and the jury found that Murphy was insane at the time of the previous bankruptcy adjudication and that the bankruptcy assignee should restore Murphy's property to him. J. W. Montgomery of East Tennessee took an opposite approach, apparently attempting to enjoy himself while his involuntary bankruptcy case was pending. The assignee claimed that Montgomery did not need an additional five hundred dollars for living expenses for which he had applied to the court. The funds were unnecessary, asserted the assignee, "as was evidenced *by the free and reckless manner in which he spend his money at the time in drinking saloons.*" The assignee set aside sixty-five dollars.[17]

In sum, as the tales of Murphy and Montgomery convey, involuntary filings in southern federal district courts involved much action and reaction on the part of creditors and debtors. Southern debtors employed various devices to attempt to defeat creditors' claims. Some, like Bodenheim and Company and Jefferson, allegedly (and, if so, fraudulently) transferred assets to others before involuntary filings took place. Other defendants, like Murphy and Montgomery, took defensive measures after creditors had filed petitions. Creditors, both northern and southern, often employed involuntary proceedings to spur settlement. The traditional depiction of the 1867 Act—and particularly involuntary proceedings—as empowering Yankee creditors to collect from debtors in the former Confederacy is not full and accurate. Southerners were not always victimized by involuntary proceedings but rather were among those who profited from them. Yet the benefits of the Bankruptcy Act of 1867 did not fall equally on all sectors of the southern population. As chapter 7 will show, southern white women and African American men and women were, with relatively few exceptions, not among the beneficiaries.

CHAPTER SEVEN

White Women and African Americans under the Bankruptcy Act

[She is] engaged in trade or business as a trader on her own account as a *femme sole.* —Involuntary bankruptcy petition against Rebecca Rothschild of Mississippi, 1874

The freedman cannot be benefited. . . . They owe no debts. —A. W. Spies, former slave from Georgia, commenting on state debtor-relief laws, 1866

In May 1868, C. A. Cogniasse petitioned for voluntary bankruptcy. The Vicksburg milliner listed herself as "Mrs. C. A. Cogniasse" but was careful to note that her debts to creditors in Memphis and New Orleans "were due by Petitioner alone." In her petition schedules, a list of those who owed her money included twenty-two women whose residences ranged from Vicksburg and Natchez, Mississippi, to Richmond, Louisiana, to Hinds County, Mississippi. Amounts owed her totaled more than twenty-five hundred dollars, while her Aetna insurance policy was worth three thousand dollars. Cogniasse, a native of France, sought to benefit from the U.S. government's beneficent Bankruptcy Act. Whether she received a discharge from her debts is unclear from the records, but she did not perceive the 1867 Act as off-limits to women. Rather, Cogniasse saw the law as an accessible avenue that she employed less than a year after it took effect.[1]

Almost five years later, in March 1873, creditors from St. Louis, Louisville, New Orleans, and Baltimore claimed that Clara Heidman of Lauderdale County, Mississippi, had committed two acts of bankruptcy and thus should be declared an involuntary bankrupt. Heidman had allegedly transferred between thirty-five hundred and four thousand dollars worth of property to R. J. Moseley, fraudulently preferring his claim over those of her other creditors. The creditors also charged that Heidman had stopped paying her commercial debts for more than fourteen days, which also provided grounds for an involuntary filing. Heidman "carried on the business of a Hotel Keeper and Bar Room and drinking saloon under the name of Clara Heidman with her own means and in her own name." She also was a "trader and dealer in the purchase and sale of liquors cigars and other merchandise." The filing parties claimed that Heidman owed them for "merchandise sold the said Clara Heidman for the use and to enable her to carry on her business." The creditors made clear that Clara, rather than her husband, was the appropriate debtor: "Said Clara Heidman is a married woman [and] Felix Heidman is her husband, but . . . the said Felix sets up no claim to any of the property in the possession of the said Clara."[2]

In February 1876, three years after the initiation of the Heidman case, eighteen creditors initiated filings against Charleston merchant John W. Linley individually and against Linley and his partner, W. W. Carpenter, as members of the firm J. W. Linley and Company. Thirteen of the creditors were from Charleston, while the remainder were New York, Maryland, and Kentucky firms. According to the creditors' petition, Linley and Linley and Company were "merchants and traders" who owed each creditor between $277.07 and $9,000. Based on 1870 census data, Linley was a retail grocer, an African American, and a South Carolina native who owned $1,000 worth of personal property six years before the bankruptcy filing against him.[3]

Cogniasse and Heidman, as white women, and Linley, as an African American man, did not represent typical bankrupts under the 1867 Act. Indeed, they are notable because they are among the very few white women and blacks (either men or women) who were involved in bankruptcy cases. Various factors contributed to these groups' general absence from bankruptcy dockets. Foremost was the fact that the individuals who owned property and dealt in the commercial arena—and, in turn, became financially distressed and needed the Bankruptcy Act—were predominantly white men. Yet how congressmen structured and how federal jurists applied the Bankruptcy Act with respect to white women and African Americans elucidates larger themes concerning the implications of post–Civil War federal economic legislation, including the Bankruptcy Act. The measure reinforced the system of federalism between the national and state governments and buttressed the South's traditional social and political hierarchy.

Congress enacted bankruptcy legislation that allowed state law to dictate how the federal measure would apply in various ways, including two principal areas: first, allowing a bankrupt to exempt from judicial seizure or execution the amount of property permitted under state law; second, following state law concerning whether and how women could act as bankrupts. As a writer for the *American Law Register* commented in 1874, "Where a woman may *owe* she may be bankrupt; where she cannot there is nothing upon which to found the proceedings." Thus, "her capacity to owe can only be determined by state legislation or interpretation; one state may establish one rule, and another a different rule; but Congress has no jurisdiction to legislate on the subject; such power was not granted in the Constitution, and is reserved to the states."[4] National legislators bowed to states' authority in areas such as women's legal status not only because of comity but also because Congress was not disposed to expand federal power to recognize greater rights for women, even during an era when federal power had been extended to unprecedented lengths to protect individuals' (particularly freedpeople's) rights. As Patricia Allan Lucie notes in her study of Congress and the courts in the 1860s, "Republicans encountered a . . . problem" in that "if they phrased definitions of civil rights for freedmen too broadly they might accidentally benefit women." Indeed, in 1866, John Bingham's original expansive wording of the federal government's power "to make laws for the equal protection of life, liberty and property" caused Robert Hale, a jurist from New York, to alert "Congress to the awful possibility that it might affect married women's property rights." Legislators and judges took no such chance under the Bankruptcy Act: "any person . . . owing debts" could file. Who actually owed debts was a key determination on which congressmen and jurists deferred to state authorities.[5]

African Americans' and white women's involvement—or lack thereof—in bankruptcy shows clearly how the Bankruptcy Act of 1867 reinforced the South's economic and thus social and political power structure. Those who profited from the legislation were from a certain race, gender, and class—white, male merchants and, less frequently, planters and professionals. No one was excluded from the Bankruptcy Act's benefits based on past service to the Confederacy. And although former slaves claimed that they had earned ownership of land through their centuries of uncompensated labor, and although some Radical Republicans, most prominently Thaddeus Stevens of Pennsylvania, agreed, urging confiscation and redistribution of land, nothing of the sort took place.[6] Instead, the 1867 Congress, dominated by Republicans devoted to taming white southerners' intransigence, passed legislation that bolstered the economic and consequently social and political security of the South's influential white men.

As discussed in chapter 1, lawmakers justified the passage of the 1867 Bankruptcy Act at that particular time by portraying the statute as economic and as divorced from the political campaign of Reconstruction. In actuality, the law was fundamentally political. Women benefited only to the extent that state authorities allowed. During the mid–nineteenth century, state legislatures and judges increasingly loosened restrictions based in the English common law doctrine of coverture, which held that married women could not own property or enter into contracts. Yet as Suzanne Lebsock establishes, southern legislators passed these married women's property acts not to empower women but rather to provide men with debtor relief, since they could then shield property by transferring it to their wives, a tactic that some voluntary bankrupts may well have used.[7] Congressmen and southern federal judges thus sustained state legislators' views concerning women's property ownership, bolstering their husbands' economic position. Likewise, as congressmen well knew, the newly freed slaves held very few assets—indeed, state law had not allowed blacks to hold property or engage in commerce during their enslavement. The great majority of African Americans, then, would be unlikely to benefit either as creditors or as debtors under the law. Lawmakers' lack of concern with this fact perhaps indicates early signs of what would become more prevalent as Reconstruction progressed: an increasing Republican inclination to turn away from the freedpeople and toward economic matters that tied the North and South together. The 1867 Bankruptcy Act thus cast aside the larger themes of Radical Reconstruction—expanded rights for citizens and a shift away from traditional state control over those rights.

Yet although legislators enacted and judges applied the bankruptcy measure in a way that benefited the established social and economic structure, various women grasped the opportunity to take advantage of the legislation. Although black men and women are virtually absent from the bankruptcy records, southern white women filed for voluntary bankruptcy and initiated involuntary claims as creditors. The relatively few women involved and the circumstances of their filing—particularly when joining male creditors in involuntary petitions—likely reflects the comparatively low number of women involved in commerce and indicates that any empowerment of women through the bankruptcy law was not broadly felt. Yet their use of the legislation and their role as involuntary bankrupts indicates, as scholars of women bankrupts under the 1800 and 1841 Bankruptcy Acts recognize, "that we have only scratched the surface in our thinking about early women's rights and opportunities within the legal system."[8] In addition, the presence of women on the dockets also portrays another group of southerners who used the 1867 Bankruptcy Act for their benefit: white women voluntary bankrupts and white women creditors. These women asserted an equal right with men to reap the benefits of the 1867 law despite the fact that the congressmen who enacted the statute did not anticipate female bankrupts and that the parameters of women's political and economic rights at the time were unsettled. The law structured the actions that these white women could take to address their economic woes, and they employed that law to fit their needs.

Under the terms of the Bankruptcy Act of 1867, bankrupts had wives: lawmakers included the requirement that "for good cause shown the wife of any bankrupt may be required to attend before the court, to the end that she may be examined as a witness; and if such wife do not attend at the time and place specified in the order, the bankrupt shall not be entitled to a discharge unless he shall prove to the satisfaction of the court that he was unable to procure the attendance of his wife." Legislators adopted this gender-restricted view of bankrupts despite the precedent of the 1800 Bankruptcy Act, which used both female and male pronouns to refer to debtors.[9] But when federal judges applied the 1867 law, women at times served as voluntary and involuntary bankrupts, depending entirely on the status of the relevant state law.

Whether a married woman could own property, engage in commerce, and sue in her own right (without the involvement or consent of her husband) was a point of contention during the nineteenth century. A widely applied legal doctrine of the time based on English common law, coverture, held that a single woman had the legal right to contract, sue, and own property but that a woman lost those rights when she married. Her rights became her husband's, and he acted in all of these respects on her behalf. As the nineteenth century progressed, increasing numbers of states passed married women's property acts that to varying degrees granted women the right to own property, sue, and contract. For example, at least seven southern states—Alabama, Arkansas, Florida, Louisiana, Mississippi, Tennessee, and Texas—had granted some property rights to married women prior to the Civil War. In 1868, three additional former Confederate states—Georgia, North Carolina, and South Carolina—conferred protection on married women's property rights.[10]

Thus, the state law with respect to women's property rights was evolving during the eleven years that the 1867 Act was in effect, and the jurisprudence of the federal bankruptcy courts reflected these developments. In 1874, an article in the *American Law Register* explained, "Impossible as it may be to reconcile the decisions on the general question of the rights and liability of married women, the duty of the Federal courts in applying the Bankrupt Law in these cases would seem to be of a simpler character." In sum, "if they determine the status of a married woman under the existing law of the state where the jurisdiction is to be exercised, and administer the Bankrupt Law upon the basis of the principles thus discovered, they have done all that can be required."[11] Yet the application was not so simple—state law evolved over time, and decisions under the bankruptcy law did not always reconcile with each other. As one federal reporter complained in 1873, "The statutory provisions in Indiana are nearly the same as in Illinois, . . . and although in both states it is held that [a woman] may engage in trade, and even employ her husband as her agent, in one state [the federal bankruptcy court] held that she may be a co-partner with her husband, and in the other [the federal court found] that she cannot."[12]

Treatise writers strove to make sense of the various decisions. An April 1867 publication, completed just a month after the law's passage, recognized the general policy that where coverture did not apply to a married woman's business dealings and contracts, "she is subject to the Bankrupt Law as fully as a *feme-sole*" (an unmarried woman).[13] But by the mid-1870s, the varying decisions in federal courts made the treatment of married women more complex. As Orlando Bump spelled out in the 1877 edition of his bankruptcy treatise, decisions primarily from federal courts in New York and Illinois (complemented by cases from California, Indiana, and Minnesota) made clear that the term "any person" in the Bankruptcy Act was "broad enough to include *femes covert*." But whether and which women were considered bankrupts depended on the status of the applicable state law and whether a woman met the law's requirements. For example, if a Minnesota woman was not abandoned or neglected by her husband and did not apply for a state license to trade, if it did not appear on the face of a note that it bound a New York woman's separate estate, or if a petition against an Indiana woman did not make clear that she had a separate estate, the married woman could "avail herself of her coverture to defeat the debt which is the basis of proceedings in bankruptcy."[14]

Women thus could benefit from not being forced into involuntary bankruptcy if coverture applied, but this benefit also represented a constriction of their rights under state law. As Lucie attests, women "could well have stood to gain from a definition of freedom which included the right to the fruits of one's labour, to make contracts, and to sue and be sued," but the federal government did not consider enacting such a general definition. Instead, federal judges bowed to state legislators and courts when determining how the Bankruptcy Act applied to married women. And state lawmakers extended these property statutes during the Reconstruction era to provide debtor protection to husbands. No wonder, as William Harris maintains, that although a married women's property measure passed during the 1868 Mississippi state convention was "a progressive innovation often cited approvingly by historians and attributed to the Radicals," it "actually received its strongest support from moderates in the convention," while "Radical Republicans, including black delegates, were seriously divided on the issue."[15]

Indeed, an example of how Mississippi federal judge Robert Hill applied the state's married women's property law displays how conservative ideas about women's economic liberty predominated and how federal judges in the South advanced the perspective of their local constituents. Although this case involved a debt collection rather than a bankruptcy, the decision illustrates Hill's attitude when he construed the same statute in the bankruptcy context. Mississippi's code of 1857 restricted the purposes for which a married woman could borrow money: a woman could bind her separate property for contracts made for family necessaries or supplies; clothing for her children or herself; her children's education; household furniture; supplies or overseer costs for her plantation; or clothing, care, maintenance, and support for her slaves. Hill stressed that Mississippi's high court had maintained "that the statute rendering the separate property of the wife liable to her contracts must be strictly construed." He held that a woman could not bind herself and make her separate property liable as a "general borrower" but rather could do so only for the purposes specifically enumerated in the statute. Hill then revealed the underlying worldview that helped dictate his decision: "For what purpose can a married woman desire to hold separate property, but for the use and benefit of herself and children; and after food and clothing, what is more dear to the heart of the mother than to see her children well educated?" The judge capped the opinion with a demeaning comparison: "The best analogy I have been able to find to the principles above stated is in the case of infants."[16]

Despite the fact that women's cases would be handled by federal judges whose outlooks could resemble Hill's and that various state statutes, like Mississippi's, were restrictive, women nevertheless employed the 1867 Bankruptcy Act to file for voluntary bankruptcy or to initiate involuntary claims as creditors. So even though state legislators might not have sought to encourage women's liberation and even though federal jurists might have possessed conservative views regarding women's rights and role in society, these women nevertheless took the available opportunities and used them as assertive instruments. The women probably did not consider the broader significance of their actions with respect to women's legal position, but as a writer for the *American Law Review* recognized in 1871, "The law of the status of women is the last vestige of slavery," and "by the married women's property acts, the first blow has been struck." Women involved in bankruptcy claims inflicted further blows by asserting their economic rights.[17]

Fourteen women filed for voluntary bankruptcy—either individually or as partners in an entity—in cases involving residents of the District of Eastern Tennessee; Warren and Lauderdale Counties, Mississippi; and Charleston and Anderson Counties, South Carolina. In twenty involuntary bankruptcy cases, fifteen women—all of whom resided in the South—filed as creditors or as members of filing entities, with four women suing more than once. One woman filed jointly with a male executor in her capacity as executrix for a deceased man. In nine involuntary bankruptcy cases, women were defendants individually or as members of firms.[18]

Just over 2 percent of the voluntary bankruptcy cases considered involved women filers, and women were creditors or partners of creditors in about 7 percent of involuntary cases.[19] The percentage of involuntary cases that involved women debtors was also small, at 5 percent. The extent to which women used the 1867 Bankruptcy Act had previously been unknown. Studies of women's use of bankruptcy laws (and, indeed, of the federal courts generally) in American history are virtually nonexistent, with one exception, a 1996 study by Karen Gross, Marie Stefanini Newman, and Denise Campbell that investigates female bankrupts under the 1800 and 1841 Acts. The authors located one woman bankrupt under the 1800 Act (under which only involuntary cases could be filed) and forty-eight women bankrupts under the 1841 statute, all but one of whom was a voluntary filer. Gross, Newman, and Campbell note that these findings prove the fallacy of the traditional separation of women's history and bankruptcy history and instead support "a cross-fertilized history of bankruptcy and women." The authors conclude that their study provides "additional support for the growing realization that although many women in 18th and 19th century America led circumscribed lives, some women were actively involved in the commercial marketplace and the world of debt and credit."[20]

The occupations of women involved in cases under the 1867 Bankruptcy Act similarly attest to women's participation in the commercial sphere. Case documents indicate occupations for five of the fourteen women who filed for voluntary bankruptcy, all of them merchants or skilled workers—two milliners, a baker, a merchant of "Window Shades & Paper Hangings," and one simply described as in the "mercantile business." Occupational data for women creditors who filed involuntary cases are scarce, but case documents identify a vocation for seven of the nine female involuntary bankrupts. Five were merchants, one—Clara Heidman—owned a hotel and bar, and one was a partner in a manufacturing corporation that produced cottonseed products.[21]

In addition to establishing that these women were involved in commerce, the filings involving women indicate a preoccupation with the changing nature of married women's rights and the legal position of women generally. This focus is not surprising, given that these topics were vital to the determination of bankruptcy cases involving married women. Although most women filers under the 1800 and 1841 Acts were unmarried, table 8 illustrates that about half of the women involved in studied cases under the 1867 Act were married.[22] And, as the figures in table 9 demonstrate, most of these women filed or were filed against as individuals rather than along with their husbands or as members of an entity. As a result—and as the cases of Cogniasse and Heidman attest—when these women were bankrupts, parties often took pains to establish that the women had the right to own property and engage in commerce and thus that the debts could properly be charged against the women under state law.

Table 8 Marital status of women involved in bankruptcy cases

Role	No. of cases involving women	No. of women involved	Single or marital status unclear	Married	Widowed
Filing for voluntary bankruptcy	14	13	5	6	2
Filing as creditors in involuntary cases	12	15	8	7	0
Defendants in involuntary bankruptcy cases	9	9	3	6	0

Note: Numbers listed in marital status columns based on the number of women involved, not the total number of cases, in filings by residents of the District of Eastern Tennessee; Lauderdale and Warren Counties, Mississippi; and Anderson and Charleston Counties, South Carolina. Some women were involved in multiple cases, and some cases involved more than one woman. Some women may have been widowed at the time of filing, although that information was not included in the case file.

Sources: Bankruptcy Case Files and Dockets (see appendix on methodology).

Petitions involving women either as voluntary or involuntary bankrupts commonly touched on the issue of the legality of women's property ownership. For example, a group of Cincinnati creditors carefully stated that the Vicksburg merchant against whom they had filed, N. Sinsheimer, was "a married woman, engaged in trade and business as a feme sole." Other filers attempted to avoid any chance that their case would fail because the female party lacked legal standing; Martha Gibbs of Warren County, Mississippi, covered any contingency by having her petition "joined and authorized by her husband A Judson Gibbs." Perhaps the most explicit petition was filed by Samuel Straus and Company of New York against "Rebecca Rothschild, wife of Samuel Rothschild" of Vicksburg. In its 1874 petition, the Straus firm stressed that Rothschild was "engaged in trade or business as a trader on her own account as a *femme sole,* under and by virtue of the Statute of the State of Mississippi, in such case made and provided, whereby a married woman is authorized to employ her money in trade or business, and whereby it is further provided that when a married woman engages in business or trade as a *feme sole,* she shall be bound by her contracts, made in the course of such trade or business, in the same manner

Table 9 Characteristics of women involved in bankruptcy cases

Role	As an individual	As member of partnership or other entity	As representative (i.e., executrix)	Listed as party with husband
Filing for voluntary bankruptcy	8	4	0	2
Filing as creditors in involuntary cases	15	3	1	1
Defendants in involuntary bankruptcy cases	6*	3	0	0

Notes: * = sole defendants. Numbers are based on the total number of times women were listed as parties in filings by residents of the District of Eastern Tennessee; Lauderdale and Warren Counties, Mississippi; and Anderson and Charleston Counties, South Carolina. One involuntary bankrupt was listed as an individual who used a company name for her business; because she had no partners, I counted her as an individual.

Sources: Bankruptcy Case Files and Dockets (see appendix on methodology).

as if she was unmarried." After that lengthy explanation, however, the creditor announced that Rebecca Rothschild carried on business "under the name and style of Samuel Rothschild, Ag't."[23]

All of these female debtors and creditors in the areas studied resided in the South. Birthplaces could not be determined for most of the women, but the 1870 census records do indicate that four of the thirteen voluntary bankrupts had been born in the South, one had been born in the Union border state of Kentucky, and one had been born in France. Although not conclusive, this information indicates that native southerners were definitely among and perhaps even formed the majority of female voluntary filers.

But a close look at filing patterns demonstrates a substantial difference in the timing of when white women employed the 1867 Bankruptcy Act's voluntary provisions as debtors and its involuntary provisions as initiating creditors. Chart 9 shows that the female voluntary bankrupts closely followed the general pattern of bankruptcy filings in the South and the rest of the country. A relatively large number of white women filed in 1868, prior to the imposition of the requirement to obtain creditor consent for discharge; the numbers subsequently dwindled. In contrast, white women more commonly filed as creditors in involuntary actions during the 1870s and particularly after 1874.

Perhaps more notable is the fact that with one exception (a white executrix who filed jointly with a male executor), white women did not initiate involuntary cases as single creditors, which the 1867 Act allowed prior to 1874 amendments that required that the plaintiffs include at least one-fourth of the debtor's creditors representing at least one-third of the amount owed. The number of creditors in involuntary cases involving white women as creditors or as members of creditor firms ranged from one to forty-six but averaged thirteen.[24] More seasoned creditors may have sought to satisfy the new requirements by persuading these women to join suits. If so, these women were not instigators of legal action but instead were participants, and thus it might not be appropriate to conclude that these female creditors used the Bankruptcy Act to aggressively enforce their rights.

One of the foremost concerns of legislators in Washington, D.C., immediately after the Civil War was ensuring the rights of freedpeople in the South. Congress passed numerous acts—from the Civil Rights Act of 1866 to statutes expanding the right to remove cases from state to federal courts—and established the Freedmen's Bureau in an effort to grant African Americans avenues for enforcing their legal rights and establishing their economic and social position as free citizens. Yet in passing the Bankruptcy Act of 1867, lawmakers did not act in the interest of freedpeople, who generally did not owe debts because state laws had restricted slaves from owning property and engaging in commerce. Instead, the law benefited white southern debtors and creditors, many of whom had recently rebelled against the U.S. government. On the surface, this action by a Republican-dominated Congress at the height of Radical Reconstruction seems incongruous. But, as discussed in chapter 1, legislators who supported the 1867 Bankruptcy Act justified its passage based on its nonpolitical, economic nature. Congressional supporters characterized the law not as a Reconstruction measure but rather as a statute meant to quell postwar economic chaos and soothe commercial wounds inflicted by the sectional conflict. Yet while the Act proved a valuable economic tool for scores of white men and a few white women, it did not provide economic or political empowerment for African Americans. As a result, the law reinforced the region's economic, social, and political hierarchy, which relegated African Americans to the bottom rung in terms of social privilege and economic well-being. In 1866, South Carolina federal Judge George Bryan noted that southern whites' property ownership put them in a more advantageous position than southern blacks. Bryan also recognized whites' other advantages. "We make, we administer the law. We judge;

Chart 9. Number of bankruptcy cases involving women

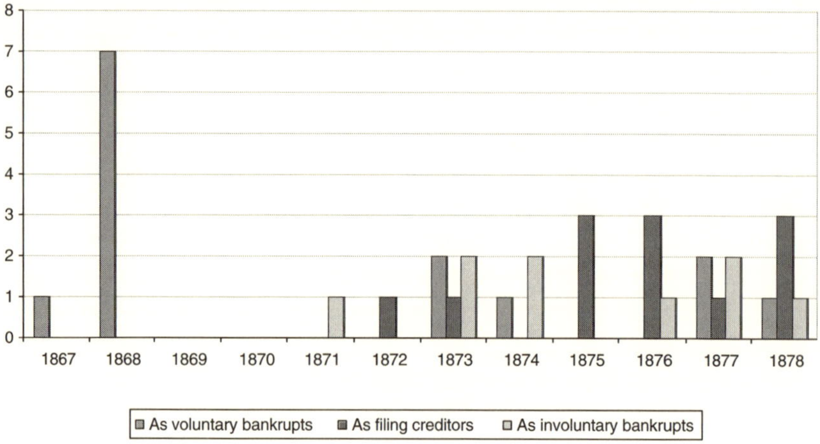

☐ As voluntary bankrupts   ■ As filing creditors   ☐ As involuntary bankrupts

Sources: Bankruptcy Case Files and Dockets (see appendix on methodology).

we have all the responsibility of superior power—*of power.*" In contrast, as Eric Foner recognizes, "In the end, most former slaves were consigned to the situation of being propertyless laborers on land owned by whites, often their own former slave owners." Thus, a wide chasm existed between African Americans' Reconstruction advances in the political and economic arenas: "There was a vast dichotomy between the very real and dramatic political gains and the failure of Reconstruction to address significantly the economic plight of the mass of black Americans."[25] The Bankruptcy Act of 1867 contributed to this state of affairs. The terms of the legislation and its effects reflected a slight of African Americans' interests by Republicans in Congress and in the federal courts, a snub that became increasingly common in the late 1860s and 1870s.[26]

A review of all case files for the District of Eastern Tennessee and files involving residents of counties in southern Mississippi and two in South Carolina yielded no African Americans who filed for voluntary bankruptcy or who served as initiating creditors in involuntary claims and only one black southerner who was an involuntary bankrupt—John W. Linley, the Charleston merchant mentioned at the beginning of this chapter.[27]

African Americans were not entirely absent from voluntary bankruptcy filings in other areas, however. Nashville, Tennessee, resident William Sumner filed for voluntary bankruptcy in the U.S. District Court for the Middle District of Tennessee in June 1875. The petition listed him as "Colored," a notation implicitly indicating that he differed from most filers. Sumner owned Nashville's Colored Fair Grounds and owed twelve unsecured debts totaling more than

$9,800, of which the largest single debts were $5,000 to Dr. W. A. Cheatham for "borrowed money to pay for the Colored Fair Grounds" and $4,000 plus interest to the Freedman's Savings and Trust Company. The latter amount had originally been secured: according to a bank officer, "The Colored Fair Grounds were mortgaged to secure this debt, but they have been sold for a prior debt without the equity of redemption." Sumner had assets worth $1,003, including seven judgments due him that ranged from $15 to $175 and four notes ranging from $50 to $200.[28]

The case documents do not indicate whether Linley's and Sumner's cases were dismissed or whether the men obtained discharges. The records also do not indicate whether Linley and Sumner were slaves or free men before the Civil War. But they clearly occupied a more fortunate economic position than did most African Americans of the era. While most freedpeople were agricultural laborers or sharecroppers with little income, Linley had established himself as a successful merchant and Sumner had engaged in a major commercial venture. Indeed, Linley's apparent business failure was in fact evidence of his achievement: his commercial dealings were expansive enough that creditors felt it was worth their while to press him for outstanding amounts.[29]

Although Sumner's and Linley's claims establish that African Americans were not entirely absent from federal court civil dockets during Reconstruction, their involvement as black southerners in bankruptcy proceedings was uncommon. The extreme dearth of blacks on the bankruptcy dockets leads to two questions. First, why did substantial numbers of cases not arise against the approximately 250,000 African Americans in the South who had been free before the Civil War and thus could have acquired assets and debts? And second, why did more freedpeople not file (or have involuntary filings against them) as time passed after their emancipation and they had the opportunity to acquire assets or to become mired in debt?[30]

Three primary factors likely help to answer both of these questions. First, African Americans used courts infrequently—their absence from court proceedings was not limited to federal bankruptcy cases. African Americans were aware of the operation of the federal courts and informed regarding which federal jurists favored blacks' interests. For example, the *Charleston Missionary Record*, a newspaper published for African American readers, listed the personnel and meeting times of the "UNITED STATES COURT IN SOUTH CAROLINA" in the paper's 1873 governmental directory. Two years earlier, South Carolina Circuit Judge Hugh Bond, who supported blacks' civil rights and staunchly opposed the Ku Klux Klan, commented that he had received superb service from blacks: "the negroes waited on us with great assiduity, because the most of them knew me."[31]

Despite this awareness, southern blacks rarely applied to federal tribunals to enforce the Civil Rights Act of 1866, which had been passed specifically to provide African Americans with legal protections. In 1867, U.S. Major William L. Vanderlip, writing from Maryland, a former slave state, informed Colonel W. W. Rogers that redress under civil rights laws "seems to be beyond the reach of the freedman" since he could not bring suit "without such expense as he is unable to meet."[32] Blacks' use of state tribunals in the late nineteenth century was likewise minimal. Robert Silverman's study of the Boston trial courts between 1880 and 1900 reveals a mere four African American defendants and six black plaintiffs in a sample of 1,445 cases. Silverman concludes that "the number of sample cases involving blacks is so small that it permits only one generalization: blacks did not sue, nor were they sued, more than a few dozen times a year." Indeed, "they were virtually excluded from the civil trial courts."[33]

In addition to a lack of funds, two factors may help to explain blacks' infrequent use of the federal courts after the Civil War. First, other avenues existed in which blacks could receive justice in a less formal setting—primarily, for a short time, the Freedmen's Bureau Courts. Established by the federal government in March 1865, these courts handled legal disputes and minor criminal offenses involving blacks. In 1865, the *Nashville Colored Tennessean* praised "the extreme prudence and evident courtesy and fairness of [various officers of the Freedmen's Bureau] to whom the enforcement of Federal authority in regard to Freedmen is entrusted." African Americans used the freedmen's courts to sue for damages and property. As a Freedmen's Bureau agent noted in 1867, "As the Negro comes to have money at his command, he is able to force matters and secure his rights" in Freedmen's Bureau courts. In 1866, in what the *Cincinnati Colored Citizen* called an "Important Case in a Freedmen's Court," Ella Freeman sued James Hallums for damages for the enslavement of herself and of her sons (who had been free) and for the recovery of lands owned by her father. She succeeded on both fronts. These courts were short-lived, however; by the end of 1866, they had transferred jurisdiction in cases involving freedpeople to the state courts. Nevertheless, the bureau's courts represented federal tribunals that African Americans might view as more accessible and receptive to their claims than state or federal courts.[34]

Second, during Reconstruction, blacks must have increasingly viewed federal courts as unaccommodating to African Americans' needs—because the tribunals became so. African Americans likely at first viewed federal authority, including federal courts, with optimism. Foner maintains that blacks identified with federal authorities during the early Reconstruction years, believing that "only outside intervention could assure the freedmen a modicum of justice." But as chapter 2 discusses, the lower federal courts in the South during

Reconstruction catered to the local interests of white southerners, which were often opposed to the interests of local blacks. In addition, by 1873, the U.S. attorney general discontinued enforcement of civil rights legislation, as Robert Kaczorowski notes, "in an effort to reduce mounting departmental expenses." Supreme Court decisions in the early to mid-1870s largely gutted various protections extended to African Americans through constitutional amendments and federal statutes. As Harold Forsythe recognizes, through these decisions, "the Court effectively removed law courts as a place of recourse for black people seeking political rights and social justice."[35] Even if African American debtors considered filing for voluntary bankruptcy, they would likely have thought twice before submitting their economic interests to a judicial authority whose support had proved so fleeting.

Yet even if African Americans or their creditors wanted to use the federal bankruptcy courts, blacks' economic condition would have dissuaded such bankruptcy filings. Right after the Civil War, most freedpeople had few debts or assets, so their ability to benefit from this legislation was minimal. African Americans' position in relation to the 1867 Bankruptcy Act thus resembled their attitude toward debt-relief measures passed by southern states after the Civil War. Black southerners resisted state legislators' proposals to legalize the delay or discharge of debts, realizing that these measures did not benefit former slaves, who owed no debts. Further, African Americans realized that any laws granting economic relief might allow employers to avoid paying their laborers and rescue white southerners from liquidation. As James W. Hood stated to North Carolinians, laws that delayed repayment of debts would profit "those who now hold lands" and would "prevent the poor people from ever getting land."[36] Thus, African Americans did not support state debtor-relief measures, which might impede the disintegration of what black South Carolinian Francis L. Cardozo called "the infernal plantation system."[37] The same arguments applied to federal bankruptcy legislation, with one exception. The 1867 Act gave precedence to the payment of laborers' earnings, providing that "wages due from [the bankrupt] to any operative, or clerk, or house servant, to an amount not exceeding fifty dollars, for labor performed within six months next preceding the adjudication of bankruptcy, shall be entitled to priority, and shall be first paid in full."[38]

Furthermore, although blacks made economic progress, such developments took time. William Harris notes that African Americans' deposits in the Freedmen's Bank in Vicksburg, Mississippi, and land purchases in that area grew between 1868 and 1870. However, according to Harris, between 1865 and 1867, the bank barely subsisted because of a lack of deposits.[39] As discussed earlier, the bulk of bankruptcy filings (and particularly voluntary filings) occurred prior to the end of 1868, when the Bankruptcy Act began requiring petitioners to obtain creditor consent before discharge could be granted. Former slaves would have had little time to become economically established or indebted before the window of opportunity closed and filing became a less user-friendly instrument.

Finally, involuntary filings against African Americans, even those who had been free before the war, were less likely than such claims against white southerners because blacks had fewer assets. Although some blacks (for example, some free blacks in Charleston prior to the war) were wealthy, African Americans on the whole held dramatically less property than whites did. Even in 1880, the average size of a white person's farm in East Tennessee was one hundred acres, but the average black-owned farm was one-fifth that size. Similarly, the average value of a black farmer's land was two hundred dollars, a quarter of the average value of a white farmer's land. And these divergences occurred in a region that was relatively poor and had fewer large plantations than the Deep South. In 1874, African Americans possessed only 1 percent of Georgia's land, and six years later, that figure had increased only slightly, to 1.6 percent. Thus, most blacks were without property, and those who did have property generally had far less than their white neighbors. Creditors had much less promising prospects of recovering assets from such debtors than from whites. As established in chapter 3, the number of involuntary filings was relatively low, so it is not surprising that so few such cases arose against African Americans.[40]

African American men and women were not among the many groups of southerners who benefited from the 1867 Bankruptcy Act, and as a result, the law arguably made freedpeople's position weaker vis-à-vis that of others in the post–Civil War South. The measure resuscitated white southerners—predominantly male merchants as well as professionals and planters and farmers—and thus reinforced their economic, social, and (increasingly in the 1870s) political dominance. African Americans struggled to establish themselves in an economically destitute region. Bereft of assets and increasingly beholden to landowners and merchants for amounts outstanding, African Americans did not benefit from laws—particularly federal bankruptcy laws—granting economic relief.

Yet even as federal legislators and judges were unwilling to recognize an extension of economic rights for white women and African Americans, congressmen and jurists expanded federal jurisdiction to accommodate the full panoply of business entities (including corporations) under the terms of the Bankruptcy Act of 1867. As chapter 8 will show, this augmentation illustrates how congressional Republicans and lower federal court jurists increasingly attended to the dominant business interests of both the North and the South during Reconstruction.

CHAPTER EIGHT

Bankrupt Partners and Corporations before the Federal Courts

> Corporations adjudged bankrupt are also made subject to the same duties as individual bankrupt debtors . . . but the emphatic exception to all those general regulations is that no allowance of discharge shall be granted to any corporation. —U.S. Supreme Court Justice Nathan Clifford, 1875

The Blue Ridge Railroad "was to be, and might have been, the great highway to the West." Charlestonians had long dreamed of connecting their eastern seaport town to the Ohio River to reap the financial rewards available as a principal port for western commerce. Commenced in 1851–52, the road was to run from Anderson in Upper South Carolina to Knoxville, Tennessee. Construction halted during the Civil War but restarted after in 1866.[1] By 1868, the governor of South Carolina, James L. Orr, described it as a "truly great public work" and stressed "the importance of a Railroad connection with the North-West to all sections of South Carolina" so that the state could "develop her great resources and keep her up with the progress ma[de] by [her] enterprising sisters." In the following year, *Brownlow's Knoxville Whig* celebrated the construction of the road. "We hail this news as good news for Knoxville," the editors proclaimed. "Within two years we hope to have continuous rail from Knoxville to Charleston."[2] But these great hopes fell flat. In January 1873, creditors filed an involuntary bankruptcy petition against the railroad. But the desire of most creditors for a return on their investments also remained unfulfilled. As Federal Circuit Judge Hugh Bond determined in 1877, "It is plain from the record in this case that at the time of the filing of the petition in bankruptcy, the bankrupt company had no property the sale of which would produce anything for its general or unsecured creditors." Indeed, "all that it owned was mortgaged greatly beyond its value."[3] Controversy and charges of corruption had plagued the railroad for years. After the Civil War, the Republican-dominated South Carolina legislature had guaranteed $4 million in bonds for the project but had later released the railroad from the state's lien that had secured this debt. Members of a conservative Tax-Payer's Convention held in Columbia in 1871 were incensed: "Such dealings . . . can only be the result of fraud, are unauthorized by law, and are void." The city of Charleston, likewise, had subscribed $1 million in gold in the company's stock. Yet by 1873, only thirty-four miles of track were in operation. As early as June 1873, six months after creditors filed the involuntary petition, the editors of the *Charleston Daily News* bemoaned what they viewed as the inevitable results of the proceedings: "Thus will go to the winds the entire amount subscribed to the capital stock by the State, the City of Charleston and individual citizens, amounting in the aggregate to between two and three millions of dollars."[4]

The fact that this involuntary filing occurred was of itself notable. The 1867 Act was the first U.S. bankruptcy legislation to allow for corporate bankruptcy. The law enabled corporations to file for voluntary bankruptcy and empowered creditors to initiate involuntary claims against such entities. Indeed, the 1867 Act represented the nineteenth-century summit of corporations' and their creditors' ability to employ the bankruptcy mechanism. Previous bankruptcy laws enacted in 1800 and 1841 had not allowed for corporate filings; the later Bankruptcy Act of 1898 permitted involuntary filings against but not voluntary petitions by corporations.[5] Scholars have recognized that the Bankruptcy Act of 1867 thus represents a landmark: one student of the 1867 Act has acknowledged the "major implications" that discussion of the influence of corporate bankruptcy and the post–Civil War influence of corporations would have on his work.[6] But an analysis of bankruptcy case files from the South makes it clear that although the legislation was a first, the corporate provisions received little use in the region. An examination of hundreds of case files from East Tennessee, from Mississippi's Lauderdale and Warren Counties, and from South Carolina's Anderson and Charleston Counties (which include the most urban and commercial counties in the three districts and thus the areas where most business entities would have been located) demonstrates that despite the liberal allowance for corporate filings, involuntary corporate bankruptcies were rare and voluntary corporate filings were virtually nonexistent. In the same southern districts, however, bankruptcies involving the other chief form of business entity—the partnership—were common, although the frequency of such filings varied from district to district: bankruptcy filings concerning partnerships were infrequent in East Tennessee but often occurred in southern Mississippi and South Carolina.[7]

Three aspects of these entity bankruptcy filings are notable. First, the pattern of corporate and partnership bankruptcy filings reflects how southerners employed the 1867 Act: it was a tool for resuscitation, not simply a device to divvy up assets among creditors. Under the law, partners could obtain discharges from their debts; corporations could not. Further, a bankruptcy case involving an individual or partnership stayed all state court proceedings against the filer, but proceedings could continue against a corporate bankrupt. Thus, filing for bankruptcy was substantially more advantageous for a struggling postwar partnership than for a corporation. Many southern corporations—from banks to railroads—were in poor shape after the war, but the cases studied indicate that these corporate entities did not take advantage of the opportunity for voluntary bankruptcy. Furthermore, when creditors initiated involuntary corporate proceedings, southerners sought to shape cases to their benefit by striving either to defeat attempts to have a corporation declared bankrupt or to tailor the involuntary proceedings to the advantage of affected southern residents.

Second, the large number of bankruptcy filings by southern business partnerships indicates a principal way that federal courts in the 1860s and 1870s served local business interests and thus adds a new dimension to the common perception of post–Civil War federal courts as serving national business concerns. As Tony Freyer discusses, between 1865 and 1900, interstate business leaders sought to avoid state courts (which these businessmen saw as biased against their interests) in favor of federal courts. "While distrustful of all government," Freyer maintains, "leaders of national business deemed the federal courts friendliest to their interests." Freyer also notes that "federal judges used their power to formulate doctrines favoring the national economy."[8] Evidence cited by Freyer and others establishes that interstate business interests crowded the federal dockets by filing suits in out-of-state federal courts against local defendants or by removing state court proceedings against the businesses into federal court. Federal courts increasingly came to be seen as tools of powerful nonresident corporations, and the South and the West reacted harshly to this perception. By the late nineteenth century, Congressman David Culberson of Texas blamed private litigation involving corporations for producing "the greatest frauds to be practiced upon the legitimate jurisdiction of these courts," clogging dockets and increasing delays.[9] Yet the federal courts' role in the South with respect to business interests was not unidimensional. During the same postwar years when nonresident businesses were filing private claims against local business interests, many local businesses employed the federal courts to file for voluntary bankruptcy. Business partnerships in the areas studied filed for voluntary bankruptcy more often than creditors filed involuntary petitions against businesses (both corporations and partnerships) in these areas. Furthermore, southerners looked to federal judges to protect interests threatened by involuntary corporate proceedings.

Thus, the pro-local-business aspects of the federal courts in the 1860s and 1870s under the Bankruptcy Act take to another level the debate noted in chapter 2 about whether federal courts served national or local interests. A principal component of the argument that these courts acted as national tribunals concerns how interstate business entities used this venue to pursue or defend themselves against private claims. Yet evidence from bankruptcy filings illustrates how local business partnerships also turned to these tribunals. In sum, eastern corporations may have preferred federal courts over state tribunals because of the supposed relative lack of bias, but southern entities also sought the federal courts for financial protection. The southern federal courts' role during Reconstruction thus was a mélange of local and national functions, even when dealing with business entities.

Third, southern entities' use of voluntary bankruptcy supported the states' rights philosophy espoused by many southerners. For decades prior to the passage of the Bankruptcy Act of 1867, congressmen had engaged in heated debates about whether the federal government had the constitutional power to regulate the dissolution of corporations through bankruptcy, given that the entities were created and regulated by states. Although proponents of federal corporate bankruptcy succeeded in including such provisions in the Bankruptcy Act of 1867, congressional deliberations concerning federal versus state power over corporate dissolution continued in the debates leading up to passage. Voluntary corporate bankruptcies were absent from the areas studied, while many filings involved partnerships. This pattern reflects not only the less advantageous terms afforded to corporate bankrupts but also how southerners—consciously or not—responded to bankruptcy provisions in a manner that supported adherence to the regional affiliation with states' rights. With respect to bankruptcies involving entities, southerners did not always succeed in fending off involuntary filings or obtaining discharge. And, as noted in chapter 3, additional business partnerships perhaps could have taken advantage of the voluntary provisions. But, in a broad sense, the pattern of filings involving entities supports a larger point advanced throughout this book: white southerners employed the Bankruptcy Act to their advantage in a utilitarian way without compromising the white South's larger goals during Reconstruction, including freedom from federal interference.

For many years before the passage of the Bankruptcy Act of 1867, southerners had promoted each state's power to determine its own affairs and had argued that the federal government should remain uninvolved. What were perceived as national authorities' unconstitutional infringements of states' rights (particularly with respect to the institution of slavery) constituted a primary reason for antebellum sectional conflict and ultimately the Civil War. During Reconstruction, calls for a return to state self-rule and withdrawal of federal influence from the region became increasingly vehement. By the mid- to late

1870s, the former Confederate states were no longer subject to federal rule: both white southerners' intransigence and northerners' frustration and increasing lack of interest led to the withdrawal of federal troops from the South and to the accession of the conservative, white Democratic Party to the helm of state governments.

In the bankruptcy context, when corporations or partnerships turned to the federal courts, the entities that filed upheld (perhaps unconsciously and somewhat ironically) the states' rights viewpoint. Key to this point is the distinction between corporations and partnerships. During the mid–nineteenth century, corporations in the United States came into existence after states passed specific legislation granting charters to conduct business. Early corporations were often quasi-public in character: for example, state legislatures granted corporations charters to build bridges or turnpikes. In these instances, corporations were, as historian David Skeel notes, "simply arms of the state." States also often granted privileges to corporations, such as the power to condemn property through eminent domain. In addition, before and after general incorporation statutes became prominent in the mid–nineteenth century (thereby allowing corporations to gain charters through applications and without specific legislative acts), states imposed various requirements on chartered corporations. Thus, state authority and corporate existence and operations were viewed as intimately related.[10] Debates concerning the application of federal bankruptcy to corporate debtors did not gain steam until some decades after the U.S. Constitution's clause enabling Congress to establish uniform laws concerning bankruptcy took effect in 1789, because relatively few corporations existed during these years and they had little economic impact. But when congressmen began debating whether a federal bankruptcy law would apply to corporate debtors in the 1820s and 1830s, stiff resistance arose, grounded on states' rights arguments. Senator Oliver H. Smith of Indiana captured the objections of many people during the debates on the Bankruptcy Act of 1841: "A power in the States to erect corporations, and a power in the Federal Government to pull them down, cannot exist at the same time." Even legal scholar and U.S. Supreme Court Justice Joseph Story, usually a strong proponent of federal constitutional power, strongly doubted whether the federal government had authority to legislate for corporations. In 1840, Story wrote to Daniel Webster concerning the proposal to apply a federal bankruptcy law to corporations: "Is it quite certain that State Rights as to the creation and dissolution of corporations are not thus virtually infringed?" Story queried. "I confess that I feel no small doubt whether Congress can regulate State corporations by any other laws than State law." These constitutional uncertainties and the resistance of states' rights adherents resulted in corporate bankruptcy's omission from the Bankruptcy Act of 1841.[11]

But by the mid–nineteenth century, the relationship between states and corporations had become less intertwined. Increased commercial activity resulted in the proliferation of business corporations that concentrated on private ventures and the decreased economic significance of entities with quasi-public purposes. The practical need to respond to a large number of applicants convinced many states to adopt general incorporation statutes. By 1867, thirty-five states or territories (76 percent) had general incorporation statutes. Further, corporate operations increasingly extended beyond state lines, which bolstered the case advanced by advocates of national bankruptcy jurisdiction. Nevertheless, opponents of federal corporate bankruptcy were still strongly arguing their position in 1867. Michigan Senator William Howard defended his motion to omit the portion of the 1867 Bankruptcy Act that permitted corporate bankruptcy: "[Corporations'] existence, all their attributes, all their liabilities, all penalties imposed upon them, the very life and being, the very soul and essence of a corporation is derived from the State statutes." Howard reasoned, "The States have full and complete control over corporations erected or created by their laws; and I have yet to learn that it is within the constitutional competency of Congress to interfere in any way whatever with the functions or operations of State corporations." But these views were no longer dominant.[12]

As a subheading of the 1867 legislation announced, the Bankruptcy Act allowed for "Bankruptcy of Partnerships and of Corporations." The logistics of a bankruptcy filing involving a partnership versus one involving a corporation differed in notable ways. Under the Act, both types of entities could file for voluntary bankruptcy or be subject to involuntary bankruptcy. Provisions concerning partnerships were more liberal, however. One partner or all partners could file to initiate a voluntary claim, while a creditor of the partners could file an involuntary petition. If only one partner filed, the partner would request that the other partners and partnership also be declared bankrupt and would submit schedules of assets and liabilities for the filer and the partnership. Each partner could receive a discharge from partnership and individual debts "as the same would or ought to be if the proceedings had been against him alone under th[e] act." Thus, the 1867 Bankruptcy Act largely treated partners as though they were individuals who happened to be jointly engaged in a business enterprise. This treatment of partner bankrupts is in accord with the law's general treatment of partners: they make up a partnership entity, but unlike a corporation, this entity is not chartered by the state or considered a separate legal entity or personality from its owners. Rather, the partners compose it and generally are jointly responsible for its losses and profits. Thus, under the Bankruptcy Act of 1867, the partners, whose life and business dealings would continue after the dissolution of the partnership, could obtain discharges from their debts.[13]

The same provision did not apply in corporate bankruptcy. "All moneyed, business, or commercial corporations and joint-stock companies" (which resembled corporations in issuing stock to their owners) could file or be filed against. Courts construed this language broadly to include insurance, railroad, and steamboat corporations. An officer of a corporation could initiate a voluntary proceeding after obtaining the approval of a majority of the stockholders, and any creditor or multiple creditors could file an involuntary petition against a corporation. The corporation and its officers were required to abide by the provisions of the Bankruptcy Act that applied to individual debtors. But unlike individuals or partnerships, neither the corporation nor any of its officers or members could obtain a discharge. The rationale behind this restriction was that a corporation was a legal entity, not an individual—an entity separate from the personality of its shareholders or officers—and thus did not have a human need for release from debt. The corporation would simply cease to exist after the proceedings. Donald Korobkin's description of bankruptcy legislation that provides "exclusively for piecemeal liquidation" aptly depicts the corporate provisions under the Bankruptcy Act of 1867: they "suggest[ed] a view of the corporation in bankruptcy as merely something to be acted upon—as a lifeless pool of assets."[14]

The inability to obtain a discharge resulted in two disadvantages. First, the filing of a petition for a corporate bankruptcy did not stay other proceedings against the corporation while the bankruptcy case was pending. As the *National Bankruptcy Register* explained in a case synopsis, "The provision of the 21st Section of the Bankrupt Act for staying any suit or proceeding to await the determination of the court in bankruptcy on the question of discharge, does not apply to a corporation, which can never receive such discharge by the terms of the said act." Further, because discharge from debts was unavailable, even if a creditor had proven that the corporation owed a certain debt and had received a portion of that amount through the bankruptcy proceeding, the creditor could still pursue the remainder of the debt in a subsequent court action. So while individuals and partnerships evaded creditor suits both during and after the bankruptcy case, corporations did not.[15]

Second, for various corporations such as railroads it was beneficial for the corporation and for those affected by it to obtain a discharge and for operations to continue. In 1874, Congress partially addressed this shortcoming by amending the 1867 Bankruptcy Act to include provisions permitting composition. These sections served as a precursor to modern corporate bankruptcy reorganization. As discussed in chapter 6, when a debtor—whether an individual or corporation—and a certain percentage of the debtor's creditors agreed to a composition agreement, the debtor would pay the creditors an agreed percentage of the amount owed and would maintain possession of the debtor's property. (This differed, then, from a standard bankruptcy proceeding, in which the bankrupt surrendered all property to an assignee.) Various requirements dictated how to treat any creditors who did not sign on to the agreement. Yet although composition provided a useful tool for individuals and entities, it was not helpful to certain corporations. Composition under the 1867 Act only allowed a debtor to restructure unsecured obligations (debts not backed by collateral). Larger corporations often possessed predominantly secured debt—for example, mortgage (secured) bonds often weighed down railroads' balance sheets.[16]

Skeel notes that the corporate bankruptcy sections "had small, mom-and-pop businesses in mind" and that this reflected the focus of the congressmen who framed the Act. "Lawmakers focused entirely on individuals and small corporations in their deliberations and the Bankruptcy Act reflected this," Skeel maintains. "The corporate bankruptcy provisions were useful only for small businesses; more substantial firms simply ignored them."[17]

The empirical data from the three federal judicial districts studied here supports Skeel's position that sizable corporations disregarded the Bankruptcy Act. But the evidence also shows that mom-and-pop corporations did not crowd bankruptcy dockets. This did not result from a lack of business corporations in the three states studied. Between 1850 and 1878, the legislatures of Mississippi, South Carolina, and Tennessee passed statutes establishing 411, 418, and 1,528 business corporations, respectively. Railroads (which were typically relatively large and complex entities) accounted for just under a quarter of these corporations in Mississippi and South Carolina and for 8 percent in Tennessee. The remainder were mainly smaller operations such as manufacturers, turnpikes, and banks. These specially chartered entities represented only a portion of the corporations in these three states; other entities had been incorporated prior to 1850, and still others were incorporated under the general incorporation statutes passed in Tennessee in 1850, Mississippi in 1857, and South Carolina in 1869.[18]

Yet despite the numerous corporations in existence, southern corporations, regardless of size or debt structure, simply did not take advantage of the opportunity to declare voluntary bankruptcy. Of the 683 voluntary bankruptcies analyzed in depth from East Tennessee, and two counties in both southern Mississippi and South Carolina, none were filed by corporate entities. Various voluntary bankrupts used the term *Company* in their firm names, but the filings indicate that these businesses were composed of a few partners and hence were partnerships rather than corporations chartered by the state that issued stock to shareholders. The absence of voluntary corporate bankrupts in these three districts does not, of course, mean that none existed across the region: the City Bank of Memphis filed a voluntary claim in the District of Western Tennessee in 1872, for example. But the findings from the three districts studied here indicate that voluntary filings by corporations were relatively—if not extremely—rare. In contrast, 113 of the 683 voluntary cases involved partnerships. In 44 of these 113 cases, the occupation of the partner or partnership was identifiable from the case files. Thirty-one involved merchants, 7 concerned skilled workers (such as artisans), and 6 involved professionals. As in voluntary cases generally (see chapter 5), southern merchants and, to a lesser degree, professionals and skilled workers who did business as partnerships took advantage of voluntary provisions.[19]

Of the 181 involuntary cases initiated against debtors in East Tennessee and counties in southern Mississippi and South Carolina, a maximum of 9 were against corporations. These involuntary bankruptcy filings included 2 cases against railroads (including the Blue Ridge Railroad proceeding in South Carolina), 4 against mining and manufacturing companies (including two against the same company), 1 against an ice company, and 2 against the same banking institution. In comparison to the sparse number of involuntary corporate bankrupts, 70 of the 181 involuntary filings (39 percent) involved partnerships.[20]

Yet this was a period of intense economic deprivation for southern corporations, just as it was for southern businesses generally. Many southern corporations were insolvent and in need of relief or, indeed, liquidation. "By the summer of 1865," Dan Carter notes, "commercial banking [in the South] had almost ceased to exist." And the strict requirements concerning paid-in capital and limitations on mortgage lending in the National Banking Act of 1865 made it difficult for southerners to establish national banks. Carter observes that "between 1865 and 1868 only 20 of the 1,688 national banks chartered were in the Deep South, and by 1869, 4 of them had closed their doors, in a failure rate six times the national average." State legislatures rebuffed banks' pleas for assistance, and the National Banking Act penalized state-chartered banks with a 10 percent tax on notes they issued. As a result, "only a handful of state-chartered banks functioned effectively in the entire region" by the middle of 1866. Southern railroads similarly suffered during the 1860s and 1870s, as wartime losses caused many railroads to default on their bonds. During the immediate postwar years, at least some railroads—such as those in Mississippi—recovered rapidly through physical repair and profitable traffic receipts. Local promoters thus retained control of these resuscitated Mississippi lines at least for a while. But the Panic of 1873 threw southern railroads into more of a downspin than roads in the North. In the 1870s, the South's railroads suffered economically, and the proportion of the nation's track located in the South fell by 20 percent.[21]

Facing such hardships, it might be expected that unwary and unknowledgeable southern corporate businesses might attempt to take advantage of voluntary bankruptcy or, more likely, that creditors would attempt to bring scores of insolvent southern corporations into bankruptcy court. But such was not the case in the studied areas. Rather, members of southern business entities did not commonly employ voluntary bankruptcy in all circumstances where it was allowed and did not passively accept creditors' attempts to impose involuntary corporate filings. Instead, southern business members took advantage of the favorable provisions concerning partnerships and shied away from relatively unfavorable corporate filings. Although Congress intended the corporate provisions to facilitate the liquidation of small operations, neither they nor more substantial corporations sought voluntary bankruptcy. In addition, when creditors attempted to use involuntary corporate proceedings, southerners sought to influence the law's application by arguing that the corporation was not a bankrupt under the terms of the 1867 Act or by seeking the most beneficial terms for those southerners affected. These efforts did not always succeed or produce advantageous results. Thus, southerners did not passively accept the terms of the Bankruptcy Act of 1867, instead attempting to strategically employ or avoid it.

Another factor that probably contributed to the application of corporate bankruptcy in the districts studied here is the post–Civil War development of a separate legal device for dealing with insolvent corporations, particularly railroads. Equitable receivership developed in response to the many late-nineteenth-century railroad failures across the country, and the doctrine eventually was applied to other types of corporations as well. Equitable receivership formed the foundation for the modern corporate reorganization process to a greater degree than the relatively unsophisticated composition provisions mentioned previously. "Just about everyone interested in the railroads agreed that troubled railroads were worth more as going concerns than in liquidation," Skeel notes. To continue railroad operations and address their financial failings, creative reorganizers combined traditional common-law doctrines to generate railroad reorganization, a process that involved two principal steps. First, a creditor, possibly friendly to the railroad's owners, would file a creditor's bill requesting the cessation of all creditors' collection efforts against the corporation and the appointment by the court of a receiver, who would continue to operate the business. The creditor would also file a foreclosure bill, which requested the sale of the corporation's assets. But the foreclosure sale was usually only a ritual and was often postponed for months or years. The real action took place behind the scenes, where creditor committees negotiated the terms of a reorganization agreement that would modify the entity's capital structure.

Once the committees agreed, they would combine to form a reorganization committee that would purchase the railroad's assets at a foreclosure sale by bidding a purchase price equal to the amount of the creditor claims. After this "sale," the purchasers would transfer the assets into a shell corporation and would distribute company securities to investors according to the terms of the reorganization plan.[22]

Beginning in the mid–nineteenth century, receiverships often took place in state court; however, at the end of the 1800s, most railroad receiverships occurred in federal courts. Between 1870 and 1900, more than seven hundred railroads across the country sought federal receivership; a quarter of the railroads that entered receivership were located in the South. Indeed, as early as 1876, more than half of the nation's railroads were controlled by receivers.[23]

Creditors' access to equitable receivership may explain the relative dearth of southern involuntary cases filed against corporations during the life of the 1867 Bankruptcy Act, since cases concerning railroads often came before federal tribunals in nonbankruptcy settings. In one June 1876 issue, under the title "Corporations in Court," the *Charleston News and Courier* described three "Important Decrees in the United States Court" concerning railroads: "The Port Royal Railroad Ordered to be Sold—Liability of the South Carolina Railroad Property to Municipal Taxation—[and Property Conveyance by] The Air Line Railway [Confirmed]."[24]

The equitable receivership process often was not friendly to locals. As Eric Foner observes, none of the numerous southern lines that fell into receivership escaped the influence of northern financial interests, thereby fixing "the regional economy even more firmly in a colonial mold."[25] Thus, even though equitable receiverships could occur collusively—as the result of a friendly creditor initiating the process with the owners' blessing—some southerners perceived receiverships as intrusive. By January 1877, resistance in Mississippi had reached such a peak that the state legislature passed a law authorizing suits against court-appointed receivers who operated railroads in the state; filings could take place without leave of the appointing court, and any judgments from such suits would be paid out of railroad assets. As Mississippi Federal District Judge Robert Hill recognized, "That this act was intended to authorize suits against receivers appointed by the United States courts, and operating railroads in this state, there is no doubt." Hill invoked the long-standing rule that state legislatures could not pass laws regulating federal courts' jurisdiction, and thus the Mississippi statute could not affect receivers appointed by the federal courts.[26] Despite the measure's failure, southerners had attempted to gain some control over the corporate reorganization process and to turn it to their advantage.

Southerners also endeavored to influence proceedings to their benefit in the context of involuntary corporate proceedings under the 1867 Act. Evidence from South Carolina illustrates that at least two devices were used. First, southerners fought to defeat involuntary filings and argued that the matters belonged more properly in state court. Two New York creditors filed an involuntary petition against the Greenville and Columbia Railroad Company in the federal court for the District of South Carolina. The creditors owned bonds and coupons of the railroad; the road had failed to make payments on these coupons. Members of the railroad resisted the petition, and South Carolina's federal judges ruled in their favor. District Judge George S. Bryan held that the railroad was not a bankrupt (meaning it did not meet the requirements for an involuntary bankrupt under the 1867 Act) and dismissed the case; Circuit Judge Hugh Bond then affirmed Bryan's decision. The *Charleston Daily News* hailed the result in an article under the title "Good News": "The decision of Judge Bryan was unquestionably sound in law, and in accord with public polity." Further, "his decision ends the attempt to wrest control of the road from the State Courts, where it properly belongs, and place it in the hands of the Federal authorities." Thus, the *Daily News* editors made a correlation that was likely shared by other southerners: in the case of involuntary corporate bankrupts, federal proceedings were improper intrusions into state matters. It is possible that the fact that New York creditors—instead of southerners—had initiated the claim contributed to the antipathy toward the proceeding. In five of the nine involuntary corporate claims initiated in the studied areas, individual southerners or a group of southerners were the initiating creditors, and they may have encountered less opposition. Yet the sentiments of the Charleston editors went beyond the claim's initiators and instead focused on whether federal or state authorities should control the resolution of corporate debts. In the editors' minds, resistance to federal control of settlement of the debts of southern corporations benefited all sides: "A decree in bankruptcy in the case of the Greenville and Columbia Railroad Company would have been injurious to the creditors and to the public at large." They exalted, "We, therefore, hail the discomfiture of the petitioners with unaffected joy."[27]

Southerners not only resisted involuntary corporate bankruptcy but also attempted to tailor involuntary federal proceedings to their advantage. The case of the Blue Ridge Railroad provides a telling example of such efforts. Southerners affected by the Blue Ridge filing attempted to influence the outcome of the case in three ways. First, Charleston journalists clamored for adequate representation of the city's interests in the bankruptcy proceeding. As the editors of the *Charleston Daily News* explained, after the bankruptcy filing in 1873, the city's million-dollar investment was "menaced with absolute extinction." The editors proclaimed, "We deem it of great public importance that the city should be represented, by counsel, when the case comes up in the District Court." The journalists warned, "At all events it is the part of prudence to watch the proceedings, so that any occasion of serving the city may be seized at once." Second, Charleston interests sought the favor of Federal District Judge Bryan. Charlestonians desired him to appoint at least one assignee who was sympathetic to the city's needs. "It is to Judge Bryan, therefore, that the citizens of Charleston look for such action as will give them a voice in the final disposal of the railroad, which for a quarter century has been the pet project of the people of the State," the *Charleston News and Courier* maintained. Third, although aware that the bankrupt line would be sold "to some moneyed and reliable railroad capitalists, with a view to its early completion," South Carolinians actively sought to effect the most beneficial outcome for local interests. The *News and Courier* encouraged its readers in June 1873 to "QUI VIVE" (remain watchful) with respect to the Blue Ridge. Residents obeyed this charge; in 1875, South Carolinians attempted to revive the Blue Ridge Railroad with a plan to have bondholders sell their shares back to the company for the lowest price possible and then to approach the state legislature for assistance and send a delegation to Washington to seek a congressional appropriation. Prominent state leaders, including former Governor Benjamin Perry and present Governor Daniel Chamberlain, approved of the plan, but nothing ever came of it. In 1876, Judge Bryan settled the protracted Blue Ridge bankruptcy litigation with a ruling that the bondholders were entitled to the property. Southerners maintained high hopes that construction on the road would resume, but almost sixty years later, "the road ha[d] never been extended, and the tunnel entering Stump Hole Mountain [along the railroad's line] ha[d] fallen in."[28]

Although the road was never completed, southern whites had sought to influence the proceeding in their favor as much as possible, treating the corporate bankruptcy of the Blue Ridge as of much greater significance than just a divvying up of assets among creditors. These efforts reflected the perspective that, in scholar Donald Korobkin's words, "whether a corporation continues and how it changes its personality affects people in ways that are not only economic." Thus, South Carolinians sought to use the opportunities afforded by the involuntary bankruptcy proceedings to influence whether and how "their old friend and first love, the great Blue Ridge road" continued and developed and whether they benefited financially as a result.[29]

When the Bankruptcy Act went into effect in 1867, southerners welcomed it as a means for gaining economic liberty. Even in the midst of this enthusiasm, however, southern corporations did not take advantage of the ability to file for voluntary bankruptcy. Whether southerners consciously avoided corporate bankruptcy to avoid impinging on an area traditionally governed by the states is unclear, since the provisions of the 1867 Act made it less advantageous for corporations to file for bankruptcy than for individuals or partnerships to do so. But regardless of the underlying reasons, the lack of voluntary corporate bankruptcies and many voluntary partnership filings highlights how southerners employed the Bankruptcy Act of 1867 to their advantage without sacrificing certain central southern tenets. Indeed, adherence to the traditional philosophy of states' rights and opposition to federal interference undergirded the increasing southern opposition to the 1867 Bankruptcy Act during the 1870s, opposition that, as chapter 9 will show, contributed to the measure's 1878 repeal.

CHAPTER NINE

Repeal of the 1867 Act

[The legislation] went down to its grave "unwept, unhonored and unsung."
—*New Jersey Law Journal*, 1878

In April 1878, Senator James R. McCreery of Kentucky introduced a bill to repeal the 1867 Bankruptcy Act. McCreery railed against the law's injurious effects. "This method of settlement has sunk lower and lower in public estimation until it is now regarded as worse than no settlement at all," McCreery maintained. "The people have borne the affliction with wonderful patience and fortitude; but so wide-spread is the evil and so contagious the example that they are calling aloud for the only measure which will stop the scourge in its desolating course." Characterizing the 1867 Act as "simply a license to prey on [the people's] substance through a betrayal of their confidence," he depicted a vast public yearning for repeal: "Surfeited and gorged with bankrupt certificates, in their stead they seek to restore 'the dollar of the fathers' to be used in the payment of debts." Fellow lawmakers apparently agreed with McCreery's negative assessment: both houses of Congress made quick work of the repealing legislation. After two days of debate in the Senate and one day of debate in the House, large bipartisan majorities in both chambers adopted the repeal bill. Signed into law in June 1878, the measure provided that no further bankruptcy cases could be filed after September 1 of that year.[1]

But notwithstanding the quick action by lawmakers in April 1878, the process of repeal had been long and circuitous. The House had passed several bills beginning in 1873 repealing the legislation, but each time the Senate had not acted on the measure.[2] Charges of high fees and incompetence and fraud by court officials (particularly those in southern federal courts) plagued the Act. Creditors complained that cumbersome bankruptcy proceedings wasted assets and meant that little was left to distribute. An 1878 contributor to the *Central Law Journal* concluded that the Bankruptcy Act "has been, and is, subject to much delay, expense, fraud and abuse." As Representative Edbridge G. Lapham of New York explained in 1878, "The result is that with a mere tithe of the debtor's property given to his creditors the debtor himself, after he obtains discharge, turns up with a wife, a brother, or a friend, with a competency on which he can rely for the remainder of his life." Federal officials in New Orleans were thought to be among the most corrupt: of eighteen hundred bankruptcy filings in the New Orleans federal court, supposedly only one rendered any sizable dividend for creditors.[3] Yet others argued that regardless of court officials' competence or honesty, the federal court system was an inefficient mechanism for handling the Act. Representative John Hanna of Indiana reflected these sentiments during the 1878 debate on repeal, maintaining that the Act had failed "because the machinery of our Federal courts is so heavy, it requires so much money to furnish the grease to run them, and the operations of those courts are so far from the men who are to be affected by the administration of the law, that in the administration of the law the property of the debtor is swallowed up by the officers of the courts, administer them as honestly and as best they may."[4] Charges of fraud and waste were so intense and lasting in effect that twenty-five years after repeal, a congressmen claimed that "the prejudices created by the abuses under the Act of 1867 make a fair discussion of any bankrupt act difficult." Wrongdoing in the southern federal courts had been endemic, a congressman asserted: those who had administered bankruptcy cases were "a lot of irresponsible carpetbag Judges who brought the Court of the United States with [sic] contempt with the people."[5]

By December 1873, thirty petitions requesting the repeal of the 1867 Bankruptcy Act had arrived in Congress from residents of states ranging from New York and New Jersey to Oregon and Iowa, including all eleven former Confederate states. In 1874, the Illinois legislature reflected the same dissatisfaction; it submitted a resolution "INSTRUCTING Her Senators and requesting her Representatives in Congress to vote for the unconditional repeal of an act of Congress known as the 'general bankrupt law.'"[6]

But not all desired repeal in 1873 and 1874: "many leading commercial men and firms of the city of New York" as well as "a great number of the principal business men of the State of Minnesota" urged curbing the worst abuses through amendment rather than repeal. As the Minnesota merchants expressed, a uniform federal law that prevented preferences and allowed for an equal division of assets among creditors was far preferable to a system of disparate state laws.[7] Similarly, the *Central Law Journal* in 1874 questioned the wisdom of repeal: "We doubt whether the present bankrupt law is worse than the system which it superceded," the authors maintained in an article on the first page of the first volume of the *Journal*, thus demonstrating the issue's centrality in legal circles. "Doubtless it has many faults and defects," the authors acknowledged. "Most of these, however, are not intrinsic, but remediable by well-considered legislation."[8] The 1874 amendments to the Act attempted to address these problems, yet these revisions did not quell dissatisfaction; four years later, a writer in the *Central Law Journal* noted, "There is evident need of amendment in many particulars before the law will work that beneficence to the commercial interests of the country that the advocates of it at the outset promised and assumed."[9]

In 1878, the 1867 Bankruptcy Act "collapsed under the weight of its inherent defects," as Peter Coleman notes. In Congress, sentiments in favor of repeal trumped. Among the foremost arguments expressed by congressmen in support of repeal was that "the day ha[d] passed for this bankrupt law," that "it ha[d] accomplished its mission; it ha[d] done its projected work," and lawmakers from the South were among those touting this position. As Senator William Pinkney Whyte of Maryland asserted, conditions at the end of the Civil War justified the passage of the bankrupt law: "After the war had closed, that great convulsion which carried down not only human life but vast wealth that had been accumulated for years past and brought to the verge of bankruptcy hundreds of thousands of our citizens, left us in a condition that business men, young and old, must have relief." Congress responded with the Bankruptcy Act to enable debtors "to wipe out with a sponge their past indebtedness, and go forth free men to work out for themselves another fortune or to go down struggling to the grave." But, he argued in 1878, "the time, in my judgment, has arrived for us to take the pruning-knife and lop off this piece of legislation and burn it with the rubbish of the past."[10] Representative Michael D. White of Indiana distinguished between those who filed right after passage in 1867—people "who had lost all their substance in the casualties of actual conflict or through accidents of war and derangements of trade," "made an honest showing of their assets," and eventually procured a discharge—and those who employed the Act in later years "as a trap to catch the honest business men of the country." White contended that the Act was "a dark shadow upon the fair face of the jurisprudence of the country."[11]

Southern lawmakers espoused similar arguments. Mississippi Representative Charles E. Hooker stressed the short-term need for the statute and that a federal bankruptcy system was properly temporary. "It was enacted originally in 1867, amid the terrible disasters of the years which succeeded the war," Hooker stated. "It was intended, as all bankrupt laws under our system of Government have heretofore been intended, to give that form of temporary relief to the embarrassed condition of the country which it requires." Hooker then criticized the woefully small dividends that purportedly flowed to creditors: "In my own State I assert that the whole history of the bankrupt law there has not shown a dividend of 2 per cent. of the assets of the debtor to the creditor." Hooker then pointed to the even poorer record in Louisiana federal courts, where, he had been informed, not "even so much as 1 per cent. has been realized." Two weeks later, another southern lawmaker, Senator Samuel D. Maxey of Texas, also recognized "that at the close of a great internecine war such as we had, when thousands of good men all over the land were broken and bankrupt in fortune without fault of their own, there was a humanity in passing such an act as that; but the great good that the act was designed to accomplish has been accomplished." Maxey contended that all those who had been economically crushed by the war and had desired to use the Bankrupt Act had done so. As a result, "The great purpose, what was conceived by the law-maker as the overwhelming necessity for the passage of the bankrupt law, has had its day in court; it has discharged its duty; and the people over this land from one end to the other now demand that this act, which has been on the statute-book for eleven years, should sleep with those which heretofore by their fiat have been sent to the tomb of the Capulets."[12]

But not all southern congressmen agreed with Hooker's and Maxey's position. On the same day that Hooker expressed his views, Senator Augustus S. Merrimon of North Carolina insisted, "I cannot understand how Senators representing Southern States, representing people who ought to have taken the benefit of this law, can stand up to-day and denounce it as machinery for the perpetration of fraud and outrage upon creditors." He insisted that the law "has done vast good all over the South." He was puzzled that lawmakers representing southerners could vote for repeal, given the continued economic stress that the region's residents suffered: "This country is not yet relieved from the business and financial embarrassments growing out of the war." Merrimon asserted, "The last hope those people have is to invoke the benefit of this bankrupt law"; "yet here are Senators representing Southern States, who ought to be able to appreciate the condition of that people, voting against extension of this law even for a brief while until those debtors with but their homestead may take advantage of it!" He concluded, "That is strange indeed to me."[13]

In the end, Hooker's and Maxey's position triumphed over Merrimon's. Congressmen from the three states studied here overwhelmingly supported repeal. Four of the six senators from South Carolina, Mississippi, and Tennessee voted in favor of repeal (the other two were absent at the time of the vote), as did eighteen of twenty-one representatives. Only two, representatives from Memphis, Tennessee, and Spartanburg, South Carolina, voted against the measure (one representative did not vote).[14] In at least one of these southern states, the state legislature had endorsed repeal. As Representative Hooker announced to the U.S. House in April 1878, "The Legislature of the State of Mississippi has unanimously passed a resolution requesting its Representatives to vote for this bill." Public sentiment in Mississippi had thus traveled a long way since March

1867, when the *Jackson Clarion* had congratulated "the public on the passage of the Bankrupt Bill."[15]

Southern support for repeal of the 1867 Bankruptcy Act and the debate among the southern lawmakers bolster the argument that southerners used the Act to provide temporary relief. Southerners initially welcomed the legislation, and many from the region filed for voluntary bankruptcy during the first year and a half after the law took effect, doing so at greater frequencies than did U.S. residents in general. Although Hooker could denounce the small dividends that creditors received from Mississippi federal court proceedings, scores of Mississippians had benefited from the Act when their debts were discharged. Voluntary filings after January 1, 1869, when the requirement that debtors obtain creditors' consent for discharge went into effect, decreased substantially nationwide but did so at a greater rate and more consistently in the South than in the nation as a whole.[16]

On the involuntary side of the docket, creditors who resided in the South initiated cases against southern debtors in the areas studied almost as frequently as did creditors who resided outside of the South, even though congressmen had expected northern merchants to be the primary creditor beneficiaries of the Bankruptcy Act. Regardless of the assets these southern creditors—mostly white, male merchants—ultimately received, they had used the federal legislation to advance their interests in ways not anticipated by Republican congressmen in 1867 or noticed by historians since.

The 1867 Bankruptcy Act, then, was not a failure from the perspective of southern whites. Although legislators and historians have repeatedly characterized the 1867 Act as a flop, debtors in the South—the most destitute region of the country after the Civil War—embraced the statute. Individuals and business entities used the legislation as a means of resuscitation, and numerous southern attorneys gladly filed claims. A high percentage of voluntary bankrupts received discharge, and numerous other southerners pressed outstanding claims as filing creditors in involuntary cases. After the mass of southern residents had reaped the benefits of the statute by employing it to serve their self-interests, southerners understandably possessed less enthusiasm for maintaining a federal bankruptcy system. Not only did the regime's alleged abuses and inefficiencies affect southerners (particularly creditors), as the petitions to Congress from all former Confederate states attest, but relatively few southerners were using the law by the late 1870s. Further, the region's residents maintained their traditional aversion to the extension of federal power into realms traditionally reserved for state governments. Federal involvement in debt-collection matters—particularly those involving citizens of the same state—was undeniably an intrusion into an area long governed by state law.[17] Senator Merrimon was surely right: destitute economic conditions continued to plague the South in the late 1870s, and the remedy of voluntary bankruptcy could have benefited residents of the region. But Reconstruction, in the sense of postwar federal enforcement of rights and governments in the South, had run its course. The last of the federal troops had been withdrawn from the South after the Compromise of 1877. Thus, southerners who might have supported a beneficent piece of federal legislation at the height of postwar economic dislocation and Radical Reconstruction in 1867 were less likely to do so in 1878. Despite Republican efforts in 1867 to frame the Bankruptcy Act as economic legislation divorced from post–Civil War political concerns, the law was thoroughly political with respect to the implicit reasons for its repeal as well as with respect to its intended beneficiaries and its actual users.

As the records from southern Mississippi, East Tennessee, and South Carolina establish, certain groups in particular profited from the 1867 Bankruptcy Act. The language of the statute both explicitly expresses and implies the type of people whom Republican legislators intended to profit from the measure: male merchants and traders. And white male merchants as well as some professionals and planters indeed reaped advantages from the Act, filing and gaining discharges as voluntary bankrupts and protecting their claims as creditors in involuntary proceedings. African Americans—women or men—were virtually absent from bankruptcy dockets, and white urban or agricultural laborers were scarce. Several white southern women employed bankruptcy proceedings to protect their interests, definitely to a greater degree than congressmen had intended, since the 1867 Act referred to bankrupts as having wives. By using the law to enforce legal rights, these white southern women made a political statement concerning their economic equality. The prevalence of white men of the merchant, professional, and planting and farming classes among those who employed the Act is not surprising, since these were generally the people who were engaged in commercial pursuits and thus would benefit from charitable economic legislation. But the predominance of these white men confirms that the Bankruptcy Act of 1867 helped to stabilize and entrench southern society's class and race structure after the Civil War. By passing a law that allowed white southern men of the merchant, professional, and agricultural classes to shake off past commercial obligations, continue to possess property exempt from bankruptcy proceedings under federal and state law, and maintain assets acquired after filing for bankruptcy, Republican legislators allowed these men to resuscitate themselves economically. No large-scale redistribution of lands owned by this class of men took place, although Radicals considered such a scheme. Other groups struggling for recognition of their rights during the 1860s and 1870s—African

American men and women and white women—found their interests largely ignored by the major piece of economic legislation passed during Reconstruction and benefiting southerners. In the interest of bolstering the economic interests of commercial classes in the North and South, Republican congressmen buttressed the economic security of white southern men. In this way, the 1867 Act contributed to what Eric Foner has termed the "unfinished revolution" of post–Civil War Reconstruction.

In 1890, Congressman Thomas C. Catchings of Mississippi stated his belief that the 1867 Bankruptcy Act had benefited residents of his state. He thought that lawmakers had repealed the statute "in pursuance of a sort of prejudice or craze which had no foundation in fact but which seemed to have taken possession of Congress."[18] Catchings's beliefs were certainly a minority position: condemnations of the deficiencies of the 1867 Act persisted for decades after its repeal, and historians have continued to agree with these negative assessments. But the records examined for this study indicate that Catchings was right in that Mississippians and other southerners profited from the bankruptcy measure. But he was likely wrong in characterizing congressional actions as based on craze or prejudice. Both southern support for the Bankruptcy Act of 1867 and southern votes for its repeal were related to immediate economic needs and entrenched political resistance. In the late 1860s, the charitable Act was practical and beneficial to franchised southerners, providing them with economic (and thus social and political) stability. By the late 1870s, however, the law had become a political lightning rod for those southerners complaining of federal inefficiency and intrusion and, implicitly, of the need for southern redemption.

APPENDIX ON METHODOLOGY

All information regarding the bankruptcy case filings in the Southern District of Mississippi, the District of South Carolina, and the Eastern District of Tennessee is taken from the following sources: Bankruptcy Case Files (1867–78), U.S. District Court, Southern District of Mississippi, 53A89, BO42/26/43; Bankruptcy Docket, Jackson, #81, U.S. District Court, Southern District of Mississippi, 53A89; Bankruptcy Case Files (1867–78), U.S. District Court of South Carolina, 52A155, BO33/22/62; Record Book: Bankruptcy, June 1867–January 1869, U.S. District Court of South Carolina, 52A155; and 1867 Bankruptcy Docket, U.S. District Court, Eastern District of Tennessee, #137, 53A643, BX24/22, and associated court documents, all in the Records of the District Courts of the United States, RG 21, National Archives and Records Administration—Southeast Region, East Point, Georgia.

The study sample included a total of 3,810 filings (3,406 voluntary and 404 involuntary) involving debtors resident in southern Mississippi, South Carolina, or East Tennessee, broken down as follows: Southern District of Mississippi, 1,477 voluntary filings, 183 involuntary filings; District of South Carolina, 1,705 voluntary filings, 188 involuntary filings; Eastern District of Tennessee, 224 voluntary filings, 33 involuntary filings. Five bankruptcy cases filed in the three southern districts could not be categorized as voluntary or involuntary filings based on the information available in court documents. In addition, the study at times focuses in depth on a subgroup of 864 filings that includes all voluntary and involuntary filings involving residents of East Tennessee; 188 voluntary and 88 involuntary filings involving residents of Lauderdale and Warren Counties, Mississippi; and 271 voluntary and 60 involuntary cases involving residents of Anderson and Charleston Counties, South Carolina.

I have used the 1870 Manuscript Federal Census Returns, Records of the Bureau of the Census, National Archives and Records Administration, Washington, D.C., to determine various pieces of information—for example, the birthplaces of debtors, creditors, and attorneys. The 1870 census, although in large measure accurate, had certain shortcomings, including underenumerating the nation's population by about 1.2 million people (or about 3.27 percent) and underreporting southerners' property values. (Indeed, the widespread underreporting led to the discontinuation of questions regarding property values in the 1880 census.)[1] These deficiencies do not seriously compromise the results presented here, although such problems may have made it more difficult for me to identify southerners in the census records and influenced calculations regarding population figures.

I have referred to John Livingston's *United States Law Register, and Official Directory for 1860* and *1868: The Law Register Comprising the Lawyers in the United States* for figures for the total number of attorneys practicing in various counties. Livingston professed to present "a correct and reliable guide of all the lawyers" in the country.² Although the listings surely were not entirely complete or accurate, they provide a valuable starting point for determining how widespread bankruptcy representation was among members of the bar in specific areas. A law firm practicing in a county in 1868 is considered as having been in business in 1860 if any member of the firm was practicing in the county in that year. The case files and dockets indicated who acted as attorneys for voluntary bankrupts and initiating creditors. Determining the total number of lawyers or firms involved in bankruptcy matters was difficult because which lawyers were in partnerships and which practiced individually shifted over time and because some bankruptcy petitions list individual attorneys as counsel, while other petitions list law partners. To avoid overstating the prevalence of bankruptcy lawyers, I have counted attorneys who were listed individually on bankruptcy petitions but who were also members of firms in 1868 in the total number of bankruptcy cases listed for that firm rather than separately as cases for those individuals. As a result, I may understate the number of solo practitioners or firms involved in bankruptcy representation. In some cases, attorneys and their clients may have resided in different counties. In an effort to verify that a listing by Livingston refers to a bankruptcy attorney, I have focused on those attorneys who both represented clients from the counties studied in depth and resided in those counties.

I have considered the initiator of a bankruptcy case to be the filer, whether an entity, a representative (such as an executor), or an individual. I have recorded those parties who were not primary filers (such as the deceased in a filing by an executor or a partner in a filing by a partnership entity), but I have not counted them in calculations unless specifically stated. In addition, if partners filed for bankruptcy for a partnership, I consider the entity rather than the partners to be the primary party. At times, an individual who belonged to a partnership sued individually; in these cases, I have considered the individual to be the primary filer but have noted that the individual was associated with an entity to indicate the type of business venture in which the filer was engaged.

The occupation of bankrupts and creditors grants a view into, in the words of the superintendent of the 1870 federal census, the "habits of a people, their social tastes, and moral standards." Various historians have devised categorizations of occupations, but the scheme used by Stephen V. Ash in his study of middle Tennessee between 1860 and 1870 is most applicable to this work because of Ash's focus on the largely rural nineteenth-century South. I have largely adopted Ash's categories, although I have created separate categories for merchants and for those with two occupations (merchants and planters and professionals and planters) and omitted the category of overseer because none were located. Like Ash, I have broadly defined "professionals" to include members of the learned professions such as lawyers and physicians as well other high-paying service-industry jobs such as bankers, engineers, accountants, manufacturers, and hotel owners. Frank Huffman, from whose dissertation Ash derives his categorization, terms this group "upper level white collar." The category of "minor professionals" includes such positions as clerks, bookkeepers, and barkeepers. I derived filers' occupations based on information in the bankruptcy case files and dockets, the 1870 manuscript census schedules, and city directories for Charleston, Knoxville, and Chattanooga published for 1870 or the closest available year. (No such directory was published for Vicksburg during these years.) Findings with respect to occupation listings in the census and city directories must be viewed with some caution because they do not necessarily indicate bankrupts' occupations at the time of filing (which might have been before or after 1870). Yet it is a safe assumption that some proportion were engaged in the activity listed in the census or city directories when the bankruptcy petitions were submitted.[3]

In chapter 3, data on total bankruptcy filings, average number of filings in U.S. courts, and average number of filings in southern federal courts include filings in U.S. lower federal courts and exclude filings in the territorial courts, which had relatively few filings. There is some overlap in data between 1872 and 1873: from 1867 to 1872, the data reflect filings by the calendar year; from 1873 to 1878, the data reflect filings by fiscal year, which ran from July 1 of the previous year until June 30 of the reported year. As a result, cases filed between July 1 and December 31, 1872, are counted twice. The available information does not permit the determination of the number of cases filed during this six-month period. Furthermore, a few districts each year did not report any data, and at times reporters used estimates, especially for the early years. Finally, data are unavailable for 1877 filings outside of the three districts studied. Despite these limitations, the data illustrate the general trend in the number of bankruptcy filings by year, with the numbers for 1872 and 1873 in accord with these trends.

The figures for 1867 reflect filings between June 1, the effective date of the Bankruptcy Act, and the end of the year; the figures for 1878 reflect filings between January 1 and September 1, the effective date of the Act's repeal.

All filing figures for the Southern District of Mississippi, the District of South Carolina, and the Eastern District of Tennessee are for calendar year. In addition, the aggregate number of filings for 1867 through 1872 (both for U.S. courts as a whole and for southern federal courts) have been corrected from those given in the U.S. Senate's *Letter from the Attorney-General, Communicating, in Compliance with a Senate Resolution of February 24, 1873, Information in Relation to the Expenses of Proceedings in Bankruptcy in United States Courts* to reflect the number of filings determined by my review of case files and dockets in the three districts studied. The corrections were as follows:

1867	Added 31
1868	Added 595
1869	Subtracted 359
1870	Subtracted 67
1871	Subtracted 50
1872	Subtracted 52

Data from 1873 on have not been corrected because case file data for this study were recorded by calendar year, while the attorney general's reports from 1873 on present the data by fiscal year.

NOTES

ABBREVIATIONS

Census Records   Manuscript Federal Census Returns, Records of the Bureau of the Census, National Archives and Records Administration, Washington, D.C.

NA RG 21   Records of the District Courts of the United States, RG 21, National Archives and Records Administration—Southeast Region, East Point, Georgia

NA RG 60   General Records of the Department of Justice, RG 60, National Archives and Records Administration, Washington, D.C.

INTRODUCTION

1. "The Stay Law: Letter from Judge Aldrich," *Barnwell (South Carolina) Sentinel*, reprinted in *Charleston Daily Courier*, July 6, 1866; Foner, *Reconstruction. Congressional Record*, 45th Cong., 2nd sess., 1878, vol. 7, pt. 3, pp. 2865, 2512, comments of Representative John Hanna of Indiana and Senator Thomas C. McCreery of Kentucky during debates on the repeal of the Bankruptcy Act.

2. Warren, *Bankruptcy*, 112.

3. Ibid., 112; Skeel, *Debt's Dominion*, 28, 26; Wiecek, "Reconstruction," 357.

4. U.S. Const., art. 1, sec. 8; Berglof and Rosenthal, "Political Economy," 3, 17; James, *Bankrupt Law*, iii; *An Act to Establish an Uniform System of Bankruptcy throughout the United States*, U.S. Statutes at Large 2 (1800): 19–36; *An Act to Establish a Uniform System of Bankruptcy throughout the United States*, U.S. Statutes at Large 5 (1841): 440–49; *An Act to Establish a Uniform System of Bankruptcy throughout the United States*, U.S. Statutes at Large 14 (1867): 517–41; *An Act to Establish a Uniform System of Bankruptcy throughout the United States*, U.S. Statutes at Large 30 (1898): 544–66; Skeel, *Debt's Dominion*, 24. For a discussion of why the 1898 Act had a long existence, unlike the earlier federal bankruptcy laws, see Skeel, *Debt's Dominion*, 23–47; Skeel, "Genius."

5. Friedman, *History*, 549. See also Watkins, " 'To Surrender,' " 208 ("there were charges of fraud, corruption, and mismanagement"). For references to complaints of fraud and waste in bankruptcy proceedings in the South, particularly in New Orleans, see U.S. Senate, *Letter*; Warren, *Bankruptcy*, 183 n.25 (referring to "the scandalous administration in New Orleans"), 113 (noting that "in New Orleans out of 1,800 bankruptcies, in only one was any substantial dividend realized").

6. Freehling, *South vs. South*, 17–20 (quotation on 17); Freehling, *Road*, 16–36. For

examples of studies of Reconstruction that consider the South to be the eleven former Confederate states, see Woodward, *Reunion;* Carter, *When the War Was Over;* Stampp, *Era;* Roark, *Masters;* Perman, *Reunion.* Works that treat at least some of the Union border states as part of the South during Reconstruction include Kaczorowski, *Politics;* Foner, *Reconstruction.*

7. Wagner, "Advantages," 227–28. See also Friedman, *History,* 550 (quoting from this report).

8. *Congressional Record,* 45th Cong., 2nd sess., 1878, vol. 7, pt. 3, p. 2860; Warren, *Bankruptcy,* 27, 30 (quotation), 83, 134, 143. For further discussion of how congressional divisions for and against bankruptcy laws have been predominately sectional, with southerners opposed, see Warren, *Bankruptcy,* 9.

9. *Congressional Record,* 45th Cong., 2nd sess., 1878, vol. 7, pt. 4, pp. 3354–55; Warren, *Bankruptcy,* 114.

10. Beman, *Selected Articles,* xxvi; Friedman, *American Law,* 598; Albert J. Beveridge quoted in Beman, *Selected Articles,* 218 (expressing the immoderate view that the Civil War "was nothing but the financial interests of slaveholders defending their unholy institution behind the breastworks of 'state rights' "); McDonald, *States' Rights* (discussing how advocates of a broad range of political beliefs adopted the cause of states' rights when doing so was in their interest).

11. Sandage, "Deadbeats," 259; Fairman, *Reconstruction,* 364. I agree with both Sandage's and Fairman's depictions but press beyond their studies to investigate the dynamics involved in further depth through empirical study and from various previously unconsidered angles.

12. Goodman, "Emergence," esp. 491 ("Their control of land left prewar elites preeminent in shaping the region's postwar destiny"); Lucie, *Freedom,* 143.

13. Foner, introduction, xviii.

14. Various scholars have examined the political nature of the law and how, even though a law may not explicitly state that it governs power relationships between parties, it does so. This phenomenon results from the fact that a law intrinsically embodies the worldview—and often the best interests—of a particular social group, frequently the group with the power to pass or rule on the law. See, for example, Horwitz, *Transformation;* Kerber, *No Constitutional Right.*

15. Scholars have recognized the importance of studying the people who employed federal bankruptcy laws. As Karen Gross, Marie Stefanini Newman, and Denise Campbell state in "Ladies in Red," 29–30, "Our findings suggest that bankruptcy history cannot be told by looking only at government data, the remarks of politicians, and outside economic events. . . . An important part of the real story gets lost. Bankruptcy history must include a look at the real people who partook of the bankruptcy system and must consider their experiences, not aggregated, but individually."

16. Cresswell, *Mormons,* 133; Fisher, *War,* 19; address of a committee of the "East Tennessee Relief Association," stated in U.S. Senate, *Message,* 3; Temple, *East Tennessee,* 201.

17. *Graver v. United States,* 3 Ct. Cl. 83, 84 (1867); Andrews, "Three Months," 241;

Trowbridge, *South*, 568, quoted in Zuczek, *State*, 12; *Charleston Daily Courier*, July 7, 1865, quoted in Zuczek, *State*, 11; Foner, *Reconstruction*, 399 (quoting northern reporter); Zuczek, *State*, 287.

18. *Jackson Clarion*, October 8, 1867, quoted in Harris, *Day*, 110; Levi Hurlbutt to niece, August 14, 1867, quoted in Fairley and Dawson, *Paths*, 68.

19. I determined the average county by using published census data to calculate the average population and property value of the counties in each state. I then chose a county that had a population and property value close to this average. Also, I attempted to pick a county that was in a different part of the district from the metropolitan county. For example, Anderson County lies in far western South Carolina, bordering Georgia, distant from Charleston County on the east coast.

20. Warren, *Bankruptcy*; Coleman, *Debtors*, esp. 18; Skeel, *Debt's Dominion*, 14; Mann, *Republic*.

21. Balleisen, *Navigating Failure*; Sandage, "Deadbeats," 4, 6.

22. Sandage maintains "that the bankruptcy debate, at its political core, was a national discussion about the meaning of freedom in nineteenth-century America" ("Deadbeats," 118). As I discuss further in chapter 1, Sandage's position has much merit: such analogies to debt slavery and freedom for debtors frequently formed part of the discussion about bankruptcy. But other political concerns—namely, disassociating the 1867 bankruptcy legislation from Reconstruction measures—also played a significant role in congressional debates (where, as Sandage recognizes, such a characterization was necessary to enable passage) and among southerners after the law's enactment. Sandage also proposes that during the nineteenth century, a bankruptcy act "faced an insuperable ideological obstacle," requiring "not only an affirmative act of Congress but also a veritable revolution in American understandings of federal power to interfere with the rights of property" ("Deadbeats," 125, 131). This astute conclusion complements my position: congressmen did not incorporate into the 1867 Bankruptcy Act terms that would enable such a revolution in federal power with respect to property relations. Nor did Americans—including southerners—believe that such a revolution had taken place. As a result, the legislation acted only as a temporary means of removing indebtedness, a short-term tool rather than a permanent system.

CHAPTER 1. *An Act of Transcendent Importance*

1. *An Act to Provide for the More Efficient Government of the Rebel States*, U.S. Statutes at Large 14 (1867): 428–30; Hyman, *More Perfect Union*, 493–94.

2. *An Act Regulating the Tenure of Certain Civil Offices*, U.S. Statutes at Large 14 (1867): 430–32; Hall, Wiecek, and Finkelman, *American Legal History*, 228–30.

3. *An Act to Amend an Act Entitled "An Act for the Removal of Causes in Certain Cases from State Courts," Approved July Twenty-seven, Eighteen Hundred and Sixty-six*, U.S. Statutes at Large 14 (1867):558; Hyman, *More Perfect Union*, 473; Kutler, *Judicial Power*, 152.

4. *Congressional Globe,* 39th Cong., 2nd sess., 1867, vol. 37, pt. 2, p. 1006; pt. 3, p. 1993; *Act to Establish a Uniform System of Bankruptcy, U.S. Statutes at Large* 14 (1867): 517–41.

5. *Congressional Globe,* 39th Cong., 2nd sess., 1867, vol. 37, pt. 2, p. 1005.

6. *Jackson Weekly Clarion,* March 7, 1867; *Charleston Daily Courier,* March 3, 1867.

7. Hyman, *More Perfect Union,* 267, 455–56, 521; Hyman and Wiecek, *Equal Justice,* 466; Lucie, *Freedom,* ii–iii, 2–3, 14–15, 53, 190; Kaczorowski, *Politics;* Paludan, *Covenant,* 47, 232–33; Hoeveler, "Reconstruction."

8. Kaczorowski, *Politics,* esp. 37 (quotation).

9. Francis W. Henry to B. E. Woffard, April 15, 1867, quoted in Harris, *Presidential Reconstruction,* 33; Foner, *Reconstruction,* 125; Goldin, "Economics," 74; Rubin, "Redefining," 287; McPherson, *Ordeal,* 475–76; *New York Times,* June 19, 1865, quoted in Harris, *Presidential Reconstruction,* 29. See also "Charge of Hon. George S. Bryan," *Charleston Daily Courier,* October 23, 1866 ("Debt, he said, was almost universal, and was at the present time a common misfortune and calamity").

10. Warren, *Bankruptcy,* 96–97. For further discussion of the extent of southerners' debts to northerners, see Watkins, " 'To Surrender,' " 207–13.

11. Sandage, "Deadbeats," 151; *Congressional Globe,* 37th Cong., 3rd sess., 1862, vol. 33, pt. 1, p. 125.

12. Simkins and Woody, *South Carolina,* 46; Harris, *Presidential Reconstruction,* 178; *Raymond Hinds County Gazette,* November 2, 1866, quoted in Harris, *Presidential Reconstruction,* 178; "The Stay Law," *Charleston Daily Courier,* June 30, 1866. For further discussion of the prevalence of such debt-collection filings in state courts, see Carter, *When the War Was Over,* 135; Bryant, " 'Settled.' " Debt collection was not common solely during Reconstruction; collection suits were the most prominent type of case before sixteen state supreme courts studied between 1870 and 1900 (Kagan et al., "Business," 137).

13. Foner, *Reconstruction,* 212; Carter, *When the War Was Over,* 135, 141; *Coffman v. Bank of Kentucky,* 40 Miss. 29 (Miss. Err. & App. 1866); *Wood v. Wood,* 48 S.C.L. 148 (S.C. 1867); Warren, *Bankruptcy,* 150; Coleman, *Debtors,* 190; Harris, *Presidential Reconstruction,* 179. For sentiment for the repeal of the South Carolina stay law, see "The Stay Law," *Charleston Daily Courier,* July 1, 1866. For criticisms of the stay laws expressed by southern judge J. H. Thomas in 1871, see quoted passage in Warren, *Bankruptcy,* 149–50. The effects of state property exemptions on proceedings under the 1867 Bankruptcy Act are discussed later in this chapter.

14. *Congressional Globe,* 39th Cong., 2nd sess., 1867, vol. 37, pt. 2, p. 952; *Congressional Record,* 45th Cong., 2nd sess., 1878, vol. 7, pt. 3, p. 2863; Bump, *Law and Practice,* 8th ed., 294; J.F.B., "Expediency," 457.

15. U.S. Const., art. 1, sec. 8; Harris, *Presidential Reconstruction,* 179.

16. *Washington News,* July 23, 1866, printed in *Charleston Daily Courier,* July 27, 1866; *Congressional Globe,* 39th Cong., 1st sess., 1866, vol. 36, pt. 3, p. 2743; *Congressional Globe,* 39th Cong., 2nd sess., 1867, vol. 37, pt. 2, p. 1192; pt. 3, p. 1193; *Act to Establish a Uniform System of Bankruptcy, U.S. Statutes at Large* 14 (1867): 517–41.

17. Warren, *Bankruptcy,* 105; *Congressional Globe,* 39th Cong., 2nd sess., 1867, vol. 37, pt. 3, p. 1708.

18. *Congressional Globe*, 39th Cong., 2nd sess., 1867, vol. 37, pt. 2, pp. 980, 1192, 984; *Congressional Globe*, 39th Cong., 1st sess., 1866, vol. 36, pt. 2, p. 1698. For comments concerning how the Act would disadvantage northern creditors by relieving southerners of their debts, see statements by Senator John Sherman of Ohio and Senator Henry Lane of Indiana in *Congressional Globe*, 39th Cong., 2nd sess., 1867, vol. 37, pt. 3, pp. 984, 1191. For examples of northern creditors' support for the bankruptcy legislation, see letters from the Boston Board of Trade and New York Chamber of Commerce read during House proceedings and recorded in *Congressional Globe*, 39th Cong., 1st sess., 1867, vol. 36, pt. 2, p. 1693. The Boston Board of Trade had submitted a memorial in 1865 proposing the postponement of enactment of a bankruptcy bill until members of the board had had time to negotiate with their debtors after the restoration of southern states. The board apparently felt that sufficient time had elapsed by 1867 (*Congressional Globe*, 38th Cong., 2nd sess., 1865, vol. 34, pt. 1, p. 292). Charles Warren notes how northern creditors served as the foremost proponents of the law (*Bankruptcy*, 106). See also Friedman, *History*, 549 ("Apparently, some Northern creditors hoped to use the bankruptcy law to reclaim at least a pittance from ruined debtors in the South").

19. Sandage, "Deadbeats," 232; Warren, *Bankruptcy*, 100–101, 107, 108; *Congressional Globe*, 39th Cong., 2nd sess., 1867, vol. 37, pt. 2, p. 1005. Senator John B. Henderson of Missouri argued that the bankruptcy law would not benefit southerners who already possessed the protection of stay laws (some of which, he failed to mention, had already been held unconstitutional by state courts), but his sentiments were in the minority; see *Congressional Globe*, 39th Cong., 2nd sess., 1867, vol. 37, pt. 2, pp. 1005, 985.

20. *Congressional Globe*, 39th Cong., 2nd sess., 1867, vol. 37, pt. 2, pp. 1005, 984, 1007.

21. Warren, *Bankruptcy*, 107; *Congressional Globe*, 39th Cong., 1st sess., 1866, vol. 36, pt. 2, pp. 1699, 1698. Agreeing with the sentiments of those who separated southerners' economic needs from their political punishment, Senator Reverdy Johnson of Maryland expressed how the justifications for applying a test oath to federal officers to ensure their loyalty "does not apply to the poor debtors who are crushed to the earth by debt, and are unable to do anything for the support of themselves or for the benefit of their country" (*Congressional Globe*, 39th Cong., 2nd sess., 1867, vol. 37, pt. 2, p. 1005).

22. *Congressional Globe*, 37th Cong., 3rd sess., 1862, vol. 1, pt. 1, p. 142.

23. Sandage, "Deadbeats," 118, 188–217; J.F.B., "Expediency," 459. For evidence of the stance of congressmen that the 1867 Act was a nonpartisan measure, see Sandage, "Deadbeats," 154 (quotation from Senator John Hale), 157 (quotation from Representative Thomas Jenckes).

24. *Congressional Globe*, 39th Cong., 2nd sess., 1867, vol. 37, pt. 2, p. 1009. Petitioners abided by this requirement; see Voluntary Petition of William T. White, filed February 29, 1868, Case #248, Bankruptcy Case Files (1867–78), U.S. District Court of South Carolina, NA RG 21, 52A155, BO33/22/62 (handwritten on a preprinted form is "and I do further make oath that I am a Citizen of the United States and that I will bear true faith and allegiance to the same").

25. Owens, "Documenting," 181, 184–85; Coleman, *Debtors*, 18–20; Skeel, *Debt's Dominion*, 43; Warren, *Bankruptcy*, 85–86, 82; James, *Bankrupt Law*, iii–iv. For discussion of

how the multifaceted debate regarding the role of debt and credit in American society led to early Congress's faltering efforts to establish a national bankruptcy system, see Weisberg, "Debt Crises."

26. Owens, "Documenting," 181, 184–85; Friedman, *History*, 269–70; Coleman, *Debtors*, 18–20, 23–24; Warren, *Bankruptcy*, 85–86, 19–20, 82. For arguments that the Constitution's framers must have intended only to authorize Congress to enact involuntary bankruptcy legislation, see comments by Senator Garrett Davis of Kentucky and Senator John B. Henderson of Missouri, *Congressional Globe*, 39th Cong., 2nd sess., 1867, vol. 37, pt. 2, pp. 981, 985.

27. *Congressional Globe*, 39th Cong., 1st sess., 1867, vol. 36, pt. 2, p. 1693; "The General Bankrupt Law," *Jackson Weekly Clarion*, March 21, 1867. See also James, *Bankrupt Law*, iv ("the author believes [the 1867 Act] will do much to place the commercial relations of this great country upon a sound and healthy basis").

28. Act to Establish a Uniform System of Bankruptcy, *U.S. Statutes at Large* 14 (1867): 517–41; Watkins, " 'To Surrender,' " 208; Warren, *Bankruptcy*, 109, 87, 104; J.F.B., "Expediency," 452; James, *Bankrupt Law*, iv. Noncitizens did use the act, as discussed in chapter 5. When noncitizens filed for voluntary bankruptcy, they were not required to swear their loyalty to the United States. See Voluntary Petition of Thomas J. Fletcher, filed February 27, 1868, Case #273, Bankruptcy Case Files (1867–78), U.S. District Court, Southern District of Mississippi, NA RG 21, 53A89, BO42/26/43.

29. Act to Establish a Uniform System of Bankruptcy, sec. 1, *U.S. Statutes at Large* 14 (1867): 517–18; *Pennington v. Sale*, 19 F. Cas. 169, 170 (D.C.N.D. Miss. 1868) (no. 10); Revised Statutes of the United States, sec. 711, *U.S. Statutes at Large* 18, pt. 1 (1873): 134–35. A party who proceeded in state court knowing that bankruptcy proceedings had begun against the debtor in federal court was, as Judge Hill expressed, in contempt, "and his proceedings must be held illegal and void so long as the injunction continues" (*Penny v. Taylor*, 19 F. Cas. 194, 195 [D.C.S.D. Miss. 1874] [no. 10,957]). An example of an injunction against parties to a state proceeding is *In re Samuel F. Spencer*, November 12, 1867, Case #4, 1867 Bankruptcy Case Files, U.S. District Court, Southern District of Mississippi, NA RG 21 ("you, your agents and attorneys, are enjoined, restrained and prohibited from any further proceedings in a certain suit by attachment in the Circuit Court of Warren County in the State of Mississippi"). For comments on how the revised statutes made the exclusive jurisdiction of the federal courts in bankruptcy explicit, see footnote 2 in *Watson v. Citizens' Savings Bank*, 29 F. Cas. 427 (C.C.D.S.C. 1874) (no. 17,279). The federal district courts had also possessed authority over bankruptcy cases under the 1800 and 1841 U.S. bankruptcy measures (Owens, "Documenting," 182). There was some discussion regarding the extent to which the U.S. circuit courts had concurrent jurisdiction with the district courts under the terms of the Act; see T.W.B., "Jurisdiction" (arguing that the circuit courts had concurrent jurisdiction in involuntary cases but no original jurisdiction in voluntary cases).

30. *Barber v. Rodgers*, 71 Pa. 362 (1872). See also "Notes of Recent Decisions," 23 (containing an annotation of the *Barber* case).

31. In an ongoing debate with Thomas Jefferson, James Madison recognized that the

bankruptcy clause allowed the federal government to expand its jurisdiction. In an 1823 letter to Jefferson, Madison explained that "federal jurisdiction is extended to controversies between Citizens of the same State." As proof, he noted, "To mention one only: In cases arising under a Bankrupt law, there is no distinction between those to which Citizens of the same and of different States are parties" (James Madison to Thomas Jefferson, June 27, 1823, quoted in Sandage, "Deadbeats," 140 n.24).

For a comment from the 1860s concerning how the Bankruptcy Act entailed extended federal jurisdiction, see remarks by Representative Halbert E. Paine of Wisconsin, *Congressional Globe*, 39th Cong., 1st sess., 1866, vol. 36, pt. 2, p. 1689 ("But, sir, if you enlarge this jurisdiction as you propose so that it shall virtually embrace the collection of debts, as between citizens of the same State, you will impose upon [mechanics and farmers in the West] a burden of expense, inconvenience, oppression, and misery, which nothing but the most urgent necessity will excuse").

32. *In re Citizens' Savings Bank*, 5 F. Cas. 738 (C.C.D.S.C. 1873) (no. 2,735). For a description of the position of a federal circuit judge, see chap. 2.

33. Act to Establish a Uniform System of Bankruptcy, secs. 11, 29, *U.S. Statutes at Large* 14 (1867): 521–22, 531–32; "The General Bankrupt Law," *Jackson Weekly Clarion*, March 21, 1867; Voluntary Petition of Newitt V. Lane, filed July 8, 1867, Case #2, 1867 Bankruptcy Case Files, U.S. District Court, Southern District of Mississippi, NA RG 21; Watkins, "'To Surrender,'" 210; *Aiken v. Edrington*, 1 F. Cas. 238, 240 (C.C.S.D. Miss. 1876) (no. 111); "Doubtful Points" (1871), 54–55. See the Newitt V. Lane file as well as others in the bankruptcy case files for details on what a debtor was required to list in the asset and debt schedules. For discussion of when a bankrupt could apply for discharge, see *In re Bodenheim*, 3 F. Cas. 792, 793 (D.C.S.D. Miss. 1869) (no. 1,594). Legal commentators differed regarding whether the one-year limit on filing for a discharge applied to all bankrupts or only to those whose proceedings did not involve any assets or debts. Compare "Bankrupt Act—Discharge," 556 (one-year limit does not apply to bankrupts with assets and debts), with "Bankruptcy—United States and State Jurisdiction," 92 (bankrupt must apply within one year). Regardless, to merit denial of a discharge, a bankrupt must have committed a forbidden act or failed to perform a required act; as Mississippi District Judge Hill noted, "Mere oversight or mistake is not sufficient" cause for denial (*In re McVey*, 16 F. Cas. 352, 353 [D.C.N.D. Miss. 1868] [no. 8,932]).

34. Act to Establish a Uniform System of Bankruptcy, sec. 29, *U.S. Statutes at Large* 14 (1867): 531–32; Certificate of Discharge of Newitt V. Lane, filed July 8, 1867, Case #2, 1867 Bankruptcy Case Files, U.S. District Court, Southern District of Mississippi, NA RG 21.

35. Act to Establish a Uniform System of Bankruptcy, secs. 39–42, *U.S. Statutes at Large* 14 (1867): 536–38; "The General Bankrupt Law," *Jackson Weekly Clarion*, March 21, 1867; Watkins, "'To Surrender,'" 211. For an example of the common provisions in an involuntary bankruptcy petition, see Involuntary Petition of Archie C. Fisk v. Philip D. Toomer, filed November 20, 1870, Case #1353, 1867 Bankruptcy Case Files, U.S. District Court, Southern District of Mississippi, NA RG 21.

36. Foner, *Reconstruction*, 125; Ransom and Sutch, *One Kind*, 51, 328 n.42 (citing statistics from an 1867 U.S. Department of Agriculture report); *Laws of the State of Missis-*

sippi, chap. 15 (1841), chap. 23 (1842); *Code of Tennessee*, chap. 4 (1858), 428–31; *Acts of the General Assembly of South Carolina*, chap. 16 (1823), no. 4041 (1851), no. 4384 (1857); Goodman, "Emergence," 493; Ford, *Origins*, 323.

37. *Laws of the State of Mississippi*, chap. 46 (1839); *Code of Tennessee*, secs. 2479, 2481–86 (1858); South Carolina Constitution, art. 14, sec. 8 (1868) (elaborated by *Acts of the General Assembly of South Carolina*, no. 220 [1870]); Goodman, "Emergence," 491; *In re Patterson*, 18 F. Cas. 1315 (C.C.S.D. N.Y. 1867) (no. 10,815); *In re Rosenfield*, 20 F. Cas. 1205 (D.C.D. N.J. 1868) (no. 12,059).

38. Warren, *Bankruptcy*, 103–4; Watkins, " 'To Surrender,' " 207; *Act to Establish a Uniform System of Bankruptcy*, secs. 14, 33, *U.S. Statutes at Large* 14 (1867): 522–24, 533. Opponents claimed that providing for property exemptions in accordance with state laws would render the 1867 Act unconstitutional because the measure would not have uniform application across the country as required by the Constitution. Nevertheless, the state exemption provision remained in effect throughout the eleven-year life of the 1867 law. In 1902, when considering the 1898 Bankruptcy Act, the U.S. Supreme Court ruled that incorporation of state exemptions was constitutional (Tabb, "History," 20). For an illustration of how bankrupts claimed both federal and state exemptions, see Petition Schedules of Elijah W. Brown, filed December 22, 1873, Case #1,535, Bankruptcy Case Files (1867–78), U.S. District Court of South Carolina, NA RG 21.

39. Warren, *Bankruptcy*, 109–10, 121; Tabb, "History," 20 n.129; *An Act in Amendment of the Act Entitled "An Act Establishing an Uniform System of Bankruptcy throughout the United States,"* sec. 1, *U.S. Statutes at Large* 16 (1870): 276; *In re Seay*, 21 F. Cas. 954 (D.C.D. Tenn. 1870) (no. 12,597); *An Act to Amend and Supplement an Act Entitled "An Act to Establish a Uniform System of Bankruptcy throughout the United States," Approved March Second, Eighteen Hundred and Sixty-seven, and for Other Purposes*, sec. 9, *U.S. Statutes at Large* 18, pt. 3 (1874): 180.

40. *An Act to Amend an Act Entitled "An Act to Establish a Uniform System of Bankruptcy throughout the United States," Approved March Second, Eighteen Hundred and Sixty-seven, U.S. Statutes at Large* 17 (1872): 334; Warren, *Bankruptcy*, 110–12; Tabb, "History," 20; Coleman, *Debtors*, 25–26; "The Bankrupt Act Amendment," *Jackson Weekly Clarion*, April 3, 1873; *Constitution of South Carolina*, sec. 32 (1868); *Acts of the State of Tennessee*, chap. 85 (1868); *Laws of the State of Mississippi*, chap. 9 (1865), chap. 25 (1870); *An Act to Declare the True Intent and Meaning of the Act Approved June Eighth, Eighteen Hundred and Seventy-two, Amendatory of the General Bankrupt Law, U.S. Statutes at Large* 17 (1873): 577. The Supreme Court never ruled on the constitutionality of applying the more generous exemption provisions against debts already existing at the time of the exemptions' enactment. But, as Charles Warren notes, one can infer that the practice was unconstitutional; in 1878, the Supreme Court ruled that southern exemption laws were unconstitutional to the extent that they applied to debts contracted prior to passage (*Bankruptcy*, 112). See also Tabb, "History," 20 (observing that some state courts held the law to be unconstitutional).

Warren refers to how the "original Act of 1867 applied to State exemptions existing in 1864; but in 1864 many of the States were regarded as out of the Union, and their Constitutions and laws illegal and of no effect" (*Bankruptcy*, 110). This view of the wartime laws in the southern states as being without effect may have reigned during the first couple of years after the Civil War. See, for example, bankruptcy scholar Edwin James's 1867 description of how state exemptions applied under the Act: "It should also be understood that no notice has been taken of . . . laws passed in the seceded States since their secession" (*Bankrupt Law*, 58). But, as explained in chapter 2, in the late 1860s and 1870s, Chief Justice Chase's decisions while holding circuit court made clear that all laws and contracts made during the Civil War in the southern states were valid as long as not in furtherance of slavery, seccession, or the war. Even before Chase's decisions, bankruptcy filers in the South claimed exemptions under state law in their petitions. See, for example, Voluntary Petition of Mrs. M. A. Stowers, filed December 30, 1868, Case #1185, Bankruptcy Case Files (1867–78), U.S. District Court, Southern District of Mississippi, NA RG 21, 53A89, BO42/26/43 (claiming 160 acres as exempt homestead).

41. J. H. Thomas, "Homestead and Exemption Laws," 149–50.

42. Gross, Newman, and Campbell, "Ladies in Red," 3.

43. *Act to Establish a Uniform System of Bankruptcy*, sec. 26, U.S. Statutes at Large 14 (1867): 529.

44. Lebsock, "Radical Reconstruction." Although Lebsock maintains that male state legislators sought largely to provide a form of debt relief for men, the passage of these state statutes nonetheless empowered married women to own property and to otherwise participate in commerce.

45. *Act to Establish a Uniform System of Bankruptcy*, secs. 26, 36, U.S. Statutes at Large 14 (1867): 529, 534–35; "Doubtful Points" (1870), 417; *Davis v. Armstrong*, 7 F. Cas. 109, 110 (D.C.N.D. Miss. 1869) (no. 3,624). In 1874, Congress made the application of the Bankruptcy Act less severe on merchants; legislators extended from fourteen to forty days the period of time that those such as merchants and traders could suspend payment of their obligations without being liable to involuntary bankruptcy proceedings (*Act to Amend and Supplement "An Act to Establish a Uniform System of Bankruptcy,"* sec. 12, U.S. Statutes at Large 18, pt. 3 [1874]: 181; "The Bankrupt Law," *Charleston News and Courier*, July 2, 1874).

CHAPTER 2. *The Federal District Courts in Bankruptcy Cases*

1. General Minutes, 1864–68, U.S. District Court, Eastern District of Tennessee, NA RG 21, #92, pp. 3–4, 53A643; General Minutes, 1864–65, U.S. Circuit Court, Eastern District of Tennessee, Knoxville, NA RG21, #71, 53A643; Brake, *Justice*, 43 (quoting Trigg's law partner, Oliver P. Temple), 41; "Judge Humphries," *Brownlow's Knoxville Whig and Rebel Ventilator*, January 16, 1872; Robinson, *Justice*, 18; Hall, "West H. Humphreys"; Hyman, *More Perfect Union*, 174.

2. "The Federal Court," *Brownlow's Knoxville Whig and Rebel Ventilator*, November 11, 1863; see also "The Federal Court," *Brownlow's Knoxville Whig and Rebel Ventilator*, January 16, 1864.

3. Randall, *Constitutional Problems*, 97 (citing *Chicago Tribune*, November 29, 1865, for indictment figures); Groce, *Mountain Rebels*, 139–40. See General Minutes, 1864–65, U.S. Circuit Court, Eastern District of Tennessee, Knoxville, NA RG21, #71, 53A643.

4. See, for example, General Minutes, 1864–65, U.S. District Court, Eastern District of Tennessee, NA RG21, #92, 53A643.

5. Minutes, U.S. District Court of South Carolina, NA RG21, vol. 394; Minutes, U.S. Circuit Court of South Carolina, NA RG21, vol. 281; Powers, "Community Evolution," 27; "United States District Court," *Charleston Daily Courier*, June 28, October 10, 1866; Robinson, *Justice*, 3, 14 (quoting a tablet on the former U.S. courthouse building concerning Magrath's closure); *Williams v. Lockhart*, Roll 31, South Carolina, U.S. Circuit Court, Law Judgments (Law Case Files with Judgments), NA RG 21, B066/11/41–71.

6. Minute Book 1866–73, District Court, Southern District of Mississippi, NA RG21, #255, 53A89, B/21/02/B, 1–17. The first volume available of the General Minute Book for the Circuit Court at the National Archives—Southeast Region does not begin until 1873.

7. U.S. Senate, *Letter*, 3–15; U.S. House, *Annual Report* (1873–78); Bankruptcy Case Files (1867–78), U.S. District Court, Southern District of Mississippi, NA RG 21, 53A89, B042/26/43; Bankruptcy Docket, Jackson, #81, U.S. District Court, Southern District of Mississippi, NA RG 21, 53A89; Bankruptcy Case Files (1867–78), U.S. District Court of South Carolina, NA RG 21, 52A155, B033/22/62; Record Book: Bankruptcy, June 1867–January 1869, U.S. District Court of South Carolina, NA RG21, 52A155; 1867 Bankruptcy Docket, U.S. District Court, Eastern District of Tennessee, NA RG21, #137, 53A643, BX24/22.

8. Law and Equity Cases (1866–1912), U.S. District Court, Southern District of Mississippi, NA RG21, B029/04/33–34; Eastern District of Tennessee Law and Equity Cases, April 1864 to the Present, NA RG21, B36/25/23; South Carolina District, U.S. Circuit Court, Equity Old Decree 1861–71, NA RG21, #71, 52A155, B036/13/11; South Carolina District, U.S. Circuit Court, Equity Cases with Final Decree, NA RG21, 52A0155, B0361361; South Carolina District, U.S. Circuit Court, Equity Cases without Decree, NA RG21, 52A0155, B0270511, B0473411, B0271313, B0271312; South Carolina District, U.S. Circuit Court, Law Case Files (Without Judgment), NA RG 21, B053/23/41; South Carolina, U.S. Circuit Court, Law Judgments (Law Case Files with Judgments), NA RG 21, B066/11/41–71.

9. Frankfurter and Landis, *Business*, 63. Bankruptcy figures based on sources cited in n.7 above. Figures for the total number of federal cases filed in a given year are not available until 1904; see Posner, *Federal Courts*, 54. But review of attorney general reports beginning in 1873 for U.S. criminal and civil cases and for private civil cases portrays how bankruptcy matters represented a significant portion of the docket (U.S. House, *Annual Report* [1873–78]). Indeed, on the opening day of its January 1876 term, the South Carolina District Court (with the exception of calling jurors) dealt solely with bankruptcy cases—ten in all (*Charleston Daily News*, January 4, 1876).

10. Jones, "Federal Power," 1392; Tachau, *Federal Courts*, 12; Hyman, *More Perfect Union*, 466.

11. For discussion of how Congress relied on the federal courts to carry out Reconstruction measures and, more generally, the expansion of federal court jurisdiction

and thus federal court power during the 1860s and 1870s, see Kutler, *Judicial Power;* Wiecek, "Reconstruction"; Lucie, *Freedom;* Hyman, *More Perfect Union,* esp. 470–80. Yet although Congress was generous in its jurisdictional grants, it was stingy in allocating funds to allow the courts to fulfill their new responsibilities. Legislators were, in Kermit Hall's words, "reluctant nationalizers"; as a result, courts and federal officials were chronically short-staffed and underfunded (Hall, "Civil War Era," 186; Gillman, "How Political Parties").

12. See, for example, Kaczorowski, *Politics;* Hall, "Political Power"; Williams, *Great South Carolina;* Trelease, *White Terror;* Cresswell, *Mormons;* Swinney, "Enforcing," 202–18.

13. Kaczorowski, *Politics,* 43, 62; Warren, "Federal and State Court Interference," 359; Hall and Rise, *From Local Courts,* 35.

14. Calculations by author from figures in U.S. House, *Annual Report* (1873). These figures are based on (1) private civil cases: 19 of 22 southern federal districts and 48 of 57 federal districts nationally; and (2) criminal cases and civil cases to which the United States was a party: 21 of 22 southern federal districts and 54 of 57 returns by 20 of the 22 federal districts nationally. I have not adjusted the figures for bankruptcy filings to reflect data from my review of case files because my calculations consider cases by the calendar year, while the 1873 attorney general report considers a fiscal year. The anomalously large number of civil cases brought by the U.S. government in the Southern District of New York principally resulted from customs and revenue cases that federal officials initiated in that commercial entrepôt.

15. Memorial to Judge Emory Spear by L. E. Bleckley, quoted in Surrency, *Quest,* 27; Testimony of David T. Corbin, Washington, D.C., June 14, 1871, in U.S. House, *Testimony,* vol. 1, pt. 3, p. 80; *Charleston News and Courier,* May 14, 1873. For an investigation of resistance to revenue laws in East Tennessee, see Cresswell, *Mormons,* 133–80.

16. *Jackson Weekly Clarion,* July 20, 1871; *Charleston News and Courier,* November 28, 1874.

17. S. C. Gardner to Senator Charles Sumner, November 19, 1866, quoted in Hyman and Wiecek, *Equal Justice,* 423–24; "Our Federal Judiciary," 553.

18. A. J. Hamilton to President Andrew Johnson, August 9, 1865, quoted in Hyman, *Era,* 56; Hyman, *Era,* 56–57; Robinson, *Justice,* 595–96; T. C. Callicott to James Speed, Charleston, South Carolina, April 13, 1866, in the personnel file of A. J. Willard, Department of Justice, Appointment Papers, South Carolina, NA RG 60. For an example of President Johnson's commission, see Judge Hill's commission dated May 1, 1866, in Minute Book 1866–73, District Court, Southern District of Mississippi, NA RG21, #255, 53A89, B/21/02/B, June 25, 1866, p. 2.

19. Kershen, "Jury Selection Act," 707–82, 711 (quotation).

20. Perman, *Reunion,* 293–96; Kaczorowski, *Politics,* 226.

21. Robert A. Hill to Salmon P. Chase, Oxford, Mississippi, August 18, 1868, in Chase, *Papers,* reel 38; Amos T. Akerman to Hon. James Jackson, November 20, 1871, pp. 3–4, Letterbooks, 1:149–61, Amos T. Akerman Papers, coll. #1165, Alderman Library, Univer-

sity of Virginia, Charlottesville; *New Orleans Daily Picayune*, June 7, 1870, quoted in Ross, " 'White Man's Flag,' " 13; McCrady, "Reorganization."

22. Cash, *Mind*, 119–21; Surrency, "Legal Effects" (summarizing state courts' political shifts during Reconstruction).

23. *Vicksburg Daily Herald*, December 25, 1868; "Radical Waste of Public Money," *Jackson Weekly Clarion*, February 2, 1871; "Give Us a Decent Judiciary," *Aberdeen (Mississippi) Examiner*, quoted in *Jackson Weekly Clarion*, January 5, 1876.

24. "The Impeachment Trial," *Charleston Daily News*, February 21, 1876; Testimony of James Chesnut, July 8, 1871, in U.S. House, *Testimony*, 1:449, 472; Address by Mr. Richard Lathers of Charleston, May 9, 1871, Proceedings of the Tax-payers' Convention of South Carolina, Columbia, May 9–12, 1871, in U.S. House, *Testimony*, 1:478.

25. Alexander, "Political Reconstruction," 69; Groce, *Mountain Rebels*, 136–38; Fowler, "Chancellor William Macon Smith," 49, 52.

26. Surrency, "Legal Effects," 164–66.

27. B. T. Johnson, *Reports*, iii–iv, xiv, quoted in Hyman, *More Perfect Union*, 288.

28. For evidence of the varied background and Republican persuasion of registers, see Testimony of Richard B. Carpenter, July 8, 1871, in U.S. House, *Testimony*, 1:226, 250, 258; Testimony of James Chesnut, July 8, 1871, in U.S. House, *Testimony*, 1:458; Testimony of Joseph W. Field, December 16, 1868, in U.S. House, *Condition*, 47, 49; *Register of the Department of Justice*, 1871, 1872, 1873, 1874, 1876 (listing how both native southerners and those from outside the South served as registers in southern Mississippi, East Tennessee, and South Carolina).

29. See Kaczorowski, *Politics*, 66–67, 77 n.40. Describing the anomaly of twentieth-century Federal District Judge Frank M. Johnson, who was an outsider to his Alabama community, Robert D. McFadden of the *New York Times* notes, "Federal district judges are usually part of the local scene: their appointments traceable to community involvement and local politics, their professional and social lives intertwined with the local power structure" ("Frank M. Johnson, Jr., Judge Whose Rulings Helped Desegregate the South, Dies at 80," *New York Times*, July 24, 1999, p. A15).

30. *Congressional Globe*, 39th Cong., 2nd sess., 1867, vol. 37, pt. 1, pp. 587, 588. The compromise, as passed, was that the district judges would appoint registers upon the recommendation of the chief justice of the United States (*Act to Establish a Uniform System of Bankruptcy*, sec. 3, *U.S. Statutes at Large* 14 [1867]: 518).

31. Gordon Adam to Charles Sumner, December 1, 1868, quoted in Hall, "Civil War," 184.

32. Sketch of R. A. Hill, R. A. Hill Subject File, Mississippi Department of Archives and History, Jackson; Hall, "Civil War," 184; *Mathews v. Springer*, 16 F. Cas. 1096, 1101 (S.C.S.C. Miss. 1871) (no. 9,277).

33. A. P. Huggins to Amos Akerman, June 28, 1871, Source-Chronological File for Northern Mississippi, NA RG 60; Amos Akerman to E. P. Jacobsen, August 18, 1871; both quoted in Cresswell, *Mormons*, 72.

34. Swinney, "Enforcing," 215.

35. Sketch of R. A. Hill; *Jackson Weekly Clarion,* June 6, 1872, July 13 or 20[?], 1871.
36. Kaczorowski, *Politics,* 68; Hall, "Civil War," 184.
37. Temple, *Notable Men,* 209; William G. Brownlow to Governor Andrew Johnson, November 30, 1864, and William G. Brownlow to Governor Andrew Johnson (telegraph), November 30, 1864, quoted in Brake, *Justice,* 45–46; James B. Bingham to Andrew Johnson, February 10, 1865, discussed and quoted in Brake, *Justice,* 46; Brake, *Justice,* 53–54; R. McPhail Smith to Circuit Judge Halmer Emmons, November 7, 1870, quoted in Kaczorowski, *Politics,* 70; George Andrews to Attorney General Williams [?], November 12, 1872, quoted in Cresswell, *Mormons,* 176.
38. Temple, *Notable Men,* 211; Caldwell, *Sketches,* 305–6; *Goodspeed's History,* quoted in Brake, *Justice,* 44; Fisher, *War,* 176.
39. Kaczorowski, *Politics,* 73 n.6; Hall, "Political Power," 935; Hugh L. Bond to Anna Bond, n.d., November 26, 1871, Hugh L. Bond Papers, MS 1206, Manuscripts Department, Maryland Historical Society Library, Baltimore; William Evarts to Hugh McCulloch, November 27, 1868, quoted in Kaczorowski, *Politics,* 69–70.
40. "United States District Court," *Charleston Daily Courier,* August 2, 1866; "Judge George S. Bryan" (appendix), *City of Charleston Year Book—1895,* 380–81 (quoting *Charleston News and Courier* article at Judge Bryan's retirement), 384 (quoting benediction at Bryan's burial).
41. Hall, "Civil War"; Hall, "Political Power," 932, 951 (quotation). In some later writings, Hall recognizes the validity of Freyer's thesis that federal courts increasingly became nationalized during the late nineteenth and early twentieth centuries (*Magic Mirror,* 229).
42. Tachau, *Federal Courts,* 191; Gillman, "Political Construction," 11.
43. Freyer, *Forums;* Freyer, "Federal Courts," 343–63. For an overview of these perspectives concerning the role of the lower federal courts, see Zelden, *Justice Lies,* 4–5.
44. Zelden, *Justice Lies,* 5, 10.
45. Freyer, *Forums,* xx.
46. *Jackson Weekly Clarion,* May 1, 1878 (quoting April 8, 1878, letter from Judge Tarbell from Washington, D.C.); Rubin, "Redefining," 280, 392–93, 395.
47. Reid, *After the War,* 221, 73.
48. Ezell, *South,* 43, 46.
49. *Congressional Globe,* 41st Cong., 2nd sess., 1870, vol. 42, pt. 1, p. 79; Harris, *Presidential Reconstruction,* 186–93, 249–50; Harris, *Day,* 487–88, 547–48, 614–15; Woodward, *Origins,* 30–31 (quoting *New Orleans Times,* February 25, 1877).

CHAPTER 3. *Southerners' Use of the 1867 Act*

1. *Congressional Record,* 45th Cong., 2nd sess., 1878, vol. 7, pt. 4, p. 3358; *Jackson Weekly Clarion,* February 28, March 7, 1867; *Vicksburg Daily Herald,* July 10, 1868; District Judge Robert A. Hill to Chief Justice Salmon P. Chase, Oxford, Mississippi, August 18, 1868, in Chase, *Papers,* reel 38. Legal historian Erwin Surrency recognizes that "southerners

were making extensive use of the statute" and concludes that "it is surprising how soon Southerners took advantage of this statute" (*History,* chap. 9, p. 3). My thanks to Professor Surrency for allowing me to review his manuscript in advance of publication.

2. See, for example, "Important Decision in the U.S. District Court of the Rights of Bankrupts," *Brownlow's Knoxville Whig,* November 13, 1867; "Amendment of the Bankrupt Law," *Brownlow's Knoxville Whig,* August 19, 1868; "The Jaynes Bankrupt Case," *Vicksburg Daily Herald,* August 18, 1868; "Important to Bankrupts and Their Creditors," *Jackson Weekly Clarion,* September 1, 1870, reprinted in *Jackson Weekly Mississippi Pilot,* September 10, 1870; "The Bankrupt Law," *Charleston News and Courier,* February 7, 1874; *Charleston Daily News,* February 2, 1874 (stating 1874 amendments to the Bankruptcy Act); "Legal Intelligence," *Jackson Weekly Mississippi Pilot,* June 5, 1875; *Jackson Weekly Clarion,* April 3, 1878 (assuring readers that repeal of the Act would not affect cases already filed).

3. *Jackson Weekly Mississippi Pilot,* December 4, 1869.

4. "The Bankrupt Law," *Charleston Daily Courier,* March 27, 1867 (numerous other advertisements for the pamphlet appeared in other *Daily Courier* issues in March 1867); "Bankrupt Blanks," *Jackson Weekly Clarion,* August 1, 1872; *Jackson Weekly Clarion,* August 1, 1872, December 6, 1876.

5. Foner, *Reconstruction,* 535.

6. Petition Schedules of Richard B. Carpenter, filed December 31, 1868, Case #1221, Bankruptcy Case Files (1867–78), U.S. District Court of South Carolina, NA RG 21, 52A155, BO33/22/62.

7. These figures do not include filings that occurred in 1877, for which no data are available. The *American Law Review* estimated a much higher number of filings—more than 103,000, with more than 22,000 filed in southern federal courts (Warren, *Bankruptcy,* 112). I rely on data in congressional documents and the annual reports of the attorney general, which began reporting information for private civil cases in federal court in 1873 (U.S. House, *Annual Report* [1873–78]). For the three judicial districts I studied in depth, the figures in these official reports largely reflect the actual number of filings each year. See appendix on methodology for more information regarding the data on which this chapter is based.

8. Calculations concerning the percentage of the nation's 1870 population that resided in the South are based on information in the Inter-university Consortium for Political and Social Research's Census Data for the Year 1870, at http://fisher.lib.virginia.edu/cgi-local/censusbin/census.pl?year=870 (accessed November 29, 2003). The consortium's database includes Colorado (which was admitted as a state in 1876) in the 1870 data; the calculations for 1870 here exclude Colorado. In addition, twenty-two of fifty-seven (39 percent) federal judicial districts (numbers that held constant during most of the period under study) were located in the former Confederate states (U.S. Senate, *Letter,* 3–15; U.S. House, *Annual Report* [1873–78]).

9. Warren, *Bankruptcy,* 112, 183 n.22 (citing the *American Law Review* 13 [1879] and the attorney general's report for these figures). Figures concerning voluntary and involuntary filings between 1867 and 1878 are incomplete because the district reports and

attorney general's reports from which I compiled these numbers often did not break down the filings into the two categories.

10. Five bankruptcy cases filed in the three southern districts could not be categorized as either voluntary or involuntary based on the information available in court documents. The District Court of Louisiana also handled a much larger number of voluntary filings (1,245) than involuntary filings (79) between June 1867 and July 1873 (Charles Claiborne, clerk, District Court of the United States for the District of Louisiana, to George H. Williams, Attorney General, September 1, 1873, quoted in U.S. Senate, *Letter*, 28).

11. Christian G. Fritz portrays a similar peak in bankruptcy filings in 1868 in northern California ("Judicial Business," p. 240, table 2).

12. Foner, *Reconstruction*, 535.

13. William Aiken to George H. Williams, Attorney General, Knoxville, Tennessee, April 2, 1873, quoted in U.S. Senate, *Letter*, 26.

CHAPTER 4. *Southern Attorneys as Bankruptcy Counsel*

1. M. P. O'Connor to General McGowan, September 1868, in O'Connor, *Life and Letters*, 33; Harris, *Day*, 111; Carter, *When the War Was Over*, 142; Waldrep, *Roots*, 112 (quoting *Vicksburg Daily Herald*, May 17, 1865); *Charleston News and Courier*, May 31, 1876.

2. *Ex parte Garland*, 71 U.S. 333, 386 (1866) (dissenting opinion of Justice Miller); Groce, *Mountain Rebels*, 140.

3. *Opinion*, 9. All of the six claims involving parties who represented themselves (five involving residents of Warren County, Mississippi, and one from Charleston, South Carolina) were voluntary. One of the Warren County case files included the phrase "No Atty," which appeared to indicate that the party involved was acting pro se, and I counted the filing as such.

4. *Vicksburg Daily Herald*, March 3, 1868. Other attorneys also advertised their ability to act as counsel in bankruptcy cases and were more forthright about the fact that such proceedings took place in federal court. Vicksburg attorney Allan MacDonnell advertised in the same issue of the *Daily Herald* as McGarr and Smedes, explaining his availability to practice in the state courts but also indicating that he practiced in "U.S. Courts and Courts of Admiralty, . . . and is prepared with the necessary books, blanks, &c., to put parties through bankruptcy" (*Vicksburg Daily Herald*, March 3, 1868).

5. Attorney advertising was customary in the nineteenth century; in the twentieth century, professional codes of ethics restricted and often set strict guidelines for the practice. See, e.g., Haywood and Jones, "Navigating," 1099.

6. See, for example, the description of the political ideology that dictated legal representation and strategy in the South Carolina Ku Klux Klan cases in Trelease, *White Terror*, 407; Hall, "Political Power," 936. Although the defense attorneys in the South Carolina cases were nationally renowned attorneys Reverdy Johnson and Henry Stanbery, who had been brought in from the North, the South Carolinians who raised the funds for legal defense, a group headed by future Redeemer governor and former voluntary bankrupt

Wade Hampton, dictated that the attorneys' foremost task was to fight for a limited role for the federal government rather than to protect the defendants.

7. O'Brien, *Legal Fraternity,* 81.

8. Skeel, *Debt's Dominion,* 34–35; Hall, *Magic Mirror,* 212–14; Friedman, *History,* 308 (describing how collection work was a staple of western attorneys' legal practices); Balleisen, *Navigating Failure,* 140–41. For discussion of the growth of large law firms (with five or more attorneys), chiefly in the Midwest and Northeast in the late nineteenth and early twentieth centuries, see Hobson, "Symbol," 3–27. None of the fourteen cities Hobson identifies as having six or more large law firms was located in the South ("Symbol," 10–12).

Paul Finkelman concludes that "Southern lawyers were perhaps more aware of national trends than other southerners" and that twentieth-century southern lawyers in particular "may have felt greater kinship with lawyers of other regions than with laymen of their own region." But he cautions that southern lawyers as well as judges and legislators were unified with their neighbors on "distinctly southern issues" ("Exploring," 116). As historian Michael de L. Landon notes in his history of the Mississippi Bar Association in the 1880s and 1890s, for nearly all Mississippi attorneys in the 1890s, "race relations and the problem of keeping the black man in his place were the overriding concern" ("Another False Start," 198). Thus, attorneys were tied to local interests in a similar way—and perhaps even more integrally—than the federal judicial officials discussed in chapter 2.

9. See Skeel, *Debt's Dominion,* 34; Balleisen, *Navigating Failure,* 140 (describing attorney representation in similar matters under the 1841 Bankruptcy Act).

10. Skeel, *Debt's Dominion,* 34–35.

11. For evidence of this fluidity, compare the members of partnerships and solo practitioners in 1860 and 1868 in East Tennessee; Charleston and Anderson Counties, South Carolina; and Warren and Lauderdale Counties, Mississippi, in Livingston, *United States Law Register,* 477, 480, 834–36, 851–61, and Livingston, *1868,* 81–82, 385, 388, 473, 477–85; see also Livingston, *1868,* preface.

12. Accurately determining attorneys' affiliations was especially challenging for Lauderdale County because of the numerous changes in groupings that occurred during the 1867–78 period, so the figures given here are approximations.

13. References to total numbers of attorneys and firms listed in Livingston, *1868,* for a certain area consider each firm (a partnership of two or more attorneys) as one and each solo practitioner as one. No attorney's name was indicated in ten voluntary filings in Charleston County, South Carolina; three such filings from Warren County, Mississippi; two such filings from Lauderdale County, Mississippi; and twenty-four such filings in East Tennessee. The attorneys' names for two additional East Tennessee filings were illegible.

14. Information about Casey and other attorneys comes from Court of Claims General Jurisdiction Case Files, 1855–1939, Records of the U.S. Court of Claims, RG 123, National Archives and Records Administration, Washington, D.C.; Dockets for Cotton Cases, 1868–90, Records of the Court of Claims Section (Justice), RG 205, National Archives

and Records Administration, Washington, D.C.; Docket—General Jurisdiction Cases, 1855–1914, Records of the Court of Claims Section (Justice).

15. Livingston, *United States Law Register;* Livingston, *1868*. Attorneys listed as "not practicing" were not counted in the totals. Livingston, *1868*, lists sixty-eight law firms or solo attorneys as practicing in Charleston County, South Carolina; thirty-seven of them (54 percent) were not practicing in the county in 1860, whereas thirty (44 percent) were. I was unable to determine whether one attorney was practicing in 1860. In Warren County, Mississippi, fifteen of the twenty-five (60 percent) firms or solo practitioners listed as practicing in 1868 were not in business in 1860, nine (36 percent) were practicing, and one was undetermined.

16. "Charles Henry Simonton," in Federal Judicial Center, "Judges of the United States Courts," at http://www.fjc.gov/newweb/jnetweb.nsf/hisj (accessed September 8, 2003).

17. See 1867 Bankruptcy Docket, U.S. District Court, Eastern District of Tennessee, NA RG 21; Livingston *1868*. Whether H. M. Aiken and William Aiken were relatives was unclear from the records.

18. Six different groups of attorneys acted as counsel in the seven involuntary claims filed in Anderson County, South Carolina. The largest number of cases handled by a firm or solo practitioner in East Tennessee was seven.

19. Census Records, Population Schedules, Warren County, Mississippi, 1870, pp. 221, 270–71; Testimony of G. Gordon Adam, June 22, 1871, in U.S. House, *Testimony,* vol. 1, pt. 11, p. 63; Neiman, *To Set the Law,* 81; Livingston, *1868,* 388; Martindale, *Law Directory,* 382; *Biographical and Historical Memoirs,* 2:805–7; "Resignation of the Clerk of the Circuit Court," *Vicksburg Weekly Herald and Mississippian,* August 8, 1868, p. 1. Speed became a prominent Vicksburg citizen, owning and helping to develop a Vicksburg suburb. He was also a high-ranking Mason and president of the community's Young Men's Christian Organization (*Biographical and Historical Memoirs,* 2:806–7). For a discussion of Adam and Speed's service as attorneys for cases before the Court of Claims, see Thompson, "Reconstructing." Although born outside of the South, both Adam and Speed engaged in what historian Christopher Waldrep terms "that most southern of institutions," the duel, during the late 1860s (*Roots,* 77–78).

20. U.S. House, *Statements,* pt. 1, pp. 43–51; Deposition of Duff Green, *Roach v. United States,* Vicksburg, April 19, 1869, Box 250, Folder 2, Records of the United States Court of Claims.

21. See, for example, Voluntary Petition of Hugh Wilson, filed March 27, 1868, Case #517, Bankruptcy Case Files (1867–78), U.S. District Court of South Carolina (quotation), NA RG 21; Voluntary Petition of John R. Watts, filed October 20, 1868, Case #841, Bankruptcy Case Files (1867–78), U.S. District Court, Southern District of Mississippi, NA RG 21.

22. Bump, *Law and Practice,* 9th ed., 248–50. One exception to the general rule that counsel fees could not come out of an estate applied to attorneys hired by the assignee of a bankrupt; in such cases, assignees could disburse fees to counsel (Bump, *Law and Practice,* 9th ed., 248). For descriptions of the various rulings concerning attorney fees,

see Bump, *Law and Practice*, 9th ed., 664–67; Moses and Shinn, *National Bankruptcy Register*, 263–64.

23. *In re Williams*, 29 F. Cas. 1324, 1325 (D.C. S.C. 1868) (no. 17,704).

24. Simkins and Woody, *South Carolina*, 29; Hugh L. Bond to Anna Bond, Charleston, South Carolina, April 22, 1873, Bond Papers.

25. Zuczek, "Last Campaign," 22–23.

26. Groce, *Mountain Rebels*, 25; *Brownlow's Knoxville Whig*, June 10, 1868; 1867 Bankruptcy Docket, U.S. District Court, Eastern District of Tennessee, NA RG 21; Caldwell, *Sketches*, 272–73.

27. *An Act Supplementary to an Act Entitled, "An Act to Prescribe an Oath of Office, and for Other Purposes,"* Approved July Two, Eighteen Hundred and Sixty-two, U.S. Statutes at Large 13 (1865): 424; Hyman, *Era*, 31–32, 159.

28. *Opinion*; Hyman, *Era*, 103–6; "United States District Court for South Carolina," *Charleston Daily Courier*, June 21, 1866; "Judge George S. Bryan" (appendix), *City of Charleston Year Book—1895*, 379 (quoting an undated excerpt from the *Charleston Daily Courier*).

29. Hyman, *Era*, 192 n.35; Robert A. Hill to Salmon P. Chase, Jacinto, Mississippi, November 14, 1866, in Chase, *Papers*, reel 25.

30. *Ex parte Garland*, 71 U.S. 333 (1866).

31. Ibid.; *Charleston Daily Courier*, n.d., quoted in "Judge George S. Bryan" (appendix), *City of Charleston Year Book—1895*, 379; Hyman, *Era*, 102; Russ, "Lawyer's Test Oath," 165. Harold Hyman points out that the only immediate effect of the *Garland* ruling was to rescind a rule of practice for the U.S. Supreme Court. But by the summer of 1867, all federal courts allowed those who had been disloyal to practice (Hyman, *Era*, 109–10, 115).

CHAPTER 5. *Voluntary Bankruptcy Proceedings in the South*

1. William Heyward to John Jenkins, July 22, 1865, quoted in Roark, *Masters*, 122; Petition of William Henry Heyward, filed April 6, 1870, Case #1,254, Bankruptcy Case Files (1867–78), U.S. District Court of South Carolina, NA RG 21, 52A155, B033/22/62.

2. Adelbert A. Ames to [?] Clous, April 4, 1866, quoted in Zuczek, *State*, 14; Petition of Wade Hampton, filed December 27, 1868, Case #1103, 1867 Bankruptcy Case Files, U.S. District Court, Southern District of Mississippi, NA RG 21. Explaining his activities in South Carolina and Mississippi, Hampton stated to a congressional committee, "This [South Carolina] is my home, though I am absent very much between here and Mississippi; I am planting in Mississippi, though I claim this as my home" (Testimony of Wade Hampton, Columbia, South Carolina, July 21, 1871, U.S. House, *Testimony*, vol. 2, pt. 3, p. 1218). My thanks to Mary Ann Hawkins, formerly of the National Archives—Southeast Division, for focusing my attention on Hampton's voluntary filing.

3. Perman, *Reunion*, 286; "Wade Hampton," *Charleston News and Courier*, September 16, 1876.

4. "Charge of Hon. George S. Bryan," *Charleston Daily Courier*, October 23, 1866; Peti-

tion Schedule of Elijah W. Brown, filed December 22, 1873, Case #1,535, Bankruptcy Case Files (1867–78), U.S. District Court of South Carolina, NA RG 21.

5. Daniel Horlbeck to George H. Williams, Charleston, South Carolina, August 7, 1873, quoted in U.S. Senate, *Letter,* 19.

6. Petition Schedules of William A. Wardlaw, filed February 29, 1868, Case #36, Bankruptcy Case Files (1867–78), U.S. District Court of South Carolina, NA RG 21; Petition Schedules of J. R. Moseley, filed August 5, 1867, Case #91,867, Bankruptcy Case Files, U.S. District Court, Southern District of Mississippi, NA RG 21; Petition Schedules of Julius Spring, filed December 17, 1867, Case #75, Bankruptcy Case Files (1867–78), U.S. District Court of South Carolina, NA RG 21.

7. *Congressional Globe,* 39th Cong., 2nd sess., 1867, vol. 37, pt. 2, p. 1012; *Congressional Record,* 45th Cong., 2nd sess., 1878, vol. 7, pt. 3, pp. 2515, 2866; Skeel, *Debt's Dominion,* 27. See also an assessment of how the lower federal courts were "practically inaccessible" for purposes of enforcing the Civil Rights Act of 1866 in Kaczorowski, *Politics,* 31, and similar complaints that the courts were "remote and infrequent" in S. C. Gardner to Charles Sumner, November 19, 1866, quoted in Hyman and Wiecek, *Equal Justice,* 424.

8. Attorney general's report for 1879, p. 34, quoted in Tabb, "History," 20.

9. See Perman, *Reunion.*

10. These percentages are based on the total number of filers, which is more than the total number of cases because certain cases involved more than one bankrupt. In East Tennessee, there were 240 voluntary bankrupts in 224 voluntary bankruptcy cases. The 188 cases involving bankrupts from Warren and Lauderdale Counties, Mississippi, placed 199 voluntary bankrupts on the docket for the District Court for the Southern District of Mississippi. A total of 281 voluntary bankrupts filed under the 271 cases initiated by residents of Charleston and Anderson Counties, South Carolina. This study located the following in the 1870 Census Records: 108 of 240 East Tennessee voluntary bankrupts; 83 of 199 Mississippi voluntary bankrupts from the two counties; and 74 of 281 voluntary filers from the two South Carolina counties.

11. Calculations based on data from the Inter-university Consortium for Political and Social Research's Census Data for the Year 1870.

12. Ibid. Findings with respect to occupation listings in the 1870 census must be viewed with some caution because the census listing does not necessarily indicate what bankrupts were doing when they filed (which might have been before or after 1870). Nevertheless, the finding that a large percentage of foreign-born voluntary bankrupts were merchants is likely to be valid. Of the forty-four identified voluntary bankrupts who were born outside of the United States, thirty-three dwelled in the districts' major urban areas, and thirty-five were merchants. The occupations of twelve of the foreign-born bankrupts were apparent from case file documents, while census data supplied occupation data for the other thirty-two filers. Data from the Charleston City Directory for 1869–70 confirmed and complemented the census data for four filers.

13. *Congressional Record,* 45th Cong., 2nd sess., 1878, vol. 7, pt. 3, p. 2866.

14. *Ninth Census.* Census data were usually collected in the jurisdictions studied in depth in June, July, or August, although the information occasionally was collected as

late as December 1870. The cutoff date of June 1, 1870, is thus a conservative approach to ensure that no filings took place after census enumerators had collected property information. Because bankrupts could keep all assets obtained after filing for bankruptcy but before discharge, it would be reasonable to include property held by those who filed prior to June 1, 1870, but received discharges after this date. However, to ensure that census enumerators did not list any property as belonging to the bankrupt even though it was in the hands of the bankrupt's assignee, the calculations take the more conservative approach of including only those who had obtained discharges before the census was taken.

15. Of the 199 bankrupts in the 188 voluntary cases filed by residents of Warren and Lauderdale Counties, Mississippi, 46 met the criteria, as did 42 of the 281 voluntary filers in the 271 cases involving residents of Charleston and Anderson County, South Carolina, and 33 of the 240 filers in 224 voluntary cases filed in East Tennessee.

16. Ash, *Middle Tennessee Society*, 260–61.

17. Petition and case file of George F. Von Kolnitz, filed January 29, 1868, Case #156, Bankruptcy Case Files (1867–78), U.S. District Court of South Carolina, NA RG 21, 52A155, B033/22/62; petition and case file of William H. Taylor, filed May 31, 1868, Case #93, 1867 Bankruptcy Docket, U.S. District Court, Eastern District of Tennessee, NA RG 21, #137, p. 93, 53A643, BX24/22; petition of Andrew D. Banks, filed December 31, 1868, Bankruptcy Case Files (1867–78), U.S. District Court, Southern District of Mississippi, NA RG 21, 53A89, B042/26/43; Census Records, Population Schedules, Mississippi, South Carolina, and Tennessee, 1870.

CHAPTER 6. *Involuntary Bankruptcy in Southern Tribunals*

1. Bill of George M. Klein, Assignee of H. Bodenheim and Company v. Leopold Baer, Abraham Baer, and Isaac Baer, filed February 2, 1877, Law and Equity Cases (1866–1912), U.S. District Court, Southern District of Mississippi, NA RG 21, B029/04/33–34.

2. Shannon and Grace to George T. Swan[n], Meridian, Mississippi, June 25, 1870, 1867 Bankruptcy Case Files, U.S. District Court, Southern District of Mississippi, NA RG 21, 53A89, B042/26/43. Other southern debtors similarly tried to defraud their creditors by transferring their assets to others. These transfers, often happening before creditors initiated involuntary bankruptcy proceedings, would constitute the "act of bankruptcy" that justified the creditors' initiation of the involuntary cases. See Petition of E. S. Keep and Sons v. Emanuel S. Cohen, filed April 27, 1877, 1867 Bankruptcy Case Files, U.S. District Court, Southern District of Mississippi, NA RG 21, 53A89, B042/26/43 (New Orleans creditors alleging fraudulent transfer by Vicksburg debtor); Petition of Weiller and Ellis v. Henry H. Badenhop, filed [?] 1872, Bankruptcy Case Files (1867–78), U.S. District Court of South Carolina, NA RG 21, 52A155, B033/22/62 (Philadelphia creditor claiming transfer in bad faith by Charleston debtor).

3. Petition of G. A. Trenholm and Son v. A. F. Chevereux, filed May 1, 1875, Bankruptcy Case Files (1867–78), U.S. District Court of South Carolina, NA RG 21, 52A155, B033/22/62;

Testimony of James L. Orr and Samuel T. Poinier in U.S. House, *Testimony*, vol. 2, pt. 3, pp. 5, 35–36.

4. *Davis v. Armstrong*, 7 F. Cas. 109, 111 (D.C.N.D. Miss. 1869) (no. 3,624).

5. Skeel, *Debt's Dominion*, 8.

6. Watkins, "'To Surrender,'" 208; "President Grant's Views," *Charleston News and Courier*, December 5, 1873; Act to Amend and Supplement "An Act to Establish a Uniform System of Bankruptcy," sec. 12, *U.S. Statutes at Large* 18, pt. 3 (1874): 181; *Barnert v. Hightower*, 2 F. Cas. 848 (D.C.N.D. Miss. 1874) (no. 1,009) (synopsis of case); "The Bankrupt Law," *Charleston News and Courier*, July 2, 1874.

7. Because multiple creditors could commence involuntary cases (indeed, multiple creditors almost by necessity had to initiate involuntary filings after the 1874 amendments went into effect), each district had a greater number of filing creditors than of involuntary cases. Thirty-seven creditors initiated the 33 involuntary cases filed in the District of Eastern Tennessee, while 304 creditors began the 88 involuntary cases filed against residents of Warren and Lauderdale Counties, Mississippi, and 257 creditors commenced the 60 cases against South Carolina debtors who resided in Charleston and Anderson Counties. It is likely that additional creditors initiated the East Tennessee cases, but because the bankruptcy case files are not available, the creditors listed in the docket—often only the first creditor listed on each petition—are the only ones that can be identified. In all, 598 creditors filed the 181 involuntary cases against residents of these areas.

8. Foner, *Reconstruction*, 13; Fisher, *War*, 19–21.

9. Of thirty-six Missouri creditors, thirty-five resided in St. Louis (with the residence of the thirty-sixth unclear); all but one of fifty-eight New Yorkers were from New York City (with the residence city of that one unclear); and twenty-one of twenty-two Ohioans lived in Cincinnati.

10. Of the 120 creditors from New York, all but four indicated their residence as New York City. Only one New York creditor filed against a debtor from Anderson County; the rest initiated petitions against debtors in Charleston County.

11. Because most creditors were entities, it was not possible to ascertain whether they were "native" to their resident regions through census information. Of the 194 individual creditors who filed (including one associated with an entity), 136 resided in the South, and birthplaces were located in census records for 35 of these people. Twenty-two were foreign-born, 9 were southern natives, and 1 came from each of the following states: Connecticut, Kentucky, Massachusetts, and New York. Again, the uncommon nature of foreigners' names makes them easier to find in census records and probably leads to the overrepresentation of the foreign-born when making these calculations. Although the number of identified creditors is not large enough to state conclusions with any certainty, the lack of northerners among those located probably indicates that the group of southern filers did not merely include northern creditors who had recently relocated to the South after the Civil War.

12. H. H. Miller to G. C. McKee, Vicksburg, Mississippi, November 28, 1870, Case File of Evans, Gardner, and Company v. Herman and Moss, Case #1355, 1867 Bankruptcy Case Files, U.S. District Court, Southern District of Mississippi, NA RG 21.

13. *American Law Review,* July 1873, quoted in Warren, *Bankruptcy,* 113; Carter, *When the War Was Over,* 142, 139, 102–3.

14. *Act to Amend and Supplement "An Act to Establish a Uniform System of Bankruptcy,"* sec. 17, *U.S. Statutes at Large* 18, pt. 3 (1874): 182–84; "The Bankrupt Law," *Charleston News and Courier,* July 2, 1874; Tabb, "History," 20–21; Bump, "I. Composition," 507; *Congressional Record,* 45th Cong., 2nd sess., 1878, vol. 7, pt. 3, p. 2514; National Board of Trade report quoted in "Summary of Events," 173. Composition proceedings could occur before a debtor was adjudicated a bankrupt (Baker, "Bankrupt Law," 274).

15. Form of Supplementary Petition, Case File of F. Von Santen, n.d., Case #1717, Bankruptcy Case Files (1867–78), U.S. District Court of South Carolina, NA RG 21 (blank form, not filled in); Petition of Robert White, filed November 9, 1876, Case #1690½, Bankruptcy Case Files (1867–78), U.S. District Court of South Carolina, NA RG 21. See also notice of White's composition agreement in *Charleston News and Courier,* November 10, 1876.

16. T. L. Brown to G. Fallin and Sons, Danville, Virginia, May 18, 1877, Case #1731, Bankruptcy Case Files (1867–78), U.S. District Court of South Carolina, NA RG 21; 1867 Bankruptcy Docket, U.S. District Court, Eastern District of Tennessee, NA RG 21, 224 (disposition of case took place on September 23, 1876).

17. *In re Murphy,* 17 F. Cas. 1030 (D.C.M.D. Tenn. 1874) (no. 9,946); Petition of Zacharia S. Zarnell v. J. W. Montgomery, filed January 9, 1877, 1867 Bankruptcy Docket, U.S. District Court, Eastern District of Tennessee, NA RG 21; 1867 Bankruptcy Minutes, U.S. District Court, Eastern District of Tennessee, NA RG21, #136, p. 299, 53A643.

CHAPTER 7. *White Women and African Americans under the Bankruptcy Act*

1. Voluntary Petition of Mrs. C. A. Cogniasse, filed May 29, 1868, Case #670, 1867 Bankruptcy Case Files, U.S. District Court, Southern District of Mississippi, NA RG 21; Proof of Debt by Jay J. Jones, F9/19/68 (listing Cogniasse's occupation as milliner). See also Census Records, Population Schedules, 1870, Warren County, Mississippi, p. 257 (confirming her occupation two years later as dressmaker). Cogniasse may have obtained a discharge; however, entries in the Mississippi Bankruptcy Docket indicated that she had not submitted a certificate of conformity (which stated that the bankrupt had complied with the terms of the 1867 Act), a prerequisite for discharge (Bankruptcy Docket, U.S. District Court, Southern District of Mississippi, NA RG21, #81, p. 32, 53A89).

2. Involuntary Petition of Darby and Day et al. v. Mrs. Clara Heidman, filed March 27, 1873, Case #1460, 1867 Bankruptcy Case Files, U.S. District Court, Southern District of Mississippi, NA RG 21.

3. Involuntary Petition of OHara Glass Company et al. v. John W. Linley et al., filed February 10, 1876, Case #1661, Bankruptcy Case Files (1867–78), U.S. District Court of South Carolina, NA RG 21; Census Records, Population Schedules, 1870, Charleston

County, South Carolina, p. 311. The listing of debts in the middle of the petition includes more creditors than the listing at the beginning of the petition but refers to the listing of debts as amounts owing to petitioners. As a result, I consider the four creditors listed in the petition but not in the initial listing of creditors to be filing creditors; all four were from Charleston. Like the 1870 Census Records, the 1870 Charleston Directory, p. 158, describes Linley as a dealer in groceries.

4. *Act to Establish a Uniform System of Bankruptcy,* sec. 14, U.S. Statutes at Large 14 (1867): 523; "Married Women as Bankrupts," 135. The authors of the *American Law Register* article compare the recognition of state exemptions with the treatment of women under the 1867 Bankruptcy Act: "This varying rule in different jurisdictions [regarding women bankrupts] is therefore not such an irregularity as the exemption clause, the constitutionality of which was at first doubted, for there is a clear underlying principle to which the various decisions may be referred, and by this they may be reconciled"— namely, "in all cases where a plea of coverture would not avail her, a married woman may be proceeded against in bankruptcy" ("Married Women as Bankrupts," 136).

5. Lucie, *Freedom,* 143; *Act to Establish a Uniform System of Bankruptcy,* sec. 11, U.S. Statutes at Large 14 (1867): 521.

6. Foner, introduction, xviii.

7. Lebsock, "Radical Reconstruction."

8. Gross, Newman, and Campbell, "Ladies in Red," 36.

9. *Act to Establish a Uniform System of Bankruptcy,* sec. 26, U.S. Statutes at Large 14 (1867): 529; Gross, Newman, and Campbell, "Ladies in Red," 3.

10. Lebsock, "Radical Reconstruction," 196; *Code of Tennessee,* secs. 2479, 2481–86 (1858).

11. "Married Women as Bankrupts," 136.

12. *In re Goodman,* 10 F. Cas. 601, 602 (D.C.D. Ind. 1883) (no. 5,540) (see note at end of decision).

13. James, *Bankrupt Law,* 27.

14. Bump, *Law and Practice,* 9th ed., 1 (quotation), 454, 57 (quotation); Moses and Shinn, *National Bankruptcy Register,* 173–74; *In re Collins,* 6 F. Cas. 113 (D.C.N.D. Ill.) (no. 3,006); *In re Slichter,* 22 F. Cas. 323 (D.C.D. Minn.) (no. 12,943); *In re Howland,* 12 F. Cas. 727 (D.C.N.D.N.Y. 1868) (no. 6,791); *In re Goodman,* 10 F. Cas. 601 (D.C.D. Ind.) (no. 5,540).

15. Lucie, *Freedom,* 143; Lebsock, "Radical Reconstruction"; Harris, *Day,* 153.

16. *Boyd v. Withers,* 3 F. Cas. 1101, 1102 (C.C.S.D. Miss. 1869) (no. 1,752) (citing Rev. Code, chap. 40, sec. 5, art. 25; the statute also allowed a husband to enter into such contracts and bind the wife's separate property, but in certain instances he could do so only with her consent).

17. "Married Women," 73.

18. One voluntary filer, Marion Van Horn of Hamilton County, Tennessee, filed once individually and once as partner in the business of Van Horn and Venable. I have considered both individual women who were involved in bankruptcy proceedings and those who were parties because they were associated with businesses that were the primary

party. In this sense, this section considers a broader number of parties than the previous sections of the book, which considered only primary filers and not people associated with the primary filers. Unless otherwise indicated, however, women were involved in bankruptcy cases as individuals.

19. Scott Sandage similarly found a small number of female bankrupt correspondents with Congressman Jenckes, the bankruptcy bill sponsor: "All but one of the 419 letters he received between 1864 and 1867 came from men" ("Deadbeats," 198).

20. Gross, Newman, and Campbell, "Ladies in Red," 10, 21–22. One question these authors posed but did not answer was "What has happened to women debtors under subsequent bankruptcy laws: the act of 1867?" ("Ladies in Red," 37).

21. Census Records, Population Schedules, Mississippi, South Carolina, and Tennessee, 1870, list another five women voluntary bankrupts as "keeping house." This census data may have been a rote response by census takers (who commonly represented all women of a certain age and particularly white women as "keeping house") and might not have represented the women's occupations at the time of filing.

22. Gross, Newman, and Campbell, "Ladies in Red," 20.

23. Involuntary Petition of A. and J. Trounstine and Company et al., filed January 26, 1877, Case #1611, Voluntary Petition of Mrs. Martha A. Gibbs, filed May 29, 1868, Case #642, Involuntary Petition of Samuel Strauss and Company v. Rebecca Rothschild, filed June 25, 1874, Case #1546, 1867 Bankruptcy Case Files, U.S. District Court, Southern District of Mississippi, NA RG 21.

24. The number of filing creditors in the twelve involuntary cases in which women were involved either as filing creditors or as members of filing entities is 1, 2, 4, 5, 6, 7, 7, 8, 18, 21, 26, and 46.

25. "Charge of Hon. George S. Bryan," *Charleston Daily Courier*, October 23, 1866 (Bryan said these words as part of a charge to the jury to fairly treat African Americans who came before the federal court); Foner, introduction, xviii.

26. Aviam Soifer investigates the shifts in federal authorities' focus during Reconstruction: "Congress vastly increased federal court jurisdiction and repeatedly enacted federal measures to protect civil and ultimately political rights across the nation. . . . But daily life soon triumphed over legal promises promulgated hundreds of miles away. The chaos of war and the political and legal battles of early Reconstruction gave way to renewed faith in the purported symmetries of private law as the infrastructure of the social order" ("Status," 1947).

27. At times, I was not able to determine whether a particular party was white or African American based on information in the case files and Census Records.

28. Voluntary Petition of William Sumner, filed June 26, 1875, Case #1789, 1867 Bankruptcy Cases, U.S. District Court, Middle District of Tennessee, Nashville Division, NA RG21, 52A351, B46/05/34; Deposition for Proof of Debt by Officer of Freedmen's Savings and Trust Company, filed July 10, 1875, Case #1789, 1867 Bankruptcy Cases, U.S. District Court, Middle District of Tennessee, NA RG21. My thanks to Mary Ann Hawkins, formerly of the National Archives—Southeast Division, for directing me to Sumner's filing.

29. Eric Foner refers to the poor economic fortunes of many African Americans during the postwar era: by 1867, "successive crop failures had left those on share contracts with little or no income and caused a precipitous decline in cash wages" (*Reconstruction*, 289).

30. M. P. Johnson and Roark, *No Chariot Let Down*, 6; Foner, *Reconstruction*, 394, 403–9.

31. "Governmental Directory," *Charleston Missionary Record*, July 5, 1873; Hugh L. Bond to Anna Bond, Columbia, South Carolina, November 26, 1871, Bond Papers; Williams, *Great South Carolina*, 51, 72, 113–22.

32. William L. Vanderlip to W. W. Rogers, Maryland, March 7, 1867, quoted in Kaczorowski, *Politics*, 35.

33. Silverman, *Law*, 24, 24 n.9, 154 (listing total number of cases in study sample).

34. Neiman, *To Set the Law*, 9; "The Freedmen's Courts," *Nashville Colored Tennessean*, August 12, 1865; Report of M. Walsh, April 8, 1867, quoted in Ash, *Middle Tennessee Society*, 220; "Important Case in a Freedmen's Court," *Cincinnati Colored Citizen*, May 19, 1866; Foner, *Reconstruction*, 149.

35. Foner, *Reconstruction*, 216; Kaczorowski, *Politics*, 79, 226; Forsythe, "Red River Blues," 3.

36. Quoted in Foner, *Reconstruction*, 326.

37. Quoted in ibid., 326–27.

38. *Act to Establish a Uniform System of Bankruptcy*, sec. 27, *U.S. Statutes at Large* 14 (1867): 529–30. Bankrupts listed debts to plantation laborers among the outstanding liabilities on petition schedules. See, for example, Petition Schedule A3 of John G. Baxter, filed February 26, 1868, Case #278, Bankruptcy Case Files (1867–78), U.S. District Court of South Carolina, NA RG 21 (listing forty-one laborers with unsecured debts for their plantation work ranging from $10.50 to $82.00).

39. Harris, *Presidential Reconstruction*, 278–79. For an example of an assessment of the lack of economic security for blacks in Reconstruction Tennessee, see Lamon, *Blacks*, 38.

40. Fitchett, "Traditions," 143; M. P. Johnson and Roark, *Black Masters*; McKenzie, *One South*, 147; Ransom and Sutch, *One Kind*, 85; Foner, introduction, xviii.

CHAPTER 8. *Bankrupt Partners and Corporations before the Federal Courts*

1. *Charleston News and Courier*, April 26, 1873; Doster, "Vicissitudes," 182; Simkins and Woody, *South Carolina*, 208–9.

2. James L. Orr to J. W. Harrison, Columbia, South Carolina, March 23, 1868, Bankruptcy Case Files (1867–78), U.S. District Court of South Carolina, NA RG 21, 52A155, B033/22/62; "The Blue Ridge Railroad," *Brownlow's Knoxville Whig*, August 18, 1869.

3. Involuntary Petition of James Low v. the Blue Ridge Rail Road, filed January 16, 1873, Case #1376, 1867 Bankruptcy Case Files, U.S. District Court of South Carolina, NA RG 21.

4. Address by Mr. Warley of the Executive Committee, Proceedings of the Tax-Payers' Convention of South Carolina, Columbia, South Carolina, May 11, 1871, quoted in U.S. House, *Testimony*, vol. 1, pt. 3, p. 499; *Charleston Daily News*, January 25, June 20, 1873.

5. Act to Establish a Uniform System of Bankruptcy, sec. 37, *U.S. Statutes at Large* 14 (1867): 535; Skeel, *Debt's Dominion*, 54; Black, "Corporations," 105–6. Although the Bankruptcy Act of 1898 originally provided only for involuntary bankruptcy for corporations, a 1910 amendment allowed voluntary corporate filings (*An Act to Establish a Uniform System of Bankruptcy throughout the United States*, sec. 4, *U.S. Statutes at Large* 30 (1898): 547; *An Act to Amend an Act Entitled "An Act to Establish a Uniform System of Bankruptcy throughout the United States," Approved July First, Eighteen Hundred and Ninety-eight, as Amended by an Act Approved February Fifth, Nineteen Hundred and Three, and as Further Amended by an Act Approved June Fifteenth, Nineteen Hundred and Six*," sec. 3, *U.S. Statutes at Large* 36, pt. 1 (1910): 839; Skeel, "Rethinking," 487 n.65).

6. Sandage, "Deadbeats," 157 n.42. Other studies include Skeel, *Debt's Dominion*; Skeel, "Rethinking"; Korobkin, "Rehabilitating Values," 746. In his analysis of the Bankruptcy Act of 1867, Sandage recognizes that the "inclusion of corporations under bankruptcy protection was a matter of such significant debate" that he chose to leave consideration of the topic for a later version of his study ("Deadbeats," 157 n.42).

7. In East Tennessee, 5 of 224 voluntary cases involved partnerships; 17 of 188 voluntary filings from Lauderdale and Warren Counties, Mississippi, concerned partners and partnerships; and 91 of 271 voluntary cases from Charleston and Anderson Counties, South Carolina, involved partnerships or partners. Because the case files for East Tennessee are not available, data are taken from the bankruptcy docket, which lists filers but may not make apparent (as a case file would) when a filing involves both an individual and partnership bankruptcy. (Filings involving partnerships could be initiated by one partner or all partners.) Thus, the number of partnership-related filings in East Tennessee may have been greater than that reported here.

8. Freyer, "Federal Courts," 345, 362. See also Freyer, *Forums*, 99–120. For discussions of the preference of corporate litigants for federal court and the results of this preference, see Zelden, *Justice Lies*, 7–8; W. G. Thomas, *Lawyering*, 31, 233–37, 253–54.

9. Congressman David Culberson, quoted in Zelden, *Justice Lies*, 7.

10. Skeel, "Rethinking," 482–84; Korobkin, "Rehabilitating Values," 745–46; Coleman, *Debtors*, 22. The current arrangement of state control over corporate organization and operations and federal control over corporate bankruptcy has caused Skeel to wonder if this separation is beneficial and to argue that both aspects of corporate law should fall under state jurisdiction, with some sort of federal disclosure requirements. See Skeel, "Rethinking."

11. U.S. Const., art. 1, sec. 8; Skeel, "Rethinking," 479–80; *Congressional Globe*, 26th Cong., 1st sess., 1840, vol. 8, p. 838; Joseph Story to Daniel Webster, May 10, 1840, in Story, *Life and Letters*, 2:332.

12. Skeel, "Rethinking," 484–87 (providing a valuable overview of these developments); Hamill, "From Special Privilege," 178; Korobkin, "Rehabilitating Values," 746; Senator William A. Howard, quoted in Skeel, "Rethinking," 486 n.63.

13. *Act to Establish a Uniform System of Bankruptcy,* subheading, sec. 36, *U.S. Statutes at Large* 14 (1867): 534–35; Bump, *Law and Practice,* 9th ed., 65–71.

14. *Act to Establish a Uniform System of Bankruptcy,* sec. 37, *U.S. Statutes at Large* 14 (1867): 535; Bump, *Law and Practice,* 8th ed., 1–2; Korobkin, "Rehabilitating Values," 746.

15. See Moses and Shinn, *National Bankruptcy Register,* 308 (stating synopsis of *Meyer v. Aurora Ins. Company,* 7 N.B.R. 191 (Ill. Cir. Ct., Cook County)); *New Lamp Chimney Company v. Ansonia Brass and Copper Company,* 91 U.S. 656 (1875). See also *Shellington v. Howland,* 53 N.Y. 371 (1873).

16. *Act to Amend and Supplement "An Act to Establish a Uniform System of Bankruptcy,"* sec. 17, *U.S. Statutes at Large* 18, pt. 3 (1874): 182–84; "New Bankrupt Act," 330–31; Tabb, "History," 20–21; Bump, "I. Composition," 515–16; Skeel, *Debt's Dominion,* 54. For further discussion of composition, see chap. 6.

17. Skeel, *Debt's Dominion,* 48.

18. Calculations from review of the State Session Laws and accompanying indexes for the three states between 1850 and 1878 (the year the Bankruptcy Act of 1867 was repealed). For Mississippi corporations prior to 1865, I referenced Humphries and Owen, *Index.* When the line between whether a corporation was a business or a philanthropic entity was unclear, the corporation was not included in the calculation. See Hamill, "From Special Privilege," 177 (for effective date of state general incorporation laws).

19. Voluntary Petition of the City Bank of Memphis, filed August 7, 1872, Case #1233, Bankruptcy Dockets, U.S. District Court, Western District of Tennessee, #119, NA RG 21, 53A507.

20. Whether a debtor was incorporated by a state was not always clear from the filing. I nevertheless counted as corporations all debtors that reasonably could be construed as incorporated entities. As a result, although I find that relatively few corporations were involved in bankruptcy proceedings, my conclusions may overstate the number of corporations involved.

21. Carter, *When the War Was Over,* 99, 100, 138; Surrency, *Quest,* 146; Harris, *Presidential Reconstruction,* 216; Foner, *Reconstruction,* 535.

22. Skeel, *Debt's Dominion,* 62, 57–59; Korobkin, "Rehabilitating Values," 747–51.

23. Skeel, *Debt's Dominion,* 61; Zelden, *Justice Lies,* 30; Foner, *Reconstruction,* 512.

24. *Charleston News and Courier,* June 16, 1876.

25. Foner, *Reconstruction,* 535–36.

26. *Laws of the State of Mississippi,* 81 (passed January 6, 1877); *Hale v. Duncan,* 11 F. Cas. 185 (C.C.N.D. Miss. 1877) (no. 5,914). An 1887 federal statute made it no longer necessary to obtain the appointing court's permission before suing a federally appointed receiver. See *Hale v. Duncan,* 11 F. Cas. 186 (describing *An Act to Amend the Act of Congress Approved March Third, Eighteen Hundred and Seventy-five, Entitled "An Act to Determine the Jurisdiction of Circuit Courts of the United States and to Regulate the Removal of Causes from State Courts, and for Other Purposes and to Further Regulate the Jurisdiction of Circuit Courts of the United States, and for Other Purposes,"* sec. 3, *U.S. Statutes at Large* 24 [1887]: 554, in a note at the end of the opinion).

174 • Notes to Chapters Eight and Nine

27. "The Greenville and Columbia Railroad" and "Good News," *Charleston Daily News*, February 14, 1873. The residences of creditors who individually initiated claims were Mobile, Alabama (one claim); Charleston, South Carolina (two claims); and Richmond, Virginia (one claim). A group of southern creditors, primarily from Mississippi, initiated the fifth claim. These findings concerning how often southern creditors initiated involuntary corporate proceedings support the broader findings in chapter 6 concerning the general prominence of southern creditors among those who initiated involuntary claims.

28. *Charleston Daily News*, January 25, 1873; "Save the Blue Ridge Railroad," *Charleston News and Courier*, July 14, 1873; "The Blue Ridge Railroad," *Charleston News and Courier*, February 18, 1876 (quoting *Anderson (South Carolina) Intelligencer*); Simkins and Woody, *South Carolina*, 221–22.

29. Korobkin, "Rehabilitating Values," 745; "The Blue Ridge Convention," *Charleston News and Courier*, May 25, 1876.

CHAPTER 9. *Repeal of the 1867 Act*

1. Warren, *Bankruptcy*, 122; *Congressional Record*, 45th Cong., 2nd sess., 1878, vol. 7, pt. 3, pp. 2512, 4232, 3882; Skeel, *Debt's Dominion*, 32 (citing Warren). The Senate adopted the repealing legislation on April 15, 1878; the House did so ten days later. See *Congressional Record*, 45th Cong., 2nd sess., 1878, vol. 7, pt. 3, pp. 2516, 2872. Historians have agreed with McCreery's assessment of citizens' disgust with the 1867 Act. Peter J. Coleman notes, "In the end, public patience was tried too long" (*Debtors*, 26).

2. Warren, *Bankruptcy*, 114–18. See descriptions of the House passage of repealing legislation and the failure of the Senate to adopt these measures in comments by Senator Francis Kernan of New York and Representative Edbridge G. Lapham of New York in *Congressional Record*, 45th Cong., 2nd sess., 1878, vol. 7, pt. 3, pp. 2513, 2861; *Charleston News and Courier*, January 21, 1873.

3. Watkins, "'To Surrender,'" 208, 213; Baker, "Bankrupt Law," 273 (Baker applies and quotes a description "generally applied against the German law based upon a similar system"); *Congressional Record*, 45th Cong., 2nd sess., 1878, vol. 7, pt. 3, p. 2861; Warren, *Bankruptcy*, 127. Complaints of high, wasteful fees charged by court officials led to a congressional inquiry. See U.S. Senate, *Letter*. One proposed solution to high court expenses was abolishing the office of register. In 1874, Democratic Senator Allen G. Thurman urged support for such a proposal, saying "that in three-fourths of the districts of the United States the judges had ample time to discharge all the duties which would devolve upon them if the office of registrar should be abolished and in consideration of the complaints from all quarters of the large amounts received by these officers as fees, he thought it a move in the right direction to abolish the office" ("The Bankrupt Law," *Charleston News and Courier*, February 7, 1874). In 1881, however, one New York merchant who pressed for a new national bankruptcy law maintained that "the dividends under the [1867 Act], bad as they were, were from twenty-five to eighty-five cents on the dollar, according to the circumstances of the case, while under state laws, during the

past two years, the dividends have been virtually nothing" (Gardner R. Colby quoted in Wagner, "Advantages," 231).

4. *Congressional Record*, 45th Cong., 2nd sess., 1878, vol. 7, pt. 3, p. 2865.

5. Quoted in Warren, *Bankruptcy*, 127 (quotation from Simon P. Wolverton of Pennsylvania, 1893).

6. Petitions listed in comments of Senator George G. Wright of Iowa, *Congressional Record*, 43rd Cong., 1st sess., 1873, vol. 2, pt. 1, p. 218; U.S. Senate, *Repeal*.

7. See comments by Senator Roscoe Conkling of New York and Senator Alexander Ramsey of Minnesota mentioning these petitions by New York and Minnesota creditors in *Congressional Record*, 43rd Cong., 1st sess., 1874, vol. 2, pt. 1, pp. 389, 469. Two years later, an article in the *Central Law Journal* expressed the same sentiment: "Notwithstanding [the defects of the 1874 amendments to the legislation], the act, as it now stands, affords the creditor class far greater protection than they would have if remitted to the race of diligence required by the wretched attachment and insolvent laws of many states" ("Current Topics" [1876], 459).

8. "The Bankrupt Act—Shall It Be Repealed?" See also J.M., "Suggestions" (laying out proposed amendments and the gains such changes would produce); "Current Topics" (1877), 377 (giving overview of petition circulated among cities in 1877 that urged amendment rather than repeal and argued that returning to a system of state insolvency laws "will prove in the very largest measure demoralizing to the business community, conduce to wide-spread fraud, derange business calculations, and cripple the now returning prosperity of the country").

9. Baker, "Bankrupt Law," 275.

10. Coleman, *Debtors*, 25; *Congressional Record*, 45th Cong., 2nd sess., 1878, vol. 7, pt. 3, p. 2514. Whyte's analogy to debtors' emancipation from slavery through the Bankruptcy Act indicates how congressmen (and surely others) continued to use the references to debt slavery and liberation that Scott Sandage identifies. See the introduction and chap. 1.

11. *Congressional Record*, 45th Cong., 2nd sess., 1878, vol. 7, pt. 3, p. 2866.

12. Ibid., pt. 3, p. 2871; pt. 4, p. 3354.

13. Ibid., pt. 4, pp. 3358–59.

14. Ibid., pt. 3, pp. 2516, 2872.

15. Ibid., 2864; *Jackson Weekly Clarion*, March 7, 1867.

16. Watkins, "'To Surrender,'" 208; Warren, *Bankruptcy*, 109.

17. Warren, *Bankruptcy*, 114.

18. Quoted in Warren, *Bankruptcy*, 128. Historical evidence is split regarding southerners' support for a federal bankruptcy regime in the period leading up to the passage of the 1898 Bankruptcy Act. David Skeel maintains that southern (and western) legislators in the late 1800s viewed a federal act as undesirable "since federal bankruptcy legislation seemed to favor northeastern commercial interests" and the "cost and inconvenience of the federal courts exacerbated this concern" (*Debt's Dominion*, 40). Peter Coleman also notes the late-nineteenth-century southern and western view that a federal bankruptcy system was "especially favored by eastern 'moneyed interests'" (*Debtors*, 28). Lawrence Friedman maintains, however, that there was general support for a voluntary bankruptcy

act toward the end of the nineteenth century (*History,* 551). At the Fourth Annual American Bar Association meeting, held in 1881, the position stated by L. H. Gardiner of New Orleans supports Friedman's position but also seems to advocate a broader law allowing voluntary and involuntary bankruptcy: "Speaking for the South and Southwest, I desire, as representing that section, to say that our people, both debtors and creditors, recognize the necessity for a national bankrupt law of equitable provisions, and alike just to the unfortunate debtor and the unfortunate creditors." Gardiner asked that the "equities between debtor and debtor, and debtor and creditor, can be established in advance by the provisions of a good national bankrupt law" (quoted in Wagner, "Advantages," 230–31).

APPENDIX ON METHODOLOGY

1. Petty, *Growth and Distribution,* 62; Ash, *Middle Tennessee Society,* 260–61.
2. Livingston, *1868,* preface.
3. Francis A. Walker, "Report of the Superintendent of the Ninth Census," in *Ninth Census,* xxxiii; Ash, *Middle Tennessee Society,* 258–59, 264–67; Huffman, "Old South, New South," 68–70.

SOURCES CITED

ARCHIVAL COLLECTIONS

Akerman, Amos T., Papers. Alderman Library. University of Virginia, Charlottesville.
Bond, Hugh L., Papers. MS 1206. Manuscripts Department. Maryland Historical Society Library, Baltimore.
General Records of the Department of Justice. RG 60. National Archives and Records Administration, Washington, D.C.
Hill, R. A., Sketch of (typescript). R. A. Hill Subject File. Mississippi Department of Archives and History, Jackson.
Manuscript Federal Census Returns. Records of the Bureau of the Census, National Archives and Records Administration, Washington, D.C.
Records of the Court of Claims Section (Justice). RG 205. National Archives and Records Administration, Washington, D.C.
Records of the District Courts of the United States. RG 21. National Archives and Records Administration—Southeast Region, East Point, Georgia.
Records of the U.S. Court of Claims. RG 123. National Archives and Records Administration, Washington, D.C.

PERIODICALS

Brownlow's Knoxville (Tennessee) Whig
Brownlow's Knoxville (Tennessee) Whig and Rebel Ventilator
Charleston (South Carolina) Daily Courier
Charleston (South Carolina) Daily News
Charleston (South Carolina) Missionary Record
Charleston (South Carolina) News and Courier
Cincinnati (Ohio) Colored Citizen
Congressional Globe
Congressional Record
Jackson (Mississippi) Weekly Clarion
Jackson (Mississippi) Weekly Mississippi Pilot
Nashville (Tennessee) Colored Tennessean
New York Times
Vicksburg (Mississippi) Daily Herald
Vicksburg (Mississippi) Weekly Herald and Mississippian

OTHER DOCUMENTS

Acts of the General Assembly of the State of South Carolina. Charleston: 1823, 1850–78.

Acts of the State of Tennessee. Nashville: 1851–77.

Alexander, Thomas B. "Political Reconstruction in Tennessee, 1865–1870." In *Radicalism, Racism, and Party Realignment: The Border States during Reconstruction,* ed. Richard O. Curry. Baltimore: Johns Hopkins Press, 1969.

Andrews, Sidney. "Three Months among the Reconstructionists." *Atlantic Monthly,* February 1866, 237–45.

Ash, Stephen V. *Middle Tennessee Society Transformed, 1860–1870.* Baton Rouge: Louisiana State University Press, 1988.

B., J. F. "Expediency of a Bankrupt Law." *American Law Register* 4 (1864–65): 449–60.

B., T. W. "The Jurisdiction of the United States Circuit Court in Bankruptcy—Original and Appellate . . ." *American Law Register* 7 (1867–68): 641–59.

Baker, John F. "The Bankrupt Law—Its Provisions and Objects—Should the Law Be Repealed." *Central Law Journal* 6 (1878): 273–75.

Balleisen, Edward. *Navigating Failure: Bankruptcy and Commercial Society in Antebellum America.* Chapel Hill: University of North Carolina Press, 2001.

"Bankrupt Act—Discharge—Limitation as to Time." *Central Law Journal* 1 (1874): 556.

"The Bankrupt Act—Shall It Be Repealed?" *Central Law Journal* 1 (1874): 1–2.

"Bankruptcy—United States and State Jurisdiction." *Central Law Journal* 3 (1876): 90–92.

Beman, Lamar T., comp. *Selected Articles on States Rights.* New York: H. W. Wilson, 1926.

Berglof, Erik, and Howard Rosenthal. "The Political Economy of American Bankruptcy: The Evidence from Roll Call Voting, 1800–1878." Available at http://web.mit.edu/polisci/polecon/www/14pe.pdf, last revised April 14, 2000.

Biographical and Historical Memoirs of Mississippi. 2 vols. 1891; reprint, Spartanburg, S.C.: Reprint Company, 1978.

Black, H. Campbell. "Corporations under the Bankruptcy Act of 1898." *Yale Law Journal* 8 (December 1898): 105–18.

Brake, Patricia E. *Justice in the Valley: A Bicentennial Perspective of the United States District Court for the Eastern District of Tennessee.* Franklin, Tenn.: Hillsboro, 1998.

Bryant, Jonathan M. "'Settled in the Old Ante-Bellum Style': Law, Power, and Justice in Georgia's County Courts, 1865–1885." Paper presented at the American Historical Association annual meeting, Boston, January 2001.

Bump, Orlando F. "I. Composition in Bankruptcy." *Southern Law Review* 3 (n.s.) (1877): 507–30.

———. *Law and Practice in Bankruptcy.* 8th ed. New York: Baker, Voorhis, 1875.

———. *Law and Practice in Bankruptcy.* 9th ed. New York: Baker, Voorhis, 1877.

Caldwell, Joshua W. *Sketches of the Bench and Bar of Tennessee.* Knoxville: Ogden Brothers, 1898.

Carter, Dan T. *When the War Was Over: The Failure of Self-Reconstruction in the South, 1865–1867*. Baton Rouge: Louisiana State University Press, 1985.
Cash, Wilbur J. *The Mind of the South*. New York: Knopf, 1941.
Chase, Salmon P. *The Salmon P. Chase Papers* [microfilm]. Ed. John Niven. Frederick, Md.: University Publications of America, 1987.
City of Charleston Year Book—1895. N.p., n.d.
Code of Tennessee. 1858.
Coleman, Peter J. *Debtors and Creditors in America: Insolvency, Imprisonment for Debt, and Bankruptcy, 1607–1900*. Madison: State Historical Society of Wisconsin, 1974.
Cresswell, Stephen. *Mormons, Cowboys, Moonshiners, and Klansmen: Federal Law Enforcement in the South and West, 1870–1893*. Tuscaloosa: University of Alabama Press, 1991.
"Current Topics." *Central Law Journal* 3 (1876): 459.
"Current Topics." *Central Law Journal* 5 (1877): 377.
Doster, James F. "Vicissitudes of the South Carolina Railroad, 1865–1878: A Case Study in Reconstruction and Regional Traffic Development." *Business History Review* 30 (June 1956): 175–95.
"Doubtful Points under the Bankrupt Law." *American Law Review* 4 (April 1870): 417–28.
"Doubtful Points under the Bankrupt Law: Unrecorded Conveyances of Chattels." *American Law Review* 6 (October 1871): 50–56.
Ezell, John Samuel. *The South since 1865*. 2nd ed. Norman: University of Oklahoma Press, 1978.
Fairley, Laura Nan, and James T. Dawson. *Paths to the Past: An Overview History of Lauderdale County, Mississippi*. Meridian, Miss.: Lauderdale County Department of Archives and History, 1988.
Fairman, Charles. *Reconstruction and Reunion, 1864–88*. Vol. 6. New York: Macmillan, 1971.
Finkelman, Paul. "Exploring Southern Legal History." *North Carolina Law Review* 64 (November 1985): 77–116.
Fisher, Noel C. *War at Every Door: Partisan Politics and Guerrilla Violence in East Tennessee, 1860–1869*. Chapel Hill: University of North Carolina Press, 1997.
Fitchett, E. Horace. "The Traditions of the Free Negro in Charleston, South Carolina." *Journal of Negro History* 25 (April 1940): 139–52.
Foner, Eric. Introduction to *At Freedom's Door: African American Founding Fathers and Lawyers in Reconstruction South Carolina*, ed. James Lowell Underwood and W. Lewis Burke Jr. Columbia: University of South Carolina Press, 2000.
―――. *Reconstruction: America's Unfinished Revolution, 1863–1877*. New York: Harper and Row, 1988.
Ford, Lacy K., Jr. *Origins of Southern Radicalism: The South Carolina Upcountry, 1800–1860*. New York: Oxford University Press, 1988.
Forsythe, Harold S. "Red River Blues: How the Colfax War of 1873 Became *U.S. v.*

Cruikshank in 1876." Paper presented at the American Historical Association annual meeting, Boston, January 2001.

Fowler, Russell. "Chancellor William Macon Smith and Judicial Reconstruction: A Study of Tyranny and Integrity." *West Tennessee Historical Society Papers* 48 (1994): 35–59.

Frankfurter, Felix, and James M. Landis. *The Business of the Supreme Court: A Study in the Federal Judicial System.* New York: Macmillan, 1927.

Freehling, William W. *The Road to Disunion.* Vol. 1., *Secessionists at Bay, 1776–1854.* New York: Oxford University Press, 1990.

———. *The South vs. the South: How Anti-Confederate Southerners Shaped the Course of the Civil War.* New York: Oxford University Press, 2001.

Freyer, Tony A. "The Federal Courts, Localism, and the National Economy, 1865–1900." *Business History Review* 53 (autumn 1979): 343–63.

———. *Forums of Order: The Federal Courts and Business in American History.* Greenwich, Conn.: JAI Press, 1979.

Friedman, Lawrence. *American Law in the Twentieth Century.* New Haven: Yale University Press, 2002.

———. *A History of American Law.* 2nd ed. New York: Simon and Schuster, 1985.

Fritz, Christian G. "The Judicial Business of a Nineteenth-Century Federal Trial Court: The Northern District of California, 1851–1891." *Western Legal History* 5 (summer–fall 1992): 217–51.

Gillman, Howard. "How Political Parties Can Use the Courts to Advance Their Agendas: Federal Courts in the United States, 1875–1891." *American Political Science Review* 96 (September 2002): 511–24.

———. "The Political Construction of Federal Judicial Power in Late Nineteenth-Century America." Paper presented at American Political Science Association annual meeting, Washington, D.C., August–September 2000.

Goldin, Claudia. "The Economics of Emancipation." *Journal of Economic History* 33 (March 1973): 66–85.

Goodman, Paul. "The Emergence of Homestead Exemption in the United States: Accommodation and Resistance to the Market Revolution, 1840–1880." *Journal of American History* 80 (September 1993): 470–98.

Goodspeed's General History of Tennessee. 1887; reprint, Nashville: Charles and Randy Elder, 1973.

Groce, W. Todd. *Mountain Rebels: East Tennessee Confederates and the Civil War, 1860–1870.* Knoxville: University of Tennessee Press, 1999.

Gross, Karen, Marie Stefanini Newman, and Denise Campbell. "Ladies in Red: Learning from America's First Female Bankrupts." *American Journal of Legal History* 40 (January 1996): 1–40.

Hall, Kermit L. "The Civil War Era as a Crucible for Nationalizing the Lower Federal Courts." *Prologue* 7 (fall 1975): 177–86.

———. *The Magic Mirror: Law in American History.* New York: Oxford University Press, 1989.

---. "Political Power and Constitutional Legitimacy: The South Carolina Ku Klux Klan Trials, 1871–72." *Emory Law Journal* 33 (fall 1984): 921–51.

---. "West H. Humphreys and the Crisis of the Union." *Tennessee Historical Quarterly* 34 (spring 1975): 48–69.

Hall, Kermit L., and Eric W. Rise. *From Local Courts to National Tribunals: The Federal District Courts of Florida, 1821–1990*. Brooklyn, N.Y.: Carlson, 1991.

Hall, Kermit L., William M. Wiecek, and Paul Finkelman. *American Legal History: Cases and Materials*. 2nd ed. New York: Oxford University Press, 1996.

Hamill, Susan Pace. "From Special Privilege to General Utility: A Continuation of Willard Hurst's Study of Corporations." *American University Law Review* 49 (October 1999): 81–180.

Harris, William C. *The Day of the Carpetbagger: Republican Reconstruction in Mississippi*. Baton Rouge: Louisiana State University Press, 1979.

---. *Presidential Reconstruction in Mississippi*. Baton Rouge: Louisiana State University Press, 1967.

Haywood, Amy, and Melissa Jones. "Navigating a Sea of Uncertainty: How Existing Ethical Guidelines Pertain to the Marketing of Legal Services over the Internet." *Georgetown Journal of Legal Ethics* 14 (summer 2001): 1099–115.

Helms' Knoxville City Directory. Knoxville: T. Haws, 1869.

Hobson, Wayne K. "Symbol of the New Profession: Emergence of the Large Law Firm, 1870–1915." In *The New High Priests: Lawyers in Post–Civil War America*, ed. Gerard W. Gawalt. Westport, Conn.: Greenwood Press, 1984.

Hoeveler, J. David, Jr. "Reconstruction and the Federal Courts: The Civil Rights Act of 1875." *Historian* 31 (August 1969): 604–17.

Horwitz, Morton J. *The Transformation of American Law, 1780–1860*. Cambridge: Harvard University Press, 1977.

Huffman, Frank J. "Old South, New South: Continuity and Change in a Georgia County, 1850–1880." Ph.D. diss., Yale University, 1974.

Humphries, Rena, and Mamie Owen. *Index of Mississippi Session Acts 1817–1865*. Jackson, Miss.: Tucker, 1937.

Hyman, Harold M. *Era of the Oath: Northern Loyalty Tests during the Civil War and Reconstruction*. 1954; reprint, New York: Octagon Books, 1978.

---. *A More Perfect Union: The Impact of the Civil War and Reconstruction on the Constitution*. Boston: Houghton Mifflin, 1975.

Hyman, Harold M., and William M. Wiecek. *Equal Justice under Law: Constitutional Development, 1835–1875*. New York: Harper and Row, 1982.

James, Edwin. *The Bankrupt Law of the United States*. New York: Harper and Brothers, 1867.

Johnson, Bradley T., comp. *Reports of Cases Decided by Chief Justice Chase in the Circuit Court of the United States for the Fourth Circuit, 1865–1869*. New York: Diossy, 1876.

Johnson, Michael P., and James L. Roark. *Black Masters: A Free Family of Color in the Old South*. New York: Norton, 1984.

———, eds. *No Chariot Let Down: Charleston's Free People of Color on the Eve of the Civil War.* Chapel Hill: University of North Carolina Press, 1984.

Jones, Jacqueline. "Federal Power, Southern Power: A Long View, 1860–1940." *Journal of American History* 87 (March 2001): 1392–96.

Jowitt's Illustrated Charleston City Directory, 1869–70. Charleston: Walker, Evans, and Cogswell, 1869.

Kaczorowski, Robert. *The Politics of Judicial Interpretation: The Federal Courts, Department of Justice, and Civil Rights, 1866–1876.* New York: Oceana, 1985.

Kagan, Robert A., Bliss Cartwright, Lawrence M. Friedman, and Stanton Wheeler. "The Business of State Supreme Courts." *Stanford Law Review* 30 (November 1977): 121–56.

Kerber, Linda K. *No Constitutional Right to Be Ladies: Women and the Obligations of Citizenship.* New York: Hill and Wang, 1998.

Kershen, Drew L. "The Jury Selection Act of 1879: Theory and Practice of Citizen Participation in the Judicial System." *University of Illinois Law Forum* 1980, #3 (fall 1980): 707–82.

Korobkin, Donald R. "Rehabilitating Values: A Jurisprudence of Bankruptcy." *Columbia Law Review* 91 (May 1991): 717–89.

Kutler, Stanley I. *Judicial Power and Reconstruction Politics.* Chicago: University of Chicago Press, 1968.

Lamon, Lester C. *Blacks in Tennessee, 1791–1970.* Knoxville: Tennessee Historical Commission, 1981.

Landon, Michael de L. "Another False Start: Mississippi's Second State Bar Association, 1886–1892." In *The New High Priests: Lawyers in Post–Civil War America,* ed. Gerard W. Gawalt. Westport, Conn.: Greenwood Press, 1984.

Laws of the State of Mississippi. Jackson: 1839, 1841–42, 1850–78.

Lebsock, Suzanne D. "Radical Reconstruction and the Property Rights of Southern Women." *Journal of Southern History* 43 (May 1977): 195–216.

Livingston, John. *1868: The Law Register Comprising the Lawyers in the United States.* New York: Merchants' Union Law, 1868.

———. *United States Law Register, and Official Directory for 1860.* New York: J. Livingston, 1860.

Lucie, Patricia Allan. *Freedom and Federalism: Congress and Courts 1861–1866.* New York: Garland, 1986.

M., J. "Suggestions of Amendments to the Bankrupt Act." *American Law Register* 12 (1873): 737–45.

Mann, Bruce H. *Republic of Debtors: Bankruptcy in the Age of American Independence.* Cambridge: Harvard University Press, 2002.

"Married Women." *American Law Review* 6 (1871): 57–73.

"Married Women as Bankrupts." *American Law Register* 13 (1874): 129–36.

Martindale, James B. *Martindale's United States Law Directory for 1874.* Indianapolis: J. B. Martindale, 1874.

McCrady, Edward, Jr. "The Reorganization of the Federal Courts." *Central Law Journal* 3 (1876): 311–12.
McDonald, Forrest. *States' Rights and the Union: Imperium in Imperio, 1776–1876*. Lawrence: University Press of Kansas, 2000.
McKenzie, Robert Tracy. *One South or Many? Plantation Belt and Upcountry in Civil War–Era Tennessee*. Cambridge: Cambridge University Press, 1994.
McPherson, James M. *Ordeal by Fire*. 2nd ed. Vol. 2, *The Civil War*. New York: McGraw-Hill, 1993.
Moses, Raphael J., Jr., and William A. Shinn, eds. *National Bankruptcy Register Digest*. New York: McDivitt, Cambell, 1875.
Neiman, Donald G. *To Set the Law in Motion: The Freedmen's Bureau and the Legal Rights of Blacks, 1865–1868*. Millwood, N.Y.: KTO, 1979.
"The New Bankrupt Act." *Central Law Journal* 1 (1874): 329–32.
Ninth Census of the United States: Population. Vol. 1. Washington, D.C.: U.S. Government Printing Office, 1872.
"Notes of Recent Decisions." *Central Law Journal* 1 (1874): 23.
O'Brien, Gail Williams. *The Legal Fraternity and the Making of a New South Community, 1848–1882*. Athens: University of Georgia Press, 1986.
O'Connor, Mary Doline, comp. *The Life and Letters of M. P. O'Connor*. New York: Dempsey and Carroll, 1893.
Opinion of the Hon. Con[n]ally F. Trigg, on the Constitutionality of the Act of Congress Prescribing an Oath on the Admission of Attorneys. Memphis: Whitmore Brothers, 1865.
"Our Federal Judiciary." *Central Law Journal* 2 (1875): 551–55.
Owens, James K. "Documenting Regional Business History: The Bankruptcy Acts of 1800 and 1841." *Prologue* 21 (fall 1989): 179–85.
Paludan, Phillip S. *A Covenant with Death: The Constitution, Law, and Equality in the Civil War Era*. Urbana: University of Illinois Press, 1975.
Parham's First Annual Directory of the City of Chattanooga. Knoxville: Whig and Register, 1871.
Perman, Michael. *Reunion without Compromise: The South and Reconstruction, 1865–1868*. New York: Cambridge University Press, 1973.
Petty, Julian J. *The Growth and Distribution of Population in South Carolina*. Spartanburg, S.C.: Reprint Company, 1975.
Posner, Richard A. *The Federal Courts: Challenge and Reform*. Cambridge: Harvard University Press, 1996.
Powers, Bernard E., Jr. "Community Evolution and Race Relations in Reconstruction Charleston, South Carolina." *South Carolina Historical Magazine* 95 (January 1994): 27–46.
Randall, James G. *Constitutional Problems under Lincoln*. Rev. ed. Urbana: University of Illinois Press, 1951.
Ransom, Roger L., and Richard Sutch. *One Kind of Freedom: The Economic Consequences of Emancipation*. Cambridge: Cambridge University Press, 1977.

"Reconstruction: The Duty of the Profession to the Times" [extract from Harvard Law School Closing Lecture by the Bussey Professor, 1864]. *Monthly Law Reporter* 26 (July 1864): 477–84.

Register of the Department of Justice. Washington, D.C.: U.S. Government Printing Office, 1871, 1872, 1873, 1874, 1876.

Reid, Whitelaw. *After the War: A Southern Tour, May 1, 1865 to May 1, 1866.* New York: Moore, Wilsatch, and Baldwin, 1866.

Roark, James L. *Masters without Slaves: Southern Planters in the Civil War and Reconstruction.* New York: Norton, 1977.

Robinson, William M., Jr. *Justice in Grey: A History of the Judicial System of the Confederate States of America.* New York: Russell and Russell, 1968.

Ross, Michael A. "'The White Man's Flag Must Be Upheld': John A. Campbell and the Legal Obstruction of Reconstruction in New Orleans, 1868–1874." Paper presented at the American Historical Association annual meeting, Boston, January 2001.

Rubin, Anne Sarah. "Redefining the South: Confederates, Southerners, and Americans, 1863–1868." Ph.D. diss., University of Virginia, 1999.

Russ, William A., Jr. "The Lawyer's Test Oath during Reconstruction." *Mississippi Law Journal* 10 (February 1938): 154–67.

Sandage, Scott A. "Deadbeats, Drunkards, and Dreamers: A Cultural History of Failure in America, 1819–1893." Ph.D. diss., Rutgers University, 1995.

Silverman, Robert A. *Law and Urban Growth: Civil Litigation in the Boston Trial Courts, 1880–1900.* Princeton: Princeton University Press, 1981.

Simkins, Francis Butler, and Robert Hilliard Woody. *South Carolina during Reconstruction.* 1932; reprint, Gloucester, Mass.: Peter Smith, 1966.

Skeel, David A., Jr. *Debt's Dominion: A History of Bankruptcy Law in America.* Princeton: Princeton University Press, 2001.

———. "The Genius of the 1898 Bankruptcy Act." *Bankruptcy Developments Journal* 15 (spring 1999): 321–41.

———. "Rethinking the Line between Corporate Law and Corporate Bankruptcy." *Texas Law Review* 72 (February 1994): 471–554.

Soifer, Aviam. "Status, Contract, and Promises Unkept." *Yale Law Journal* 96 (July 1987): 1916–59.

Stampp, Kenneth M. *The Era of Reconstruction, 1865–1877.* New York: Knopf, 1978.

Story, William W., ed., *Life and Letters of Joseph Story.* Vol. 2. Boston: C. C. Little and J. Brown, 1851.

"Summary of Events—Bankrupt Law." *American Law Review* 12 (October 1877): 173–74.

Surrency, Erwin C. "The Legal Effects of the Civil War." *American Journal of Legal History* 5 (1961): 145–65.

———. The Quest for Constitutional Justice: A History of the Federal Courts in Georgia. Paper in possession of author, University of Georgia School of Law, 2000.

Swinney, Everette. "Enforcing the Fifteenth Amendment, 1870–1877." *Journal of Southern History* 28 (May 1962): 202–18.

Tabb, Charles Jordan. "The History of the Bankruptcy Laws in the United States." *American Bankruptcy Institute Law Review* 3 (spring 1995): 5–52.

Tachau, Mary K. Bonsteel. *Federal Courts in the Early Republic: Kentucky, 1789–1816.* Princeton: Princeton University Press, 1978.

Temple, Oliver P. *East Tennessee and the Civil War.* 1899; reprint, Johnson City, Tenn.: Overmountain, 1995.

———. *Notable Men of Tennessee from 1833 to 1875.* Comp. Mary B. Temple. New York: Cosmopolitan, 1912.

Thomas, J. H. "Homestead and Exemption Laws of the Southern States." *American Law Register* 19 (1871): 1–17, 137–50.

Thomas, William G. *Lawyering for the Railroad: Business, Law, and Power in the New South.* Baton Rouge: Louisiana State University Press, 1999.

Thompson, Elizabeth Lee. "Reconstructing the Practice: The Effects of Expanded Federal Judicial Power on Postbellum Lawyers." *American Journal of Legal History* 43 (July 1999): 306–30.

Thorndale, William, and William Dollarhide. *Map Guide to the U.S. Federal Censuses, 1790–1920.* Baltimore: Genealogical Publishing, 1987.

Trelease, Allen W. *White Terror: The Ku Klux Klan Conspiracy and Southern Reconstruction.* New York: Harper and Row, 1971.

Trowbridge, John T. *The South: A Tour of Its Battlefields and Ruined Cities.* 1866; reprint, New York: Arno Press, 1969.

U.S. House. *Annual Report of the Attorney-General of the United States for the Fiscal Year Ending June 30, 1873.* 43rd Cong., 1st sess., 1873. H. Ex. Doc. 6.

———. *Annual Report of the Attorney-General for the Fiscal Year Ending June 30, 1874.* 43rd Cong., 2nd sess., 1874. H. Ex. Doc. 7.

———. *Annual Report of the Attorney-General of the United States.* 44th Cong., 1st sess., 1875. H. Ex. Doc. 14.

———. *Annual Report of the Attorney-General of the United States.* 44th Cong., 2nd sess., 1877. H. Ex. Doc. 20.

———. *Annual Report of the Attorney-General of the United States.* 45th Cong., 2nd sess., 1877. H. Ex. Doc. 7.

———. *Annual Report of the Attorney-General of the United States for the Year 1878.* 45th Cong., 3rd sess., 1878. H. Ex. Doc. 7.

———. *Condition of Affairs in Mississippi: Evidence Taken by the Committee on Reconstruction.* 40th Cong., 3rd sess., 1869. H. Misc. Doc. 53.

———. *Statements, Letters, and Testimony Relative to Captured and Abandoned Property, before the Committee on Expenditures of the Treasury Department.* 44th Cong., 1st sess., 1876. H. Misc. Doc. 190.

———. *Testimony Taken by the Joint Select Committee to Inquire into the Condition of Affairs in the Late Insurrectionary States: South Carolina.* 42nd Cong., 2nd sess., 1872. H. Rep. 22.

U.S. Senate. *Letter from the Attorney-General, Communicating, in Compliance with a Senate Resolution of February 24, 1873, Information in Relation to the Expenses of*

Proceedings in Bankruptcy in United States Courts. 43rd Cong., 1st sess., 1874. S. Ex. Doc. 19.

———. *Message of the President of the United States Transmitting an Address of a Committee of the "East Tennessee Relief Association" on the Condition and Wants of the People of East Tennessee,* 38th Cong., 1st sess., 1864. S. Ex. Doc. 40.

———. *Repeal of General Bankrupt Law. Resolution of the Legislature of Illinois.* 43rd Cong., 1st sess., 1874. S. Misc. Doc. 112.

Wagener, Johann Andreas. *South Carolina: A Home for the Industrious Immigrant.* Charleston: J. Walker, 1867. Reprinted in Simkins and Woody, *South Carolina.*

Wagner, Samuel. "The Advantages of a National Bankrupt Law." In *Report of the Fourth Annual Meeting of the American Bar Association, 1881.* Philadelphia: E. D. Markley and Son, 1881.

Waldrep, Christopher. *Roots of Disorder: Race and Criminal Justice in the American South, 1817–1880.* Urbana: University of Illinois Press, 1998.

Warren, Charles. *Bankruptcy in United States History.* Cambridge: Harvard University Press, 1935.

———. "Federal and State Court Interference." *Harvard Law Review* 43 (January 1930): 345–78.

Watkins, Beverly. " 'To Surrender All His Estate': The 1867 Bankruptcy Act." *Prologue* 21 (fall 1989): 207–13.

Weisberg, Robert. "Debt Crises, Commercial Morals, and Federal Law: A 200-Year Perspective." Paper in possession of author, Stanford Law School.

Wiecek, William M. "The Reconstruction of Federal Judicial Power, 1863–1875." *American Journal of Legal History* 13 (1969): 333–59.

Williams, Lou Falkner. *The Great South Carolina Ku Klux Klan Trials, 1871–1872.* Athens: University of Georgia Press, 1996.

Woodward, C. Vann. *Origins of the New South, 1877–1913.* Baton Rouge: Louisiana State University Press, 1951.

———. *Reunion and Reaction: The Compromise of 1877 and the End of Reconstruction.* Boston: Little, Brown, 1951.

Wyld, James. *Map of the Southern States of North America.* London: James Wyld, 1865.

Zelden, Charles L. *Justice Lies in the District: The U.S. District Court, Southern District of Texas, 1902–1960.* College Station: Texas A&M University Press, 1993.

Zuczek, Richard. "The Last Campaign of the Civil War: South Carolina and the Revolution of 1876." *Civil War History* 42 (March 1996): 18–31.

———. *State of Rebellion: Reconstruction in South Carolina.* Columbia: University of South Carolina Press, 1996.

INDEX

Aberdeen, Miss., 40
Adam and Speed, 69. *See also* Speed, Frederick
Adam, G. Gordon, 43, 69
Admiralty, Courts of, 161 (n. 4)
African Americans: and antebellum free blacks, 117, 120; economic condition of, 116, 117, 119–20, 171 (n. 29); and economic rights, 6; and federal courts, 117, 118–19; and political/economic Reconstruction experience, 116; population shifts by, 3; property of, 108; and property rights, 89, 107; recognition of rights of, 115; Reconstruction policies toward, 115, 116; and state debt-relief laws, 119; and use of courts, 117–18
—and Bankruptcy Act of 1867: 6–7, 105–8, 115–20, 141, 170 (n. 27); lack of benefit to, 115–16, 120; use of, 82, 116–20, 140–41. *See also entries for specific jurisdictions*
Aiken, H. M., 66, 163 (n. 17)
Aiken, William, 66, 163 (n. 17)
Air Line Railway, The, 131
Akerman, Amos, 39, 44
Alabama, 99
Alexander, Thomas, 41
American Bar Association, 3, 176 (n. 18)
American Law Register, 13, 17, 21, 22, 28, 106, 109, 169 (n. 4)
American Law Review, 24, 27, 29, 101, 111, 160 (n. 7)
Anders, George, 45
Anderson County, S.C., 9, 149 (n. 19); attorneys in, 63
—and Bankruptcy Act of 1867: and corporate bankruptcy filings, 122, 124, 128–29; and filing creditors, 97–98, 100–101, 167 (n. 7); and filings involving women, 111–15; and partnership bankruptcy filings, 122, 124, 129, 172 (n. 7); voluntary bankruptcy attorneys in, 61, 63, 64–65, 163 (n. 18); voluntary bankrupts from, 85–92
Anderson, S.C., 121
Appomattox, Va., 32
Army, U.S., 34, 50
Ash, Stephen V., 144
Assignee, in bankruptcy, 24–25, 104; fees for attorney for, 162 (n. 22)
Atlantic Monthly, 8
Attorney General, U.S., annual reports of, 33, 156 (n. 9), 160 (n. 7)
Attorneys
—bankruptcy, 11, 58; bar of, 62; diverse tasks of, 62; fees of, 69–70, 163–64 (n. 22)
—in Midwest: practice of, 62, 162 (n. 8)
—in nineteenth century, 60, 62, 161 (n. 3)
—in Northeast: practice of, 62, 162 (n. 8)
—in South, 59–72, 162 (n. 8); advertising by, 60, 161 (nn. 4, 5); competition among, 59; ideology of, 61–62; local interests of, 162 (n. 8); professional affiliations of, 65; in small firms, 62; as solo practitioners, 62; and state courts, 60, 161 (n. 4). *See also entries for specific jurisdictions*
—southern bankruptcy: 59–72, 143–44; advertising by, 60, 161 (n. 4); and bankruptcy practice, 60–61; former Confederates and redemptionists among, 70–71; involuntary bankruptcy representation by, 63; political beliefs

Attorneys (*continued*)
of, 70–72; and pro se legal representation, 60, 161 (n. 3); professional affiliations of, 63; voluntary bankruptcy representation by, 63. *See also entries for specific jurisdictions*

Balleisen, Edward, 10, 62
Baltimore, Md., 15
Bankruptcy Act of 1800, 1, 2, 21–23, 29, 62, 109, 122; criticisms of, 2, 22; and federal court jurisdiction, 152 (n. 29); repeal of, 2; and women, 112. *See also* Bankruptcy acts, nineteenth-century federal
Bankruptcy Act of 1841, 1, 2, 21–22, 23, 29, 62, 122; and corporate bankruptcy debates, 125; criticisms of, 2, 22; debates concerning, 4; and federal court jurisdiction, 152 (n. 29); repeal of, 2. *See also* Bankruptcy acts, nineteenth-century federal
Bankruptcy Act of 1867, 1, 2, 62; amendments to, 27–28, 97, 102–3, 136–37, 155 (n. 45); beneficiaries of, 6; congressional debates concerning, 14, 18–21; congressional views of, 1, 2, 4; as contributor to postwar stability, 42; and creditors, 24–25, 27; criticisms of administration and expense of, 2, 101, 135–36, 141; and debt slavery, 10, 20–21, 52, 149 (n. 22), 175 (n. 10); and discharge, 6, 24–25, 27, 42, 122, 126–27, 153 (n. 33); as economic measure, 6; and federal court jurisdiction, 15, 23–24; and federal property exemption, 6, 25–26; and federalism, 106–7; and filings nationally, 54–55, 57, 145, 160–61 (nn. 7–10); gendered wording of, 28–29, 108–9; historians' views of, 1–2; and influence on federal courts' role, 47–49; and laborers' wages, 119, 171 (n. 38); and loyalty oath, 19–20, 21, 151 (n. 24); merchants and, 29, 139, 140, 155 (n. 45); and northern creditors, 18–19, 139, 151 (n. 18); passage of, 14, 17–18; political natures of, 28–29, 107–8, 140; portrayed as politically neutral, 5–6, 14, 20–21, 107, 115, 149 (n. 22); property subject to creditors under, 26–27; reception of, 22–23; and Reconstruction, 3–4, 5–7, 11, 141; and state property exemptions, 25–26, 27–28, 106, 140, 154 (n. 38), 154–55 (n. 40); as temporary measure, 137–39, 149 (n. 22); terms of, 23, 24–30. *See also* Bankruptcy Acts, nineteenth-century federal; Repeal of Bankruptcy Act of 1867; *and entries for specific jurisdictions, topics, or groups*
—in South: as bolstering political and social hierarchy, 6, 12, 27, 89, 106–8, 115, 120, 140–41; and discharge rates, 84–85, 139; filings under, 33, 53–54, 57–58, 145, 160–61 (nn. 7–10); and former Confederates, 6, 14, 19, 107; political nature of, 5–7, 12; popularity of, 14, 52–53, 133; postwar role of, 54–56; as providing economic assistance, 15, 51, 139; as serving self-interests, 3–4, 5, 15, 49, 51, 58, 134, 139, 141; southern debtors as beneficiaries of, 18–21; southerners' benefit from, 5, 14, 139; southerners' views of, 3, 4, 49, 58, 124; and states' rights, 5, 51, 124; whites' use of, 3, 5, 11, 52–58, 82, 139. *See also entries for specific jurisdictions, topics, or groups*
Bankruptcy Act of 1898, 2, 22, 62, 122, 154 (n. 38); and corporate bankruptcy, 172 (n. 5); debates concerning, 4–5; and southerners' sentiments for, 175–76 (n. 18)
Bankruptcy acts, nineteenth-century federal, 1–2, 4–5, 6; and federal jurisdiction, 152–53 (n. 31); and opposition to expanded federal power through, 149 (n. 22)

Bankruptcy Clause, U.S. Constitution, 2, 17–18
Bankruptcy, study of, 148 (n. 15)
Banks, Andrew D., 90
Banks, southern, 129
Baxter, Champion, and Ricks, 70–71
Baxter, John M., 70–71
Beecher, Henry Ward, 40
Beveridge, Albert J., 148 (n. 10)
Bingham, John, 107
Blue Ridge Railroad, 121–22, 131–32
Bodenheim, Henry, and Company, 93–94, 95, 104
Bond, Hugh Lennox, 24, 46, 65, 70, 121; and African Americans, 117; in corporate bankruptcy ruling, 132; representing national/Republican interests, 47. *See also* Federal judges
Boston Board of Trade, 151 (n. 18)
Boston, Mass., 15
Brown, Elijah W., 74
Brown, T. L., 103
Brownlow, William G., 31, 41, 45, 70–71
Brownlow's Knoxville Whig, 31, 71, 121
Bryan, George S., 32, 37, 38, 52, 65, 69–70; and attorney's loyalty oath, 71–72; background of, 46; conduct of, on bench, 46; and corporate bankruptcy cases, 132, 133; serving conservative local interests, 43, 46–48; southerners' opinions of, 47; and southerners' postwar debt, 150 (n. 9); and white southerners' power, 115–16. *See also* Federal judges
Bump, Orlando, 17, 69, 102, 110
Business entities, and Bankruptcy Act of 1867, 120, 121–134. *See also* Composition, under Bankruptcy Act of 1867; Corporate bankruptcy; Corporate bankruptcy, and Bankruptcy Act of 1867; Corporate bankruptcy, in South, and Bankruptcy Act of 1867; Partnership bankruptcy, and Bankruptcy Act of 1867; Partnership bankruptcy, in South, and Bankruptcy Act of 1867; *and entries for specific jurisdictions*

Caldwell, A., 66
California, court decisions in, 110
Campbell, Denise, 112, 148 (n. 15)
Captured and Abandoned Property Act, 64
Cardozo, Francis L., 119
Carpenter, Richard, 53
Carpenter, W. W., 106
Carter County, Tenn., voluntary filings in, 82
Carter, Dan T., 101–2, 129
Casey, Joseph, 64
Cash, Wilbur J., 40
Catchings, Thomas C., 141
Central Law Journal, 38, 40, 135, 136, 137, 175 (n. 7)
Chamberlain, Daniel, 133
Charleston Chamber of Commerce, 4
Charleston County, S.C., 9, 149 (n. 19); attorneys in, 63, 65
—and Bankruptcy Act of 1867: and corporate bankruptcy filings, 122, 124, 128–29; and filing creditors, 97–98, 100–101, 167 (n. 7); and filings involving women, 111–15; involuntary bankruptcy attorneys in, 61, 67, 68; and involuntary filings, 100; and partnership bankruptcy filings, 122, 124, 129, 172 (n. 7); voluntary bankruptcy attorneys in, 61, 63–66, 162 (n. 13), 163 (n. 15); voluntary bankrupts from, 82, 85–92, 161 (n. 3)
Charleston Daily Courier, 9, 14, 47, 53, 72
Charleston Daily News, 122, 132–33
Charleston Missionary Record, 117
Charleston News and Courier, 37, 41, 47, 59, 74, 131, 133

Charleston, S.C., 8–9, 32, 82, 86, 121–22; and Blue Ridge Railroad bankruptcy, 132–33; and commercial ties to New York, 99–100; filing creditors from, 100; involuntary bankrupts from, 68; voluntary bankruptcy attorneys in, 65

Chase, Salmon P., 39, 44, 52, 72, 73; and postwar legal stability, 42, 155 (n. 40)

Chattanooga, Tenn., 82, 86; voluntary bankruptcy attorneys in, 65

Cheatham, W. A., 117

Chesnut, James, 41

Chevereux, A. F., 94

Cincinnati Colored Citizen, 118

Cincinnati, Ohio, 100, 113, 167 (n. 9)

Circuit Courts, U.S., 43, 152 (n. 29)

City Bank of Memphis, 129

City of Charleston Year Book, 47

Civil Rights Act of 1866, 115, 118

Civil rights laws, 35, 39, 119

Clifford, Nathan, 121

Cogniasse, C. A., 105, 106, 112, 168 (n. 1)

Colby, Gardner R., 174–75 (n. 3)

Coleman, Peter, 10, 22, 28, 137, 174 (n. 2), 175–76 (n. 18)

Commerce, between North and South, 15–16

Composition, under Bankruptcy Act of 1867, 102–3, 127–28

Compromise of 1877, 140

Confederate currency, 1

Confederate States of America, 3

Confiscation, proposals for, of southern land, 6, 89, 107

Conkling, Roscoe, 83, 175 (n. 7)

Conner, James, 70

Cooke, Jay, and Company, 96

Corbin, David, 37

Corporate bankruptcy, 122–28; jurisdiction over, 172 (n. 10)

—and Bankruptcy Act of 1867, 120, 122–34; and bankrupts, 129; and filing creditors, 132, 174 (n. 27); and states' rights, 124, 125, 134. *See also* Business entities, and Bankruptcy Act of 1867; *and entries for specific jurisdictions*

—in South, and Bankruptcy Act of 1867, 122–34. *See also* Business entities, and Bankruptcy Act of 1867; *and entries for specific jurisdictions*

Corporations, 29, 125–26, 128, 129

Court of Claims, U.S., 64, 69

Coverture, 107, 109, 110. *See also* Women, married, property rights of

Cowan, Edgar, 83

Creditors, filing. *See* Corporate bankruptcy, in South, and Bankruptcy Act of 1867; Involuntary Bankruptcy; Involuntary bankruptcy, in South, under Bankruptcy Act of 1867; Women, southern white, and Bankruptcy Act of 1867; *and entries for specific jurisdictions*

Culberson, David, 123

Davis, Garrett, 152 (n. 26)

Debt relief, in South, 16–17

Debt-collection suits. *See* State courts, southern

Doolittle, James, 20

East Tennessee. *See* Tennessee, East

Eastern Tennessee, Federal District of. *See* Tennessee, Eastern, Federal District of

Economic stress, in 1870s, 53, 56

Edgefield County, S.C., 16

Edmonds, George, 21

1868: The Law Register, 63–64, 65, 143

Emancipation of slaves, 1, 15

Enforcement Acts, 35, 36, 37, 44, 45, 46, 61–62

Entities, in bankruptcy. *See* Business entities, and Bankruptcy Act of 1867; Composition, under Bankruptcy Act of 1867; Corporate bankruptcy; Corporate bankruptcy, and Bankruptcy Act of 1867; Corporate bankruptcy,

in South, and Bankruptcy Act of 1867; Partnership bankruptcy, and Bankruptcy Act of 1867; Partnership bankruptcy, in south, and Bankruptcy Act of 1867; *and entries for specific jurisdictions*
Equitable receivership, 130–31
Europe, 86
Evans, Gardner, and Company, 101
Evarts, William, 47
Ewing, Thomas, 17
Ex parte Garland, 72, 164 (n. 31)
Ezell, Samuel, 50

Fairman, Charles, 6, 148 (n. 11)
Fallin, G., and Sons, 103
Federal Census, 1870, 90, 143, 149 (n. 19), 160 (n. 8), 165 (n. 12), 165–66 (n. 14), 170 (n. 21)
Federal courts: bankruptcy caseload of, 36, 156 (n. 9), 157 (n. 14); criticisms of, 37–38; and enforceability of wartime legal actions, 41–42; and interstate business interests, 123; jurisdiction and roles of, 23–24, 35, 155, 156–57 (n. 11), 170 (n. 26); postwar caseload of, 36, 157 (n. 14); and private suits, 33, 35–36, 48, 123–24; and pro se representation, 60; proximity of, 82–83; resistance to, in South, 15, 49; U.S. civil and criminal cases before, 35–36
—southern, 31–51; multifaceted roles of, 7–8, 34–36, 48; postwar caseload of, 33, 36, 156 (n. 9), 157 (n. 14); reasons for positive views of, 40–49; as serving local and national interests, 47–49, 123–24, 159 (n. 41); southerners' mixed views of, 35, 36–42; southerners' use of, 39–40; southerners' use of, in bankruptcy, 7, 34, 49–51, 74; and whites' local interests, 118–19
Federal government, in South, 49–51

Federal judges, congressmen's views of, 136; serving conservative local interests, 34, 42–49, 110, 158 (n. 29). *See also entries for specific judges*
Federal receivers. *See* Receivers, federal
Federalism, 23–24, 106–7
Fem[m]e covert, 110
Fem[m]e sole, 105, 110, 113
Fessenden, William Pitt, 20, 43, 46
Finkelman, Paul, 162 (n. 8)
Fisher, Noel, 46
Florida, 35, 59
Foner, Eric, 7, 16–17, 53, 116, 118, 131, 141, 171 (n. 29)
Forsythe, Harold, 119
Foster, LaFayette, 16
France, 114
Frankfurter, Felix, 33
Freedman's Savings and Trust Company/Bank, 117, 119
Freedmen's Bureau, 34, 37, 50, 115; courts of, 118
Freedpeople. *See* African Americans
Freehling, William H., 3
Freeman, Ella, 118
Freyer, Tony, 48, 123, 159 (n. 41)
Friedman, Lawrence, 2, 5, 176 (n. 18)
Fritz, Christian G., 161 (n. 11)

Gardiner, L. H., 176 (n. 18)
Gardner, S. C., 165 (n. 7)
Gibbs, A. Judson, 113
Gibbs, Martha, 113
Gillman, Howard, 48
Goodman, Paul, 26–27
Goodspeed's History of Tennessee of 1887, 45–46
Grant, Ulysses S., 96
Greenville and Columbia Railroad Company, 132
Greenville County, S.C., 82
Gross, Karen, 112, 148 (n. 15)

Habeas Corpus Acts of 1863 and 1867, 35
Hale, John P., 21
Hale, Robert, 107
Hall, Kermit, 35, 47, 157 (n. 11), 159 (n. 41)
Hallums, James, 118
Hamilton, A. J., 38
Hamilton County, Tenn., 82
Hampton, Wade, 73–74, 161–62 (n. 6), 164 (n. 2)
Hanna, John, 136
Harris, William, 9, 18, 110, 119
Harvard Law School, 59
Heidman, Clara, 105–6, 112
Heidman, Felix, 106
Henderson, John B., 151 (n. 19), 152 (n. 26)
Henry, Francis W., 15
Herman and Moss, 101
Herman, Joseph, 101
Heyward, William, 73–74
Hill, Robert A., 23, 24, 29, 32, 38, 52, 73, 74, 93, 101; and attorney's loyalty oath, 72; background of, 43–44; and business of federal courts, 39; and enforcement of federal laws, 44; and federal court bankruptcy jurisdiction, 152 (n. 29); and federal receivers, 131; and federal-state relations, 131; and involuntary bankruptcy, 95; serving conservative local interests, 43–44, 48; southerners' opinions of, 44–45; and women's economic rights, 110–11. *See also* Federal judges
Hobson, Wayne K., 162 (n. 8)
Homestead exemptions. *See* Property exemptions, state
Hood, James W., 119
Hooker, Charles E., 137, 138, 139
Horlbeck, Daniel, 74–75
Howard, Jacob M., 1, 14, 17, 19
Howard, William, 126
Huffman, Frank, 144

Humphreys, West H., 31. *See also* Federal judges
Hyman, Harold, 164 (n. 31)

Ideology, southern. *See* States' rights.
Illinois, 110, 136
Indiana, 110
Insolvency laws, state, 17–18
Involuntary bankruptcy, 22; and Bankruptcy Act of 1867, 2, 25, 54
—in South, under Bankruptcy Act of 1867, 92, 93–104; debtors' actions in, 7, 103–4, 166 (n. 2); filing creditors in, 7, 95–101, 115, 139, 140, 167 (n. 11); and incidence of filing by geography, 97–100; interactions among parties in, 95, 104; logistics of, 25; number of cases of, 95, 96; occupations of debtors in, 100–101, 144–45; and out-of-court settlement of, 95, 101–3. *See also entries for specific jurisdictions*

Jackson, Miss., 82
Jackson Weekly Clarion, 9, 14, 22, 37, 40, 44, 52, 53, 139
Jackson Weekly Mississippi Pilot, 52
James, Edwin, 155 (n. 40)
Jarnagin, H. T., 103
Jarnagin, T. J., 103
Jefferson, Thomas, 152–53 (n. 31)
Jefferson, W. W., 94, 95, 104
Jencks, Thomas A., 20, 170 (n. 19)
Johnson, Andrew, 13, 31, 38, 43, 45
Johnson, Frank M., 158 (n. 29)
Johnson, Reverdy, 151 (n. 21), 161–62 (n. 6)
Jones, Jacqueline, 34
Judges, 43
Judiciary Act of 1869, 47
Jurisdiction and Removal Act of 1875, 35

Kaczorowski, Robert, 15, 35, 39, 43, 44, 46, 119
Kentucky, 48, 97, 114

Kernan, Francis, 174 (n. 2)
Kershaw County, S.C., 41
Kershen, Drew, 38
Knoxville, Tenn., 65, 82, 86, 121
Kolnitz, George Von, 90
Korobkin, David, 127, 133
Ku Klux Klan, laws punishing. *See* Enforcement Acts

Lamar, Lucius Q. C., 49–50
Landis, James, 33
Landon, Michael de L., 162 (n. 8)
Lane, Henry, 151 (n. 18)
Lapham, Edbridge G., 135–36, 174 (n. 2)
Lathers, Richard, 41
Lauderdale County, Miss., 9; attorneys in, 64
—and Bankruptcy Act of 1867: and corporate bankruptcy filings, 122, 124, 128–29; and filing creditors, 97–101, 167 (n. 7); and filings involving women, 111–15; involuntary bankruptcy attorneys in, 61, 67, 68; and involuntary filings, 99–100; and partnership bankruptcy filings, 122, 124, 129, 172 (n. 7); voluntary bankruptcy attorneys in, 61, 63–64, 65, 67, 162 (nn. 12, 13); voluntary bankrupts from, 85–92
Law, political nature of, 148 (n. 14)
Lebsock, Suzanne, 107–8, 155 (n. 44)
Lee, Robert E., 32
Lexington County, S.C., 16
Lincoln, Abraham, 31, 32, 43, 70
Linley, J. W., and Company, 106
Linley, John W., 106, 116, 117, 168–69 (n. 3)
Livingston, John, 143–44
Local Prejudice Act of 1867, 13, 35
Louisiana, 99–100; courts in, 38–40; federal courts in, 136, 137, 161 (n. 10)
Loyalists. *See* Unionists

Loyalty oaths, 38, 42, 60, 61, 71–72, 164 (n. 31). *See also* Bankruptcy Act of 1867; and entries for specific judges
Lucie, Patricia Allan, 6, 107, 110

MacDonnell, Allan, 161 (n. 4)
Madison, James, 152–52 (n. 31)
Magrath, A. G., 32, 70
Mann, Bruce H., 10
Marion County, Tenn., 82
Married women's property acts, 26–27, 92, 107–8, 109, 110, 155 (n. 44)
Maryland, 97
Maxey, Samuel D., 5, 138
McCreery, James R., 135, 174 (n. 1)
McCulloch, Hugh, 47
McFadden, Robert D., 158 (n. 29)
McGarr and Smedes, 60, 161 (n. 4)
McKee, George C., 101
McMahon, John A., 4
Memphis, Tenn., 138
Meridian, Miss., 86, 100
Merrimon, Augustus S., 52, 138
Middle Tennessee, Federal District of, 46, 104, 116
Military Reconstruction Act of 1867, 13, 14, 39
Miller, H. H., 101
Miller, Samuel F., 59–60
Minnesota, 110
Mississippi, 8, 9; antebellum economy of, 56; attorneys in, 72, 162 (n. 8); and Captured and Abandoned Property Act, 64; corporations in, 128; debt relief laws in, 17; democratic control of, 40; 1868 state convention in, 110; federal courts in, 43, 137; postwar conditions in, 9; postwar federal aid to, 50; property exemptions in, 26, 28; state courts in, 40; support for repeal of 1867 Bankruptcy Act in, 138–39; women's property rights in, 26, 28, 110–11
Mississippi Bar Association, 162 (n. 8)

Mississippi, Northern, Federal District of, 44
Mississippi, Southern, Federal Courts of the District of, 32
Mississippi, Southern, Federal District of, 8, 33
—and Bankruptcy Act of 1867: bankruptcy attorneys in, 61; bankruptcy filings in, 33, 55–58, 145; corporate bankruptcy filings in, 122, 124, 128–29; discharge rate in, 84–85; and filing creditors, 97–101, 167 (n. 11); filings involving African Americans in, 116–17; filings involving women in, 111–15; involuntary filings in, 56, 58, 96, 97–101, 167 (n. 7); Mississippians' benefits from, 139; partnership bankruptcy filings in, 122, 124, 129, 172 (n. 7); voluntary bankruptcy attorneys in, 63–65; voluntary bankrupts in, 85–92; voluntary filings in, 56–57, 76–77, 82–84, 165 (n. 10)
Missouri, 97
Montgomery, J. W., 104
Mortgaged bonds, 128
Moseley, R. J., 105
Moseley, Robert J., 75
Moss, Lewis, 101
Murphy, Alonzo, 103–4

Nashville Colored Fair Grounds, 116–17
Nashville Colored Tennessean, 118
Nashville, Tenn., 45
Nathans, J. N., 68
National Banking Act of 1865, 129
National Bankruptcy Register, 127
National Board of Trade, 102
New Jersey Law Journal, 135
New Orleans Picayune, 39
New Orleans Times, 51
New York: filing creditors from, 68, 98–99, 100, 167 (nn. 9, 10); merchants in, 15, 174–75 (n. 3); state court decisions in, 110

New York Chamber of Commerce, 22, 151 (n. 18)
New York, Southern, Federal District of, 36, 157 (n. 14)
New York Times, 15
Newman, Marie Stefanini, 112, 148 (n. 15)
Northern states, 3. *See also* Union states

Oaths, loyalty. *See* Loyalty oaths
O'Brien, Gail Williams, 62
O'Connor, M. P., 59, 62
Ohio River, 121
Orr, James L., 121

Paine, Halbert E., 153 (n. 31)
Panic of 1873, 50, 56, 96, 129
Partnership bankruptcy, and Bankruptcy Act of 1867, 122–23, 126–28. *See also* Business entities, and Bankruptcy Act of 1867
—in South, and Bankruptcy Act of 1867, 122–24, 125, 128–29, 130, 134. *See also* Business Entities, and Bankruptcy Act of 1867; *and entries for specific jurisdictions*
Partnerships, 29, 125, 126
Pennsylvania, 23
Perman, Michael, 38–39, 85
Perry, Benjamin, 133
Philadelphia, Pa., 15
Poland, Luke, 14, 19, 20, 43
Pomeroy, Samuel, 19
Port Royal Railroad, 131
Porter and Conner, 70
Property exemptions, state, 6, 17, 25; in South, 26, 27–28, 154–55 (n. 40)
Property values, and voluntary bankruptcy, 82

Radical Reconstruction, 6, 18, 34, 140. *See also* Reconstruction
Radical Republicans, 13–14, 15, 89, 110. *See also* Reconstruction

Railroads, 50, 128, 129; and voluntary bankruptcy, 83–84
Ramsey, Alexander, 175 (n. 7)
Receivers, federal, 131, 193 (n. 26)
Reconstruction, 7; and congressional legislation, 13–14; economic components of, 1; outcome of, 124–25, 140. *See also* Radical Reconstruction; Radical Republicans; Republican congressmen, during Reconstruction
Register, in bankruptcy, 24, 42, 43, 158 (n. 30), 174–75 (n. 3); and bankruptcy counsel, 66; in District of Eastern Tennessee, 55–56. *See also* Bankruptcy Act of 1867
Reid, Whitelaw, 50
Repeal of Bankruptcy Act of 1867, 2, 135–41; arguments against, 136–37, 138, 174–75 (n. 3), 175 (nn. 7, 8); bills calling for, 135, 174 (n. 2); criticisms leading to, 135–38, 174–75 (n. 3); debates concerning, 5, 136–38; passage of, 135, 174 (n. 1); popular support for, 136; as serving southerners' interests, 134, 139–41; southerners' support for, 3, 5, 136, 137–39. *See also* Bankruptcy Act of 1867; Bankruptcy Act of 1867, in South
Republican congressmen, during Reconstruction, 7, 108. *See also* Reconstruction
Revenue laws, 36, 37, 47
Richmond, Va., 50
Rifle Clubs, in South Carolina, 70
Rise, Eric, 35
Rogers, W. W., 118
Rothschild, Rebecca, 105, 113–14
Rothschild, Samuel, 113–14
Rubin, Anne, 50
Russ, William, 72

Sandage, Scott, 10, 16, 170 (n. 19); and corporate bankruptcy, 172 (n. 6); and debt slavery, 21, 149 (n. 22), 175 (n. 10); and depiction of 1867 Act, 5, 148 (n. 11); and federal bankruptcy power, 149 (n. 22)
Secured debt, 128
Self-interest, 3, 4; and states' rights ideology, 4, 5. *See also* States' rights
Senate, U.S., *Letter from the Attorney-General . . .* , 145
Sequestration, writ of, 94
Shannon and Grace, 94
Sharkey, William L., 39
Sherman, John, 18–19, 151 (n. 18)
Sherman, William T., 75
Silverman, Robert, 118
Simonton, Charles H., 65
Sinsheimer, N., 113
Skeel, David, 10; and Bankruptcy Act of 1898, 175 (n. 18); and bankruptcy legal practice, 62, 63; and corporate bankruptcy, 128, 172 (n. 10); and corporations, 125; and court accessibility, 83; and involuntary bankruptcy, 96; and opposition to federal bankruptcy, 1–2; and railroads, 130
Slaves. *See* African Americans
Smith, Oliver H., 125
Sneed, William H., 60
Soifer, Aviam, 170 (n. 26)
South Carolina, 8–9; antebellum economy of, 56; attorneys in, 72; and Captured and Abandoned Property Act, 64; corporations in, 128; debt relief laws in, 17; federal officers in, 38; legislature of, 121; postwar conditions in, 8–9; postwar federal aid to, 50; property exemptions in, 26, 28; state courts in, 16, 41; women's property rights in, 26, 28
South Carolina, Federal Courts of the District of, 32, 47–48
South Carolina, Federal District of, 8, 33
—and Bankruptcy Act of 1867: bankruptcy attorneys in, 61; bankruptcy filings in,

South Carolina, Federal District of (*continued*)
33, 55–58, 145; corporate bankruptcy filings in, 122, 124, 128–29, 132; discharge rate in, 84–85; and filing creditors, 97–98, 100–101, 132, 167 (nn. 7, 11); filings involving African Americans in, 116–17; filings involving women in, 111–15; involuntary filings in, 56, 58, 96, 97–98, 100–101, 167 (n. 7); partnership bankruptcy filings in, 122, 124, 129, 172 (n. 7); voluntary bankruptcy attorneys in, 63–65; voluntary bankrupts in, 85–92; voluntary filings in, 56, 57, 78–79, 82–84, 165 (n. 10)
South Carolina Railroad, 131
South, U.S.: definition of, 3; and 1873 depression, 53; postwar destitution in, 1, 15, 16, 53, 59, 74, 150 (n. 9); property values in, 15, 26. *See also* Southerners; *and entries for specific jurisdictions*
Southern attorneys. *See* Attorneys, in South; Attorneys, southern bankruptcy
Southern Mississippi, Federal District of. *See* Mississippi, Southern, Federal District of
Southerners: as bankruptcy filing initiators, 61, 64; definition of, 3; opposition to federal bankruptcy laws from, 1–2; opposition to Reconstruction legislation from, 14, 15; and postwar federal benefits, 50–51; postwar federal employment of, 50; property values of, 1; reception of 1867 Act by, 14. *See also* South; *and entries for specific jurisdictions*
Spartanburg County, S.C., 82
Spartanburg, S.C., 138
Spear, Emory, 36. *See also* Federal judges
Speed, Frederick, 69, 163 (n. 19)
Speed, James, 38
Spies, A. W., 105
Spring, Julius, 75

St. Louis, Mo., 100, 167 (n. 9)
Stanbery, Henry, 161–62 (n. 6)
State courts, 23–24
—southern: bias in, 14; debt-collection suits in, 16, 150 (n. 12); southerners' views of, 38–41, 71
State insolvency laws, 17–18
State property exemptions. *See* Property exemptions, state
States' rights, 51; as buttressing slavery, 4; and federal court jurisdiction, 161–62 (n. 6); interaction of, with self-interest, 4, 5; as southern ideology, 3, 4, 124–25. *See also* Self-interest
Stay laws, 16–17
Stevens, Thaddeus, 19, 20, 107
Stewart, William, 18
Story, Joseph, 125
Straus, Samuel, and Company, 113
Sullivan County, Tenn., 82
Sumner, Charles, 19, 37, 43, 165 (n. 7)
Sumner, William, 116–17
Supreme Court, U.S., 39
Surrency, Erwin, 159–60 (n. 1)
Swinney, Everette, 44

Tabb, Charles Jordan, 27
Tachau, Mary K., 34, 48
Tarrant's Effervescent Seltzer Aperient, 53
Tax-Payer's Convention, Columbia, S.C., 1871, 41, 121–22
Taylor, William H., 90
Temple, Oliver, 45, 46
Tennessee: and Captured and Abandoned Property Act, 64; corporations in, 128; political control of, 41; property exemptions in, 26, 28; state courts in, 41; women's property rights in, 26
Tennessee, East, 8; antebellum economy, 56; attorneys in, 63–64, 72; characteristics of, 99; property ownership in, 120; unionism in, 8, 99

Tennessee, Eastern, Federal Courts of the District of, 31–32, 45, 60
Tennessee, Eastern, Federal District of, 8, 33, 46
—and Bankruptcy Act of 1867: bankruptcy filings in, 33, 55–58, 145; corporate bankruptcy filings in, 122, 124, 128–29, 132–33; discharge rate in, 84–85; and filing creditors, 97–101, 167 (nn. 7, 11); filings involving African Americans in, 116–17; filings involving women in, 111–15; involuntary filings in, 56, 58, 96, 97–101, 167 (n. 7); partnership bankruptcy filings in, 122, 124, 129, 172 (n. 7); voluntary bankruptcy attorneys in, 61, 63–66, 162 (n. 13), 163 (n. 18); voluntary bankrupts in, 85–92; voluntary filings in, 56, 57, 80–84, 165 (n. 10)
Tennessee, Middle, Federal District of, 46, 104, 116
Tennessee, Western, Federal District of, 46, 129
Tenure of Office Act, 13
Thomas, J. H., 150 (n. 13)
Thurman, Allen G., 174 (n. 3)
Trenholm, G. A., and Son, 94, 95
Trenholm, George A., 94
Trenholm, William, 94
Trigg, Connally F., 31, 60, 104; and attorney's loyalty oath, 71; conduct of, 46; as serving conservative local interests, 43, 45–46, 48; southerners' opinions of, 45; unionist background of, 43, 45. *See also* Federal judges
Trowbridge, L. S., 66
Trumbull, Lyman, 43

Union states, border slave, 3, 97
Unionists: in East Tennessee, 41, 45; in South, 20
United States Law Register, and Official Directory for 1860, 143

Unsecured debt, 128
U.S. Army, 34, 50
U.S. Supreme Court, 39

Van Horn and Venable, 169 (n. 18)
Van Horn, Marion, 169 (n. 18)
Vanderlip, William L., 118
Vicksburg Daily Herald, 40, 52, 59, 60, 161 (n. 4)
Vicksburg, Miss., 9, 82, 86, 100, 119; bankruptcy attorneys in, 65
Voluntary bankruptcy, 2, 22
—under Bankruptcy Act of 1867, 73–92; logistics of, 24–25; number of filings of, 54; out-of-court settlement of, in South, 103; use of, in South, 139. *See also entries for specific jurisdictions*
Voluntary bankrupts, southern, under Bankruptcy Act of 1867: birthplaces of, 84–87; characteristics of, 74–92; destruction of records of, 75; factors influencing filing rates of, 82–84; foreign born among, 86, 152 (n. 28), 165 (n. 12); incidence of, by geographic area, 75–84; number of, 54, 75; occupations of, 86–89, 140, 144–45, 165 (n. 12); property owned by, after discharge, 89–90, 166 (n. 14); property owned by wives and mothers of, 26–27, 90–92; small estates of, 74–75. *See also entries for specific jurisdictions*

Wardlaw, William A., 75
Warner, Willard, 50
Warren, Charles, 10; and 1867 Bankruptcy Act, 19, 22, 151 (n. 18), 154–55 (n. 40); and opposition to federal bankruptcy, 1, 4, 5; and opposition to federal courts, 35; and state debtor relief laws, 17
Warren County, Miss., 9; attorneys in, 59, 63, 69
—and Bankruptcy Act of 1867: and corporate bankruptcy filings, 122,

Warren County, Miss.—and Bankruptcy Act of 1867 (*continued*) 124, 128–29; and filing creditors, 97–101, 167 (n. 7); and filings involving women, 111–15; involuntary bankruptcy attorneys in, 61, 67, 68; and involuntary filings, 99; and partnership bankruptcy filings, 122, 124, 129, 172 (n. 7); voluntary bankruptcy attorneys in, 61, 63, 65, 67, 162 (n. 13), 163 (n. 15); voluntary bankrupts from, 85–92, 161 (n. 3)

Washington News, 18

Webster, Daniel, 125

Western Tennessee, Federal District of, 46, 129

Westerners, 1–2

Whaley, William, 71–72

White, Michael D., 83, 87, 137

White, Robert, 103

Whyte, William Pinkney, 102, 137, 175 (n. 10)

Wiecek, William, 2

Williams, George H., 74

Women: economic and political rights of, 6, 89; and federal bankruptcy, 112, 170 (n. 20); postwar Congress's attitude toward, 107

—and Bankruptcy Act of 1867: and state property laws, 106–7, 109–11, 169 (n. 4); and women's rights, 6–7, 106–11. *See also entries for specific jurisdictions*

—married, property rights of, 26, 92, 106–7, 107–8, 109–10, 112

—southern white, and Bankruptcy Act of 1867, 6–7, 105–16, 140–41; characteristics of, 112–14; as creditors, 115, 170 (n. 24); as debtors, 114–15; as involuntary bankrupts, 111–14; and involvement in commerce, 112; use of, 108, 111–15, 122, 169–70 (n. 18), 170 (n. 19). *See also entries for specific jurisdictions*

Woodward, C. Vann, 51

Zelden, Charles, 48–49

Zuczek, Richard, 70